The Maternal Drama of the Chechen Jihadi

NANCY HARTEVELT KOBRIN, Ph.D.

The Maternal Drama of the Chechen Jihadi

ISBN#: 978-1-885881-13-7

MultiEducator, Inc.
Publishers since 1994
New Rochelle, NY 10805
www.multieducator.net

THE CHECHEN NATIONAL ANTHEM

Death or Freedom

We were born at night when the **she-wolf whelped**,
In the morning, to lion's deafening roar, they named us
There is no god but Allah

In eagles' nests our mothers nursed us,
To tame wild bulls our fathers taught us.
There is no god but Allah

Our mothers raised us to dedicate ourselves to our Nation and our Homeland,
And if our nation needs us we're ready to fight the oppressive hand.
There is no god but Allah

We grew up free as eagles, princes of the mountains.
There is no threshold from which we will shy away.
There is no god but Allah

Sooner will cliffs of granite begin to melt like molten lead,
Than any one of us shall lose our **honor** in life's struggles.
There is no god but Allah

Sooner shall the Earth be swallowed up by the broiling sun,
Than we emerge from a trial in life without our **honor**!
There is no god but Allah

Never to bow our heads to anyone, we give our sacred pledge,
To die or to live in freedom is our fate.
There is no god but Allah

Our sisters heal our brothers' bloody wounds with their songs,
Lovers' eyes will supply the strength of arms.
There is no god but Allah

If hunger weaken us, we'll gnaw on the roots of trees,
And if thirst debilitates us, we'll drink the dew from the grass.
There is no god but Allah

For we were born at night when the she-wolf whelped.
We pledge our lives to God, Nation and Vainakh homeland.
There is no god but Allah

IN MEMORY OF

Brendan Mess, Erik Weissman, Raphael Teken

Murdered on the tenth anniversary of 9/11 in Waltham, Massachusetts

Krystle Marie Campell, Lu Lingzi, Martin William Richard

Murdered on April 15, 2013 in Boston

Massachusetts Institute of Technology Police Officer Sean Collier

Murdered on April 18, 2013

and

For the 95% of Chechen, Dagestan, Ingushetian and Russian people

who wish to live in peace

TABLE OF CONTENTS

ACKNOWLEDGMENTS

I wish to thank my friend and colleague Dr. Joan Jutta Lachkar for her motivation and insights. She was the inspiration behind my making the initial contact with International Psychotherapy Institute e-books' publisher, Jay Aronson, M.D. I wish to thank him for encouraging me to pursue the concept of the maternal platform for terrorism studies.

Special tribute and thanks to Anonymous, whose help and concern for the Chechen people and whose contribution made this book more informative. His correspondence was a gift.

Again I owe a debt of gratitude to the fine mind, eye, and editing of Joanne Freeman, who helped this book see the light of day.

I also am immensely grateful to my former doctoral student Dr. David Van Dyke for his help and friendship. He coined the phrase "maternal drama" to characterize the jihadi dependency on the mother.

My life partner, Professor Yitzhak Reiter—chair of Land of Israel Studies at Ashkelon Academic College and senior researcher at the Truman Institute for Peace and Reconciliation, The Hebrew University of Jerusalem, and the Jerusalem Institute for Israel Studies—has been of immeasurable help. He is one of Israel's leading authorities on the Arab minority, and I could not have written this book without his wisdom, support, kindness, and love—although I take full responsibility for any errors it contains.

Finally, special thanks to my children and grandchildren for their love, support, and the joy they bring to my life.

ABOUT THE AUTHOR

Nancy Hartevelt Kobrin, Ph.D., is a psychoanalyst and counterterrorist expert. She is a fellow of the American Center for Democracy and has a doctorate in comparative literature, specializing in translation theory, semiotics and aljamía, Old Spanish in Arabic script, focusing on Islam and Hadith. She holds a B.A. and an M.A. in Spanish and Portuguese, which she studied in Mexico, Brazil, and Portugal. She also studied Hebrew, receiving a Bachelors of Judaic Studies prior to her doctoral work. Her post-doctoral work included training at the Chicago Institute of Psychoanalysis, where she became the first woman from the Upper Midwest with a doctorate in a non-medical field to graduate from the Institute. At the same time, Dr. Kobrin was appointed director of graduate studies for the department of comparative literature and also taught Jewish Studies. In the 1980s she independently began to focus on the psychological mindset of the terrorist, drawing from her own "internal terrorist." After the train attacks in Madrid, she presented (in Spanish) to the Madrid police. She has also presented to NATO, as well as to law enforcement and military in Sri Lanka, throughout the United States, England, and Israel. Because of her expertise in this field, she was invited to conduct interviews with Somali prisoners, which led to her becoming a specialist on Somali culture.

After 9/11 the U.S. Army at Fort Leonard Wood asked Dr. Kobrin to help them understand the relationship between the devalued female in Arab Muslim shame-honor culture and the spawning of Islamic suicide terrorism. Her analytic training allowed her to develop a theory for the suicide attack that explained its unconscious derivatives within the scope of the family. This was published in her 2010 book, *The Banality of Suicide Terrorism*, available from Potomac. The Hebrew translation appeared in 2013 with a forward written by professor emeritus Gideon Kressel, one of Israel's leading experts on the Bedouins. Her second book, *Penetrating the Terrorist Psyche*, published in 2013 and available at multieducator.com, explains the importance of early childhood development and expounds on the onset of terrorism as it occurs during maternal attachment and bonding. It focuses on the interlocking links of domestic violence, domestic terrorism, and political violence. Dr. Kobrin is a graduate of the Human Terrain System program in Leavenworth, Kansas.

Dr. Kobrin immigrated to Israel in 2010, where she lives with her partner, Professor Yitzhak Reiter, one of Israel's leading authorities on the Arab minority. Together they have eight grandchildren.

INTRODUCTION

The aim of this book is to demystify terrorist behavior from a psychoanalytic perspective for the lay public, the military, law enforcement, as well as therapists who may have difficulty understanding how terrorism works. It sheds light on the combustible combination of factors inherent in being raised in a shame-honor culture and religion. Its intent is to help readers understand terrorist behavior using the tools and insights drawn from psychoanalysis. This knowledge will facilitate better and earlier interventions for terrorism rather than feed the existing cycle of violence.

In this book I use the phrase volcanic iceberg mentality to describe the behavior of the Chechen jihadi in general and the Tsarnaev brothers in particular. In Iceland the icebergs have active volcanoes beneath them, with the potential to make a global impact on the environment.[1] I appropriate this image as a metaphor for Chechen jihadis, who appear cold as ice, while simultaneously lurking below the surface is a violent, murderous personality that is undetectable to the untrained eye. The volcanic iceberg mentality is a narrative descriptor of the Chechen jihadis' lack of empathy; their obsession with warrior weaponry, fire, and rage; and their murder and maiming of innocent men, women, and children. Of utmost importance is understanding the impact of a shame–honor culture and religion such as that in Chechnya, and how problematic child-rearing practices unintentionally prevent children from acquiring empathy.

The volcanic iceberg mentality is a psychotic adaptation, a result of children having been treated as objects when they were infants, a vicious cycle transmitted across generations. While the metaphor presents a dialectic of a frozen cold image, underneath there lies a seething cauldron of rage ready to explode, This mentality also encompasses the dynamic of psychic splitting, which fits with paranoid thinking, as frequently occurs in "nice guy" psychopaths who turn out to be serial killers.

In this book, the term Chechen is sometimes used in place of Chechen terrorist or jihadi. This does NOT imply that all Chechens are terrorists or identify with leaders who perpetuate this kind of violence. It is not my intent to stereotype the Chechens, who have had a very difficult and traumatic history in relation to Russia. However, with the spread of global terrorism, the "Chechen" jihadi has become famous, almost on the order of having its own "brand." My aim is to disclose its seductive nature by explaining the psychodynamics.

The inspiration for this book came about following the tragedy of the Boston Marathon Bombing in April 2013. The attack was committed by two radicalized half Chechen and half Avar brothers, Tamerlan and Dzhokhar Tsarnaev, who were living in America. At this writing, Tamerlan is dead and Dzhokhar is awaiting trial. Their act emboldened the "brand" of Chechen jihad. Others now emulate them, including Doku Umarov, who is considered to be the most wanted Chechen terrorist. Umarov vowed to attack the Winter Olympics 2014 in Sochi, Russia, Putin's pet project. Symbolically the choice of Sochi highlights the long-standing conflict of the Caucasus with Russia. Sochi is a Black Sea resort in view of the Caucasus mountains. During the Soviet era, Sochi was a favorite retreat for the Communist Party honchos.

> Integrating the North Caucasus, a region of unique ethnic and religious diversity, has always been a challenge for Russia. During the Caucasian War (1817-64), the Russian military used extreme violence, razing villages and deporting entire communities. Krasnaya Polyana, located in the mountains less than 50 kilometers from Sochi, was the site of the war's final bloody battle, marking Russia's subjugation of Circassia, the westernmost country of the Caucasus. In February, Krasnaya Polyana will be a center for snowboarding and skiing events

Some Circassian activist groups today argue that Russia's actions in the 19th century should be recognized as genocide; they plan to publicize their cause at the Olympics. But the greatest mobilization has come from a more menacing source: Islamist fighters. In July 2013, the leader of the North Caucasus insurgency, the Chechen separatist Doku Umarov, threatened to disrupt the Olympics, urging his fighters to attack Russia by any means.[2] Northern Caucasus terrorists are said to be planning to attack the Olympic Games.[3]

THE UNCONSCIOUS MESSAGES OF CHECHEN TERRORIST BEHAVIOR

The volcanic iceberg metaphor as an unmentalized experience offers a window of opportunity to explore the unconscious underpinnings of a group of rageful men engaged in jihadism, empowered by their manipulated/distorted image of the females, whom they hate and devalue.

The Chechen jihadis unconsciously attach themselves to their enemies, targeting them and brutally killing their innocent victims. Where does this kind of violent attachment originate? The first attachment in life is the bonding between the mother and infant. Consider, if the Chechens project their hatred onto the female, rage then becomes the replacement for a loving, healthy dependency on her. As much as they hate the mother and repudiate her, they are still fused with her in a parasitic bond. In fantasy she is characterized as a "heroic" angel, while at the same time she remains the devalued female in the stark reality of a brutal shame–honor culture. This über-idealization is a defense against how they utterly disregard her.

Members of a shame–honor culture or religion lack the awareness to realize that shame is a counterproductive, crippling dynamic during children's development. In this type of society, children learn to repress, as opposed to express, their feelings. As a consequence, internal rage boils within the personality. Shame-honor cultures embrace child-rearing practices that control the child through submission. This is not intended to sound pejorative in any way since many of these practices are covert and not done intentionally. Rather, they are an unconscious expression of the parents' own internal terrors, enactments that they project into the innocent child. In shame–honor cultures these dynamics are transmitted from one generation to the next, perpetuating the trauma. It becomes a generational catch-22 cycle and is very difficult to break because to discuss shaming is experienced as shaming itself rather than an opportunity to promote change. Therefore, these inherent traumas surrounding shame cultures are reenacted. They are not viewed as traumatic for the child or necessitating intervention for they become complicit with the societal norms, and there is never the opportunity to work them through. This is the ground floor of building a functioning personality. Further complicating this, as we shall see, is the trauma of war—and in the case of the Chechens, exile from their homeland during Stalinist times, with many dying during the transports. Compounding this communal tragedy were the two Chechen Wars in the 1990s, in which many lost family members. This additional trauma among the Chechens adds to understanding the perpetuation of cycles of violence.

The mother becomes the target of blame/shame, and the object of unconscious hatred from the moment her power as nurturer and sexual prowess becomes a threat. The mother is NOT to be blamed, for none of this is her fault. She has been prescribed and preprogrammed under extreme adversity, and in this state she must raise her children. This presents a double bind: on the one hand she is idealized as a powerful object, and on the other she is devalued; her power becomes perceived as toxic and must be destroyed. This bitter paradox has been grossly underestimated and the central role it plays on the political stage has been disregarded. The essence of the envy and hatred of the female leads to violence as the Chechen jihadists believe they must destroy her.

It is well known, and confirmed by many researchers, that the female is vital to the early development of the baby's brain. While there are still many environmental and genetic factors that remain unexplored, generally it is agreed that the internal stress of being the constant shame/blame, hated object severely jeopardizes the capacity for a healthy maternal attachment bond. In my first book, *The Banality of Suicide Terrorism*, I wrote extensively about this, emphasizing how terrorism is shaped by culture and religion, and by extension its treatment of the female and children through its prescribed child-rearing practices.[4]

This book further focuses on the critical centrality of the mother–infant relationship, the quality of that maternal attachment, and its use as an indicator of the seemingly undetectable potential in political violence. Unlike the healthy maternal attachment, which is soothing, calming, and harmonious, the unhealthy maternal attachment leads to confrontation and violence. This dynamic plays itself out as a thematic motif with an accompanying concrete image or icon that courses through the violence, which I refer to as the maternal cameo. This flawed maternal relationship forms the launching pad for jihadi violence. I am grateful for psychoanalytic analysis, which provides the tools for detecting the seemingly undetectable. The jihadis' volcanic iceberg personality erupts erratically without conscious awareness, especially in the absence of early soothing and empathic containment by the mother. People are viewed merely as objects, not as whole human beings with feelings, needs, and desires, which are considered shameful.

The psychoanalytic approach I use has been grossly under-regarded and poorly understood both in counterterrorism circles as well as in the Middle East. Freud himself had a profound and scholarly understanding of Islam and Al Andalus (medieval Islamic Spain) and identification with Middle Eastern culture.[5] Moreover, Muslims who are themselves psychoanalysts—such as Vamik Volkan, Abdelwahhab Boudhiba, Fethi Benslama, and Salman Akhtar, to cite only a few that do not include those psychoanalysts who continue to practice but must remain anonymous due to death threats, as in the case of Lebanon—have found psychoanalytic thinking to be an amazing adjunct to the understanding and awareness of aggression and rage.[6] They also acknowledge that the key conflict stems from Islamic unconscious envy and hatred of the female. Obviously, such unconscious hatred impacts and influences the development of the mother and her maternal attachment with the baby.

The five percent or so of Chechens who commit heinous acts of terror suffer from myopia and lack awareness of how transparent, stark, and revealing their unconscious behavior is. They are unaware of how utterly dissociated they are from their unconscious rage as result of dysfunctional family psychodynamics, fueled by patriarchal elders who encourage, teach, and demand that they seek revenge and shed blood in order to save face, thereby "cleansing" their honor and relieving their shame.

It is not an easy task for highly skilled psychoanalysts, let alone for the lay public, to connect the dots and understand from where this aberrant behavior arises and what its "drivers" are—externalized and projected through repression and unconscious murderous rage. I seek to show how Chechen behavior is inextricably linked to the early maternal relationship by undertaking a psychological X-ray of their behavior, their own internal terrorists, how and why they choose targets unconsciously, and how they view and misuse people as mere objects. This cultural context is further exacerbated when coupled with an extremist complaint, reading and adherence to Islamic ideology.

The Chechen jihadi offers a unique window on this kind of concrete, delusional thinking, acting out, and unacceptable antisocial destructive behaviors targeting women, children and infants. While I often use the word "he," we shall also see how the Chechen female jihadis play an important role in this maternal drama. By delving into a series of terrorist acts that they have committed, their behavior is propelled by their seeking justification for the shame/blame role into which the female has been cast. The image of the mother in Chechen culture is the embodiment of the chronically devalued female emanating from a shame–honor culture. One can see the dialectic jihadi struggle to have security and intimacy while bonded to concepts like blood vengeance.

Terrorism is complex, comprising multifaceted aspects that defy simple explanation. Yet the spread of the toxic conditions that characterize jihadism can be globally disorganizing and devastating. It precipitates a pull into a chaotic world, a whirlpool of psychotic trauma. Part of the reason terrorism exists is because people in regressed groups are coerced into forming an identification with the aggressor. This kind of collusion further blinds and cripples the capacity to devise appropriate interventions and to set boundaries in order to protect the civilian population.

Chechens who become involved in jihad have a myriad of inner conflicts fueled by their psychopathology and the demands of a shame–honor culture. They are Muslim but not Arabs. Chechens are by and large mountain people. For an outstanding short video on the trials and tribulations of Chechen mountain life, see "Crying Sun: The Impact of War in the Mountains of Chechnya" by documentary maker Zarema Mukusheva.[7] At the beginning of this video in its initial statement she writes that "Two wars between separatists and Russian federal forces have turned Chechnya into a land of devastation and impurity. In this republic of 800,000 people, thousands have been killed and hundreds of thousands uprooted."

Chechens have long been an embattled people, feuding among their own *teips* or clans and especially with the Russians. The long, historical negative interaction with the Russians adds yet another difficult layer to understanding such recalcitrant violence. Russian culture, too, is essentially still very much a shame–honor culture and by no means monolithic. When two shame–honor cultures engage, the interlocking links of conflict are more difficult to untangle. Russia has not dealt wisely with countering terrorism. It has been too heavy handed and as a result has taken the Chechen warrior bait. This has poured oil on the fire rather than promote separation, and the two cultures remain violently bonded to each other.

HOW THE STUDY OF THE CHECHENS AND THEIR CULTURE CAME ABOUT

My interest in the Chechens originated when I was in Tel Aviv in October 2002, when the horror of the Moscow Theatre Hostage Crisis occurred. This terrorist event, discussed in more detail in Chapter 5, was the first Chechen terrorist attack that received global media attention post 9/11. At the same time, Israel was experiencing a surge in Palestinian suicide bombings.[8]

At that time I was also working informally with Yoram Schweitzer, who held the portfolio on Osama bin Laden. He acknowledges me in his book *The Globalization of Terror: The Challenge of Al Qaeda and the Response of the International Community* published in 2003.[9] I related the story about how I became involved in the subject of political violence, terrorism, and counterterrorism in my second book *Penetrating the Terrorist Psyche.*[10] I had been researching trauma and terrorism on my own since the early 1980s. Prior to formal training in psychoanalysis, my academic career focused on understanding the communal traumas of the three predominant Abrahamic faith communities—Jewish, Christian and Muslim in medieval Spain, Sepharad (in Hebrew) and Al Andalus (in Arabic). When I began my training at the Chicago Institute of Psychoanalysis I merely shifted my long-standing research on communal trauma to individual trauma.

I had made contact with Schweitzer before 9/11 and began lecturing internationally on the subject of political violence, a category that experts prefer to hold sacred. I view political violence as an abstract, artificially constructed category that inhibits a critical analysis of the roots of its violence. As a practical person I have always believed that theory is worthless if it cannot be deployed in practice, on the ground in real time. In order to gain more insight, I began working with the military and the police and did open-ended prison interviews on early childhood experience of trauma and violence. The majority of the interviewees were East African, Somali and Sudanese. The Somalis also come from a Muslim shame–honor, clan-dominated culture. Over the course of some twenty years, thousands of Somalis were resettled as political refugees in the Twin Cities of Minneapolis/St. Paul. I also was invited to train some FBI and more than 300 sheriff's deputies on radical Islam. Interestingly enough, it was the sheriff's unit that invited me on "ride alongs" with them because of domestic violence in the immigrant Somali community. These officers found my work of interest because I linked political violence to violence occurring in the home.

After 9/11 the U.S. Army at Fort Leonard Wood contacted me. They were looking for someone to explain to them the role of the devalued female in the Islamic suicide attacks. They had had a British commander who led a special multinational strike mission to the Middle East and had lectured his troops about his belief that the Islamic suicide attack was nothing more than a form of murder-suicide writ large and was related to domestic violence, although he never wrote about his ideas. I surmised that most likely he had been educated and influenced by the British School of Object Relations. This theory is one of the most suitable to explain aggression and rage and how one relates and attaches to one's "objects." Lest we forget, Freud fled Nazi Germany for England along with other psychoanalysts such as Melanie Klein, the founder of British Object Relation Theory. Three other famous psychoanalysts and contributors of object relations theory also had military backgrounds—Winnicott, Fairbairn, who actually served in Palestine, and Bion, a tank commander—who had had intimate experience with war, decades prior to the escalation of global jihad.

The U.S. Army has been using my work ever since, including *The Banality of Suicide Terrorism* as a textbook. Indeed, my work contributed in part to the reason why such great attention has been given to bolstering literacy and prenatal care for females in Iraq and Afghanistan. Both, it should be noted, are also Muslim shame–honor cultures. I also had wanted to deploy to Afghanistan as I have an interest in IEDs (improvised explosive devices or roadside bombs, the kind that the Boston Bombers made), and am writing a dictionary about the terrorist use and misuse of objects called *The Dictionary of Desperanto.* I was accepted into the controversial Human Terrain Program run by BAE Systems and worked as a contractor. I graduated from the program and also completed an intensive course at the University of Nebraska in Omaha on Afghan culture. The Human Terrain System program was specifically developed to connect with local Muslim shame–honor clans[11] and peoples. Yet the program was rife with sexism, racism, homophobia and anti-Semitism and, ironically, had difficulties connecting with its own personnel.

In addition, I traveled to both Moscow and Central Asian Uzbekistan in 1977. The terrorism organization IMU, the Islamic Movement of Uzbekistan, affiliated with Al Qaeda, is yet another example of a shame–honor culture arising out of Islam. Back in 1977, Islam was quiet in Uzbekistan and Chechnya, at least on the surface. The mosques were monitored by the Soviets. This experience would help me understand the underlying tensions between the Chechens and the Russians.

At this time I had the privilege to meet and correspond with the world-renowned Israeli Chechen scholar, Professor Moshe Gammer, who unfortunately died of cancer at age 62 on April 16, 2013, the day after the Boston Marathon attacks, about which I blogged.[12] I wondered what Professor Gammer would have said about the attacks and the fact that Tamerlan Tsarnaev's wish list at Amazon.com included Professor Gammer's *The Lone Wolf and the Bear: Three Centuries of Chechen Defiance of Russian Rule.*[13] Also on

Tamerlan's list were a Chechen dictionary and phrase book, indicating that he did not know the language that well. Yet he maintained a strong identification to the ethnic identity of his father as opposed to his Avar mother. The Avars are an ethnic people in neighboring Dagestan, where he traveled hoping to join the jihad. Being only half Chechen and not having grown up there, he became Chechen by choice, showing the pull and undertow of its warrior culture and the perfect fit of jihad and Chechen history.

The mother's ethnicity questions the fairness of considering the Tsarnaevs[14] as Chechen. Chechens, like Somalis, fear that they will be stereotyped, and that a backlash will occur when a few bad apples are caught murdering innocent people in the name of Allah. Indeed, in the *Rolling Stone* article on Jahar (Dzhokhar, Tamerlan's younger brother), a Chechen woman named Anna Nikeava, who befriended the family, put it this way: "Underneath it all, they were a screwed-up family. They weren't Chechen—they had not come from Chechnya, as she and others had—and I don't think the other families accepted them as Chechens. They could not define themselves or where they belonged. And poor Jahar was the silent survivor of all that dysfunction. He never said a word. But inside, he was very hurt, his world was crushed by what was going on with his family. He just learned not to show it."[15]

I wanted to know more about the Chechens and their culture after the Moscow Theater attack and started to read everything I could find on the subject. The more I read, the more I associated the Chechens with the Basque people. I am an expert on medieval Spain by doctoral training and have knowledge of the Basque in northern Spain, where I had traveled. The Basque have been locked in an intractable conflict with Spain over their independence, and to a degree against the French, since the Basques straddle the geopolitical border between these two countries. In addition, the Muslims had advanced all the way north in Spain toward the Basque region, conquering and converting vast portions from 711 AD until they were defeated and pushed back to North Africa in 1492. According to Islam, which adheres to irredentism, once a land is conquered it remains theirs even if they no longer live there; such is the case with Spain, known as Al Andalus in Arabic. Like the Basque, the Ummah, the Muslim worldwide community, has a similar grievance with the Spaniards. These two mountain peoples shared this "underdog mentality."

ETA (Euskadi Ta Askatasuna, Basque Homeland and Freedom), the Basque terrorist organization, arose from an environment reminiscent of that of the Chechens. They were also mountain people. Like the Chechens they had first been converted to Christianity, although the Chechens were then subsequently converted to Islam. The Basque would have been converted to Islam, too, if the Moorish invasion had not been stopped in the northern realm of the Iberian peninsula by 714 AD. The Moors, the invading North African Muslims, were slowly pushed back, though not before reaching Tours, France. History is still being written. It is hard to say what inroads Islam might make in Basque country in the future. Like the Chechens, the Basque are a shame–honor culture in which the female is strictly controlled. Perhaps this is less true today under the influence of education and modernization, but at the height of ETA violence it was still very clan oriented. The Basque have their *tukkum* (clan), while the Chechens have their *teip*.

The similarities between Basque and Chechen terrorism and their respective cultures are striking. Both were initially characterized as ethnic nationalist separatist movements to gain independence from Spain and Russia, respectively. However as Chechnya became increasingly "Islamized," the violence was justified as *fil sabil Allah*, i.e., fighting in the path of Allah. In fact, there is the Chechenization, like the Palestinization, of geographic areas being coopted by radical Islam and its global jihad, similar to Iraq and Afghanistan.[16]

When I was in Basque Country in 2004, I met with a leading civil rights lawyer whose name I do not recall. I asked if he thought the tactic of suicide bombing could be adopted by the Basque even though they are Catholic. He candidly said yes and confirmed it was possible due to the sense of desperation and honor. However, he did not mention shame.

Another association is their respective languages. To someone who doesn't speak Basque or Chechen, the languages look alike when they are transcribed into English, because x, y, and z are used often in their orthography. In Basque, or as they call their mother tongue *Euskara*, the names are very long. I discovered that one of the theories postulated for explaining the roots of *Euskara*, linked it back to the Caucasus, even though this theory generally has not been upheld by linguists.[17]

I came across a real case of a known Al Qaeda terrorist, a former member of the Basque ETA named Yussuf Galan (José Luis Galan Gonzalez). Galan is his mother's surname. He was one of the rare terrorists of Spanish origin in Iraq and was arrested in Spain in April 2002. He was questioned by Judge Baltasar Garzon for the 9/11 inquest into Al Qaeda. He had belonged to ETA for a long time before his conversion to Islam.[18] So we see that the Basques can relate to the violence of Islamic terrorism. There have been many Al Qaeda terrorists fighting in Chechnya and now Dagestan.

This brings us back to the Tsarnaevs, who had never lived specifically in Chechnya. Yet the brothers and even the Dagestani Avar mother, Zubeidat, self-identified with the Chechen jihad. The most famous eighteenth century jihadi, named Shamil, who fought Russia, was Avar. Furthermore Stalin deported many Chechens en masse in 1944 to Kazakhstan from where two of Dzhokhar Tsarnaev's Muslim friends came. Because of this persecution, a special psychological tie exists between the Muslims of the Caucasus and Kazakhstanis. Ultimately the Chechens were permitted to return home in 1957. The deportation was thought to be due in part to collaboration with the Nazis during World War II. Some did collaborate, but Aleksandr Nekrich, who witnessed the deportation by the Russians, characterized it as brutal and wrote an extensive history about it in his *The Punished Peoples*. The deportation strengthened their religious ties to Islam. The Muslim clergy functioned to a degree as a shadow state.[19] Russian animosity and brutality continue to this day in the extra-judicial treatment of Chechens, who are summarily executed. An op-ed in *The Wall Street Journal* recently foregrounded the lack of justice for these people.[20]

However, no matter how persecuted a people are, murdering innocent victims through suicide bombing or other bombing attacks is psychotic behavior signaling that an early developmental problem has gone untreated. In September 2012, I was interviewed for a Canadian Montreal documentary directed and produced by Doina Harap on this developmental problem, which has been repeatedly missed by most counterterrorist experts. Called *The Body Does Not Lie*, the film deals with imagery and the body language of terrorists and why they lack empathy, important considerations for airport security. It specifically focuses on the Ben Gurion Airport in Tel Aviv, perhaps the airport most famous for its tight security and its young women screeners, who are exceptionally good at reading body language. This book offers a few more pieces of the puzzle regarding the nonverbal and verbal language of the terrorist, especially the Chechen terrorist attacks in Boston, Moscow, and Beslan.

Harap had read my first book, *The Banality of Suicide Terrorism: The Naked Truth About Islamic Suicide Bombing*, in which I stated that the murder-suicide of Western-style domestic violence is Islamic suicide bombing's lowest common denominator, its template. My findings were that the vast majority of the jihadis manifest something akin to a malignant form of autism, as well as a disorganized maternal attachment disorder. Harap's film also included interviews with neuroscientist Professor Marco Iacoboni, whose groundbreaking work on mirror neurons suggests why jihadis lack empathy:

In order to develop mirror neurons for empathy, maternal attachment must be optimal.

Professor Jonathan Matusitz, a specialist on terrorism and communication, argues that culture shapes terrorism. I extend that argument to early child-rearing practices such as threatening a child by beating his or her mother. In shame–honor cultures, the female struggles to maintain a relaxed, healthy attachment to her baby despite having grown up and continuing to live under a real, not imagined, death threat.

The issue of domestic violence has extreme relevance for the Boston Marathon Bombings because Tamerlan had a documented history of domestic violence involving his girlfriend, as well as his future wife, Katherine Russell. Domestic violence is an aggressive attachment. I have long argued that the elephant in the room is the underlying interlocking terrorisms of domestic violence and the early childhood development of these jihadis, who are exposed to wife beating of their mothers. This negative environmental factor is not the entire story but an important aspect. Children in the Islamic world often witness their mothers being abused, if not beaten according to Sura 4 of the Quran. Abu Zubaydah, a Palestinian who is imprisoned in Guantanamo for his participation in Al Qaeda, wrote the following self-revelatory observation of the abuse and the significance of the role of the mother in embracing political violence. In short, this drama is really about protecting the defenseless abused female:

> The Palestinian national trauma is an inherited memory; it's the personal injuries of his childhood that most haunt him—like the moment he saw his father beating his mother, who had become embroiled in a fistfight with her sister-in-law, as Abu Zubaydah and his older brother, Mahir, screamed for the adults to stop.
>
> After that moment, Abu Zubaydah recalls, he never witnessed "a happy day" in his family. He seems to remember only "yelling, crying, and weeping." Sometime

> later, his mother and father argued again, and he was standing next to his mother in the kitchen and saw tears in her eyes. "Perhaps I was ten, and for the first time I see my mother crying like a child as she was telling me things that I didn't understand …To be a child and see my mother crying, that was so tough for me …" That image traumatized him. It forced "my tears to fall and fall and fall."
>
> One of the first entries of his diary, dated June 7, 1990, begins, "A picture of me at five or perhaps six years old; if only I could wipe out all my past since the moment I was born until this moment, by God, I will not hesitate one bit." He had been in India for a year and apparently growing more desperately depressed by the day.[21]

As we listen to the jihadis closely with our third ear, they reveal how their problems developed early in life, but they are unable to connect these psychological traumas to their violent rage. This denial stems from a psychological splitting, a defense that projects their rage outwards. This is the tip of the volcanic Iceberg mentality.

ACTING OUT VIOLENCE AS PSYCHIC ADAPTATION

Terrorists do not feel their *terror*; they become it. A good example is a psychotic who sits on a psychiatric ward like an iceberg. The psychotic is emotionally freezing to death but does not know how to communicate this verbally, instead communicating this frozen mental state through nonverbal behavior.[22] The nonverbal communication of a terrorist works in a similar way. Terrorists literally paint the fantasies and rage they feel on the canvas of the crime scene they create. They take their psychotic fantasies for reality and act them out. This somewhat abstract, autistic, horrifically graphic painting of blood and guts is an intrapsychic adaptation to their internal conflicts, which emanate from the inability to separate psychological from their mothers. They have not gained psychological maturation. Their *in extremis* psychotic behavior is under the alleged guide of political violence and the ideologies to which they cling. The jihadi is like the psychotic iceberg patient but with one major difference: he is a volcanic Iceberg. Beneath the surface he is boiling with rage that erupts into violent murder.

In *The Banality of Suicide Terrorism: The Naked Truth about Islamic Suicide Bombing*, I enhanced the idea of play therapy as initiated by Melanie Klein, and transposed it to the behavior of terrorists. I found myself stepping back and asking what these terrorists were communicating about their own terrors. Obviously they are not playing, yet all of human behavior is potentially understandable; we are more alike than we are different. As Abu Zubaydah tells us, they did not have happy childhoods; they did not experience healthy play. They never learned to distinguish the difference between playing (fantasizing) and reality. They grew up acting out their aggression and rage and have no filter between their violent thoughts and their actions. They developed a perverse way of engaging the world and bonding to people violently. They are terrified, become their terrors, and in turn terrify us.[23]

In Chapter 1 we will turn our attention to the importance of maternal bonding, the infant's first attachment experience in life. By focusing on the mother, we discover that she has extreme significance in Avar and Chechen shame–honor cultures as the platform and launching pad for terrorism. To know her psychic mind is to know a good portion of the challenges and possible solutions to the violence. This book explores beyond the role of Zubeidat Tsarnaeva, Tamerlan's mother, who helped radicalize her son, to more fundamental issues regarding early childhood development and maternal attachment and how that fuels the flames of political violence. In many ways one could conceptualize the problem as the opposite of what Rosemary M. Balsam describes in her excellent book *Sons of Passionate Mothering* (a free download at the International Psychotherapy Institute) as Zubeidat's passionate mothering proved to be ineffective, if not malignant.

We will also examine the ineffectiveness of Anzor as a father, and the terrorists' relationship to sisters Alina and Bella. The father left the mother when she and the eldest son became increasingly religious and returned to Dagestan. The mother was picked up on charges of shoplifting, and rather than face prosecution she fled to Dagestan and reconciled with her ex-husband. As we see again the reoccurring theme of traumatic bonding, it gives us a better sense of sliding back into an abusive relationship.[24] The developmental stumbling blocks are in the details.

CHAPTER 1

THE SHAME–HONOR CULTURE AS CAULDRON OF THE VOLCANIC ICEBERG MENTALITY

What is learned in childhood is like carved in stone.

—*Chechen Proverb*

We cannot make all of the Chechen people out to be bandits and thieves—or, for that matter, Islamic extremists, as the Russians have done over the course of generations. As a Jew, I am acutely aware of stereotyping and would not wish that people view Jews as evil, as does radical Islam. As with any people, there are good and bad apples among the Chechens, and the Islamic extremists are in the minority. This book argues that the problem of jihadi violence arises mostly out of the setting in the home and its dysfunctional psychodynamics. We are still in the early stages of understanding the biology of violence, but a problematic early childhood development can tip the scales toward violent enactments.

For the "bad apples" who become violent jihadis, the familial situation is the most severe. With multifactorial aspects coming into play, these five per cent manifest what I refer to as a volcanic iceberg mind, a prerequisite for those who commit these heinous crimes. For example, the "normal" mind allows one to say "I feel cold" or "I feel sadness due to the death of my mother." A person with a psychotic or autistic-like mind will "become" the volcanic iceberg. These are the emotionally frozen ones who, specifically in the case of the terrorists, will act out their pent-up rage and aggression like a volcanic explosion, expressing through a violent nonverbal pantomime what they cannot articulate through the use of language. They become enraged and attacking, but will cloak their volcanic iceberg mind under the banner of jihad, justifying what they cannot express emotionally. Ironically, the Sochi Olympics have been described using the same explosive imagery that defines my concept of the volcanic iceberg mind: "So far as anyone can remember, this is the first time that any Olympic Games has been held so close to such a bleeding insurgency or a *volcano about to explode* [emphasis mine]. In addition, the skating facility is 29 miles outside of Sochi, and other venues also are scattered around. One might bet that the safest place would be on the rocky beaches with the ladies in their bras."[25]

While we are still driving a Model T Ford as far as the interplay between genetics, neuroscience, and psychodynamics, we can still speculate as to what the terrorists are trying to communicate through their behavior. They are not developing empathy. Their terrors blind us as spectator/victims of the trauma that they inflict. We, too, can become like icebergs with regard to denying this unconscious process. It is our denial defending against our own deepest terrors of vulnerability and our own internal terrorist abuser. Through examining this unconscious and unspoken dialogue, terrorism in general and Chechen terrorism in particular can be demystified, and more appropriate interventions can be made.

Central to this discussion is the role that shame bears in the highly traumatizing shame–honor culture/religion, which has yielded a devastating history of generations of deprivation and warring. Even discussing the concept of shame in this book is for a shame–honor people like washing their dirty laundry in public. This places them in a double bind from which it is nearly impossible to extract themselves from the shame, turn the corner, and look at themselves in a non-judgmental light. The female has been brutally devalued, and yet she is creating the brain of the baby of the future jihadi. She is NOT to be blamed but to be understood as working under a severe handicap in this shaming culture, which is predicated on the devaluation of the female. We can surmise that an outcome is the creation of a volcanic iceberg mentality: Act out your rage rather than containing and understanding it.

The Pew Center undertook a survey concerning violence in the Caucasus and found the number of jihadis was small. Yet there remain fears of radicalization.[26] This book focuses on understanding from a psychoanalytic perspective why there is violence emanating out of this region. Unfortunately, the Chechens were placed on the psychological map of Americans because of the Boston Marathon Bombings in April 2013, similar to the way the Saudi Hijackers of 9/11 captured our attention after the attacks on the Twin Towers, the Pentagon, and the air crash in Shanksville, Pennsylvania.

A Short History of the Caucasus: War as Paranoia[27]

Chechnya is located in the Caucasus and is a crossroads between Europe and Central Asia. There are a series of nations, but here we limit the discussion to Chechnya, Dagestan, and Ingushtia of the Northern Caucasus. Technically, Chechnya is a federal subject of Russia and has been even as far back at the writings of Tolstoy, who in his famous novel *Hadji Murat* memorialized the relationship between Russia and Chechnya as highly conflicted and a thorn in "Mother" Russia's side.[28]

While Chechnya has a limited autonomy, it feels that it remains largely controlled by the Russians, and to a large degree this feeling is grounded in reality. Listen to what the photographer Monteleone had to say about the region:

> Monteleone first travelled to the Caucasus in 2001, as part of a wider investigation of Russia and its citizens' relationship to power. He returned most recently in January, 2013, well over a decade after the official end of the second Chechen war, which resulted in Chechnya losing its hard-won independence when Vladimir Putin installed the Kremlin-friendly leader Akhmad Kadyrov to power. Akhmad's son Ramzan, the current leader—whom Monteleone describes as a young, uneducated megalomaniac—rebuilt Grozny and attained relative peace, although sporadic attacks by separatists continued. Though Chechens now speak their once-banned language, practice Islam openly, are permitted to practice Chechen traditions, and

> enjoy relative freedom from Russia, Chechnya is still a republic within the Russian Federation. As Monteleone says, "Everything is controlled by the authorities that give to the people as they please. A state of comforting stagnation …. The physical violence that was so much part of the post-conflict years … seems to have decreased. The Chechens are so frightened that these acts of violence are almost no longer necessary. The violence is now psychological, a form of brainwashing that starts with the youngest generations."[29]

Russia conquered the Caucasus in the seventeenth century under Tzar Peter the Great. Russia annexed Chechnya in the 1870s. It is as if the Russians and the Chechens have been violently wedded to each other, and the Chechens want a divorce. The War of Resistance that took place in 1785–1864 caused the death of half the Chechen population. Many fled to Jordan and Turkey. Then there was the First Chechen War from December 1994 through August 1996, with its fierce battle for Grozny. The Second Chechen War followed three years later, lasting until April 16, 2009. It is against this background of warring that the Chechen jihadi became venerated and their violence sanctioned by clan feuds, cultural blood vengeance, and even the habit of domestic violence.

THE CHECHEN HISTORICAL TRAUMA: MASS DEPORTATION BY STALIN

Nekrich, in his book *The Punished People*, relates how the Chechens were forcibly deported to Kazakhstan en masse in late 1943.[30] He claims that the enforced exile strengthened the religion. Some of the deportees had collaborated with the German occupation authorities during WWII. Late in 1943 and early 1944, after the Nazi invasion of Russia had been turned back, the Soviets invaded the Caucasus without warning and brutally deported one million Chechens, Ingush, Balkars, Kavachi Kalmyks, and Tartars to Central Asia, Kazakhstan, Kyrgystan, and Siberia. The Soviets executed hundreds, while thousands died of malnutrition, exposure, and harsh treatment. Aleksandr Nekrich was in Crimea and witnessed the brutal deportation. Under Khrushchev's regime there was a reversal in policy and the deportees were permitted to return. Many carried the bones of their relatives back to Chechnya from Kazakhstan.[31]

> In Dagestan, a traditionally Islamic republic bordering Chechnya, school principal Temirmagomed Davudov said the Tsarnaev family came to Dagestan in 2001 from the Central Asian republic of Kyrgyzstan. During World War II, Stalin deported most of the population of Chechnya to Central Asia.[32] The family spent one year in 2001 in Makhachkala, Dagestan where all four children attended school. They then immigrated to Turkey and from there came to the U.S. We can surmise that the family carried this intergenerational trauma forward without having learned to process the emotional impact the displacement had upon them.

THE ONLY INDEPENDENCE MOVEMENT OF ITS KIND IN POST-SOVIET RUSSIA

The Chechen Rebellion had been attributed to largely "clannish loyalties, economic interests, and the spillover of internal Russian rivalries into Chechnya."[33] Karny, who traveled extensively throughout Caucasus and wrote about the region, explored the spiritual dimension and insisted that the Chechen quest for separation from Russia was influenced by the Sufi *tariqa*, or lodges. Sufism stresses the mystical dimension of Islam and is known to harbor moments of violent outbursts. Yet, charismatic leaders have always played an important role in Sufism and can be traced back to eleventh century saints in Baghdad who guided the *zikr* performers.[34]

Ro'i described sufism in the Soviet Union as an unofficial parallel to Islam. Unlike the mosques, it was not registered within the state apparatus. One wonders if one could conceptualize it as an underground movement of sorts, a way of preserving control over one's own communal sense of self. Sufism in Chechnya acted as a kind of syncretistic fusion of ethnic and religious practices, including especially the *zikr* dance of its mysticism, which induces an altered state of consciousness and is experienced as being free from earthly endeavors and from the restrictive monitored state-sanctioned Islam that preceded the rise of a violent radical Islam. Karny believes that the Soviets and now Russians completely underestimated the importance of mystical spirituality as a kind of glue for Chechen cultural ethnic and religious identity. They retained more than just ethnic food habits or a few exotic dances; rather, the sense of communal identity was bolstered. Its leaders all tended to be charismatic. Winnicott, the Object Relations theorist who developed the concept of the true and false self, may have thought of Sufism to be the truer sense of communal self, one that was more hidden from the surveillance eye of the Soviets. While not an in-depth report of its leaders, here are some of the influential icons.

- Kunta Haji: the most venerated Sufi leader, was born in the 1820s and died in 1867. He believed in nonviolence and was the leader of the Qadariya Tarika movement. He was so popular and his following so great that Imam Shamil, mentioned below, felt threatened.[35]
- Hagi Murad: inspired Tolstoy's last novel, which romanticized the Chechens as warriors and their leader. Hagi is an honorific bestowed upon one once he has completed the haj, the holy pilgrimage to Mecca, one of its five pillars of faith. Ironically, Haji Murad was an Avar like Zubeidat Tsarnaeva. There are two famous anecdotes told about Hagi Murad: one in which he reversed the shoes on horses to throw off the tracking of his pursuing enemy, and the second in which he attempted to commit suicide by leaping over mountain precipices, dragging soldiers with him, but he only broke his leg.[36] However, it has generally been overlooked that the latter anecdote encapsulates the template of murder–suicide also found in Islamic suicide terrorism. Hence, it can be said that inscribed in the Chechen warrior tradition is this underlying template, which is venerated.

Legend also has it that if one were a coward, his eyes would be gouged out for betrayal. Psychologically we know that a basis for the experience of feeling shame is the accusatory eye of the mother.[37] In a shame–honor culture, the eye takes on a central importance and assumes the status of a cultural obsession. This thread runs throughout the shame–honor culture, in which the female is under surveillance to preserve her sexual purity.

- Imam Shamil: "another famous warrior, also technically was not a Chechen as he was born in Dagestan. He lived from 1797 to 1871 and was considered a scholar of the Quran. Shamil was said to have been a born leader, commander, diplomat, and politician, who repeatedly outmaneuvered the Russians in battles. Contrary to Russian propaganda, he was far from extremism or blind fanaticism."[38] Griffin records that Shamil was called "an Islamic Mountain warrior."[39] Shamil was also famous for whipping his own mother, Bahou Messadou, in public because she had been manipulated to try to get Shamil to surrender to the Tzar.[40] The psychological message this communicates is counterproductive to raising healthy, nonviolent children. Yet, this cultural narrative continues to be venerated as honorable rather than seen for its destructive potential. Moreover, Imam Shamil captured an ethnic Armenian teen and took her as his bride. Hostage taking, about which we will read more below, is also socially sanctioned behavior; it is a fusion, related to murder–suicide, as the murderer takes his victim hostage, then after murdering his victim kills himself. Shamil's bride ultimately converted to Islam during her years of captivity. The theme of conversion in Islam points to the concept that conversion does not have to be of free will; it can be coerced. No one held in captivity converts of his/her own volition. Shamil, in turn, was captured by the Tzar and exiled to Russia, where he was held captive.
- Shamil Basayev: took his name from Imam Shamil. Born Shamil

Salmanovich Basayev in 1965, he died at age 41 in a 2006 explosion. Basayev, Russia's most wanted terrorist, was implicated in numerous terrorist attacks, especially the three central attacks involving a maternity hospital, the Moscow Theatre, and a school, which will be addressed in the following chapter.[41] He was known for his bloody and brutal beheadings of six Russian soldiers in the Dagestan Massacre in 1999, a video of which was made and disseminated. He was also the classic example of a villainous, charismatic leader with a defect.[42] He had only one foot, having lost the other in battle.[43] Basayev also experienced a personal tragedy. He lost many members of his family when the Russians aerial-bombed a relative's home. I quote at length from an interesting article that appeared in the *Los Angeles Times*:

> MOSCOW—Shamil Basayev, the guerrilla commander holding hundreds of hostages in a hospital in southern Russia, inherited a long and proud ancestral tradition of suicidal resistance to invaders of his native Chechnya. Central to that tradition was the Basayev family's two-story stone house—built in the year 1010 and now reportedly destroyed by Russian bombs—in the mountain village of Vedeno. In its defense, one Basayev ancestor fought the 14th-Century Central Asian warlord Tamerlane.
>
> A great-great-great-grandfather died in wartime service as a deputy to Imam Shamil, for whom Shamil Basayev was named. The imam fought to create an independent Islamic state, held off the czar's army for four decades and made a last stand at Vedeno before surrendering in 1859. A great-grandfather was killed fighting the Bolshevik army, and his son died when Soviet dictator Josef Stalin deported 800,000 Chechens to Kazakhstan and Siberia in cattle cars in 1944. "If the Russians come in here and take our home, what's the point of living?" Shamil Basayev's father, Suleyman, asked a visitor to the stone house last winter after the Russian army had again invaded Chechnya to crush its latest drive for independence.

> Tragedy befell the Basayev household in a Russian air raid late in May. And after losing his village, his home, his mother, two children, a brother, a sister and six other kin, Basayev did last week what no ancestor—and no other Chechen warrior—had ever done. He took vengeance outside his homeland. He struck in spectacular fashion, storming Budennovsk—a town of 54,000 people—with no more than 75 guerrillas who slipped in undetected, seized government buildings, grabbed as many as 2,000 hostages and herded them into a hospital, demanding nothing less than a Russian surrender in Chechnya.
>
> "We are sick of watching our villages being bombed and our women and children being killed," the bearded commander explained from the city's hospital, which was surrounded by Russian troops, armored personnel carriers and sharpshooters. "Let them come and storm the place. It does not matter to us when we die. What matters is how we die. We must die with dignity."[44]

Interestingly enough, the counterterrorist expert on Chechnya, A. Dolnik, cited this incident of loss in passing, noting that other counterterrorists had thought that this may have been the tripwire for Basayev, who then unleashed his reign of terror—engaging in hostage taking. murder, and suicide bombings as revenge. Basayev seized the Budennovsk Maternity Hospital, the Moscow Theatre and then a school in Beslan.[45] Similarly, Zarqawi, the Palestinian Al Qaeda leader in Iraq, went on his beheading rampage after he lost his mother to cancer.[46]

However, the counterterrorist experts seem to minimize the ramifications of maternal loss on the undoing of the terrorist psyche. When we later examine Basayev's terror attacks and their link to the repudiated mother, we find his behavior is consummately concrete. While counterterrorist experts often point to the strategic choice of the target, it is not mutually exclusive that there is an unconscious choice deriving from unresolved conflicts in early childhood that actually drives the conscious strategic choice. Indeed, this synergistic dimension of doubly induced volcanic rage blinds us from seeing the earlier unconscious driver of maternal loss. We are sucked into the psychotic world of the terrorist and remain in denial because it is just too terrifying to think that the problem lies buried in early childhood development, embedded in the family.

What has also been overlooked is the intervening, underlying cultural practices of hostage taking—ranging from bride stealing to clan hostage taking for revenge. This is yet another link in the imagery of fusion. Taking a hostage is an attempt to re-fuse with the mother in a shame–honor culture where one is not permitted to separate from her. Hostage taking is a fusion that harkens back to the maternal fusion, the first fusion in life. The intervening fusions replay the trauma of not having the emotional, psychological, and cognitive capacities to be independent. These cultural practices easily mask the underlying developmental problem. Another aspect is that the individual never learns to accept loss and genuinely mourn. Instead, he resorts to turning the tables and merely inflicting his loss on the hostage, thus perpetuating the trauma, rage, and violence.

Shamil's life ended violently like his mother's. Below is an incomplete list of other Chechen leaders, many of whom died a violent death:

- Dzhokhar Dudayev (1991–1996): Ex-Soviet air force officer, killed by a missile homing in on his telephone
- Zelimkhan Yandarbiyev (1996–1997): Radical poet and ex-Chechen president, killed by Russian agents in Qatar in 2004
- Aslan Maskhadov (1997–2005): Ex-Soviet artillery officer elected president in 1997, killed by Russian special forces
- Abdul-Khalim Saydullayev (2005–2006): Radical cleric killed in a gun battle with FSB (Russian Federal Security Service) and pro-Russian Chechen forces
- Salman Raduyev: Warlord, who died of internal bleeding in 2002, in a Russian jail

- Khattab: While not Chechen but an Arab from Saudi Arabia, this warlord gained central notoriety as a jihadi, He was killed by a poisoned letter in 2002.

CHECHEN CULTURE

The name "Chechen" first appeared in Arabic during the eighth century,[47] although the people prefer to refer to themselves as the Vainakh nation, meaning "our nation/our people." The term generally refers to both Chechen and Ingush peoples.[48] The Chechens have a long-standing tradition of being embattled and fighting. They are the only peoples who turned back the Mongol invaders, including Tamerlan[49] (after whom the eldest Boston jihadi was named) twice during the thirteenth and fourteenth centuries. The Mongols, while Islamized, merely laid the ground for a later reception of Islam during Chechen contact with the Ottoman Empire in order to curry favor with them against the Russians. There was nominal conversion to Sunni Islam, and a form of Sufism evolved. Prior to the reception of Islam into this religion, there was pagan worship, which became fused through a kind of syncretism with Christianity. Islam in part was embraced as a way in which to distinguish Chechen identity from that of Christian Orthodox Russia.[50]

As memorialized in its national anthem, the Chechen culture exhibits the reoccurring theme of the struggle for freedom. We can speculate that the iconic imagery of the Chechen nursing mother as the potentially violent she-wolf haunts the group's unconscious psyche. In the maternal relationship, a mother starts feeding her infant as soon as the baby enters the culture of seeking honor and warding off shame. "Our mothers pledged us to our people."[51] This verse of the anthem fits hand in glove with their cultural practices. To give one brief example concerning the mother, it is the mother's family even more than the clan (*teip*) that decides if a son goes to fight or not.[52] Because its religion is intricately interwoven into a shame–honor culture, and its ideologies cannot be separated from cultural practices. They are part and parcel of the communal identity formation process.

The Chechens, like the other groups in the North Caucasus, are extremely conservative, reminiscent, for example, of the Bedouins in the south of Israel. Many will say that the female's lowly, unconsciously despised position in society is a matter of cultural and historical traditions rather than Islam. Unfortunately, this perspective is short-sighted because it dismisses discussion of the role Islam plays in keeping the cultural milieu both conservative and stifling. Rarely is it asked why Islam, the religion of peace, does not put an end to violence? The wish is for peace, but the praxis involves an entirely different aspect of psychological thinking. It involves jihad as a fundamental unconscious pillar of faith.

In a region completely preoccupied with shame and shaming practices, the female—as in all shame–honor clans, tribes, societies, and patriarchal families—is devalued and psychologically, if not physically, controlled to the point where she has been coopted. She has been brainwashed and trained from birth to accept this inferior status—although she, herself, may think she is "free" in the sense of choosing to become a female jihadi, a Black Widow as they are called. The devaluation of the female by male authority figures is merely a defense against their inability to be emotionally independent and free standing. They rely on their mothers to split off and guard against vulnerability in adult relationships with females. This point is not well understood by counterterrorist experts who are not grounded in early childhood development.

The group is highly fused, regressed, and enmeshed. In fact, just as we hear in the greeting of "peace," shalom/salaam in the Middle East, we note that there is none. And yet there is this verbal obsession for it, a desperate wish for peace with little acknowledgement of how to bring it about and an ineptitude to achieve peace because a functional psychological infrastructure is lacking. Similarly, the Chechens are obsessed with freedom because they have none psychologically because they are trapped in their inherited shame–honor structure. They are also terrified of freedom because it would entail giving up their externalized hatred and being unable to contain their negative feelings about themselves. The external hated object in their unconscious allows them to stabilize an inherently fragile personality.

The entry of the female infant into this life is particularly fraught with complexities, mainly because she comes culturally prescribed as a devalued, meaningless being within the status of the clan. From birth she has internalized this cultural communication and fantasy, which is an unconscious nonverbal message that her womb and even her mother's womb are of virtually no importance.

With the bearing of a son comes honor to offset the shame of having a vagina. In this kind of environment not only is the vagina seen as being worthless, it is also an object of terror. I use the word "fantasy" because paradoxically, without the female, the clan cannot reproduce. Therefore she is feared because of this power, and the males remain dependent on her. So the male honor code has evolved to maintain control over this terrifying, all-powerful female. Even though the mother is larger than life, she assumes the role of subservience, diminishing herself almost as if she were not female. In psychoanalytic terms one could interpret "to diminish the woman and her power" as merely a defensive cover-up for the male's dependency, his reliance on needing her for his existence.

Let me further define what is meant by a shame–honor society. The primary tool for gaining control over children is the inculcation of shame, on the one hand, with ridicule and ostracism, including bullying, on the other. In short, it would constitute child abuse in Western terms because it is a very aggressive and violent environment in which to grow up. Having said this, I hasten to point out that in the West there are shame–honor families that fit this profile of child abuse. The lowest person on the totem pole in a shame–honor culture, society, or clan is the female baby. Honor is the word used to project worthiness, respectability, and above all purity, e.g., the virginity of the female. Her vagina is the locus of shame.

Shame is one of our earlier feelings such as "interest and enjoyment (positive feelings); surprise (a re-setting feeling); and distress, anger, fear, shame, disgust, and dissmell (negative feelings). Babies have the capacity to respond to their surrounding with these nine signals."[53] Hence babies very early on experience shame, especially in a shame–honor culture.

Shame is inextricably linked to saving face.[54] Honor is often the code word to guard, protect, and control the female, hovering over her to "protect" her purity, a defense against male fears of weakness, impotence, psychological fragility, and seething rage. The adhesive that holds the family together is often extended to the brother, who becomes the replacement father for the family. In part, the father has never disengaged and separated from his own mother. What this means is that the son as brother and in place of the absent father is tasked with placing his sisters under constant surveillance. This is evident in the case of Tamerlan Tsarnaev, who was described by a high school class mate as "tailing his little sister" all the time to guard the family honor Abdul-Khalim Saydullayev.

In a shame–honor society, unlike in Western cultures, one is never psychologically encouraged or permitted, for that matter, to go through the normal separation process from one's mother. There is a special word for not being allowed to grow up: neotenization. The males in particular remain psychologically and emotionally infantile, never learning how to relate to the female and, by extension, to others outside of their culture. This causes ambivalence and confusion, especially about one's identity, that keeps men psychologically held back in childhood, in a kind of time-warp mentality. The male remains emotionally glued to a maternal object, who is needed and therefore must be repudiated.

Shame gives rise to the need to protect oneself within a group functioning in a controlled manner to meet the needs of the males. It is power and control predicated on abusing the female. In addition, in shame–honor cultures, there must be constant purging of the group's aggression through a "safety valve," the emotional escape hatch of scapegoating. The scapegoat is always the female or a male who has been feminized and hence shamed. The other is always feminized.

Some may ask, "But what about the father?" He may be better understood if discussed from the viewpoint of the son. The authoritarian father in shame–honor cultures is a symptom of the underlying problem of the devalued female who only gains honor via the birth of her first male son. She misuses the son as her narcissistic object, if not as a crutch for her self-esteem. In shame–honor cultures, it is a cultural taboo to separate from the mother, including when a man marries. The son remains tightly bound to the mother. We see this in the Chechen proverb: "The son gets married, the back of the mother bends; the daughter marries, it becomes straight." This proverb shows us the attachment between mother and son. She will bend at all costs to support him, to cover for him, and to remain glued to him. The daughter is essentially unconsciously despised property until she has a son, and then she too can bend. It is out of this suffocating relationship of mother and son in this highly patriarchal society and clan that "freedom" gains a special unconscious meaning. The patriotic freedom the Chechens have long sought, and about which they sing, is really the attempt to break free of a stifling shame–honor culture that perpetuates violence. Note that this also is applicable to all other ethno-nationalist separatist terrorist movements.

Shame is the grid against which social relations are conducted and experienced. Honor is really a code word for the male hovering over the female body like an adhesive because his identity is so weak and dependent. This is a later-life compensation for when the mother hovered over him as a baby. It is a reversal and a replay of an aspect of traumatic bonding. It is an attempt at mastery of that which was suffocating. Think of the expression in English of the over-involved helicopter mom always hovering over her children. In the West, we at times share many similarities with these shame–honor cultures but to a different degree. In a shame–honor culture, the brother becomes obsessed with his sister's sexuality, as is mandated by the culture. The male who is charged with guarding the sexuality of the female is the brother who then grows up to become the father. Should the sister dishonor the family, her brother is tasked with taking her life in an honor killing.[55] It is culturally sanctioned domestic violence. A society can only advance as far as its females are genuinely free.

There are many converts to Islam who become radicalized. It can be surmised that they grew up in extremely dysfunctional, controlling, shame-oriented families. In the West we find pockets of shame–honor families. Perhaps Katherine Russell, Tamerlan's converted wife, came from just such a family. While they were upper middle class and her father a doctor, one wonders to what degree she may have been subtly and perhaps not so subtly controlled, manipulated, and emotionally abused. We speculate here because as of yet few details have emerged concerning her family history. However, it is well known that doctors can be notoriously controlling and exceedingly passive aggressive.[56] Furthermore, most likely there was some kind of an early problem in her personality formation that led her to seek out a man who was known to abuse her. We can further imagine that the message communicated to her by Tamerlan was that of the classically abused partner: if she were to leave him, he would kill her. This is a recycling of an early traumatic bonding with her mother, who may have been a devalued female as well.

Some readers may be more familiar with the specific terminology of shame–honor in Arab Muslim culture. Male honor is called *Sharaf*. It can be reinstated if lost, through willfully shedding blood, which functions as "cleansing" the stain of the shame brought upon the family, clan or tribe. It should also be noted that *Sharaf* is a term used to designate the bloodline descendants of the Prophet Muhammad. Recall the famous Egyptian actor Omar Sharif, his last name indicates a link to the holy lineage of the Prophet and shares the same root sh-r-f.

In contrast, female honor is called *'ird.* It means pubis, the anatomical site of the vagina. If the female's honor is stained, she must be killed, repudiated to the point of being erased from life. There are a series of words in Arabic for shame: *'Awrah, mahāshim* and more commonly *'ayb.* All three refer to private anatomical parts.[57] This is how the shame–honor culture functions. *'Awrah* comes from *'ār* and carries the connotation of an intense shame

> triggered by committing deeds that are in extreme opposition to moral values and social norms. Typical situations that lead one to feel it is betraying one's country or a single woman committing adultery. It is not unheard of in some rural areas in the Arab world that a father kills his daughter in public because she committed adultery. Moreover, 'ār is quite intense that can cause one to *commit suicide* [emphasis added]. One may put an end to his/her life to escape suffering. This is related to the fact that 'ār is everlasting. No matter what a person does he/she cannot undo the 'ār that is inflicted on him/her. If someone does something that classifies as 'ār, then dies, this 'ār will be associated with the name of his/her family forever.[58]

The following remarks concerning shame and honor in Chechen culture were obtained through a colleague who asked to remain anonymous but who spoke with native Chechen informants about how they talk about shame and honor. I am deeply grateful for his help in accessing this important information and for those Chechens who were willing to speak with him. For me to discuss the shame–honor dynamics is a complicated matter because it may be experienced as shaming. Here is a paraphrase of what Anonymous related to me:[59]

> "Honor" is called "Seey." When I asked my friend to give me an example of the use of this, she gave me something like: "She brought dishonor to her (enlarged) family". So I asked her, whether the concept could only be used in case of women who are perceived as having brought dishonor to their families (the entire tribe...). She answered that it could, in theory, also be a man. Meaning it is mostly used to blame women for wrong conduct... I can only guess what that means.
>
> "Shame" is called "eakh," where the "e" is like in "leg" and the "a" like in "dusk"—together they form a diphthong, like the "ee" sound and the "e" together form the "ye" in e.g. yes. (Or like the old Jewish grandmothers expressed their disapproval or disgust: Eakh!) Whether "eakh" also means body parts, I did not dare ask. I am not that close with the ladies... I would guess, though, it has something to do with that, as it does in other languages. Chechens are very modest. e.g., my good friend, a smart and strong lady, age 46, one of eight siblings, told me that she never saw her father without a shirt, even a t-shirt on. It is not done. *Girls would rather die of a busted bladder than go to the bathroom, if a man can see where they are heading... I had to move away from sight of bathrooms – many times* [emphasis mine].
>
> There is another phrase: "Yu arzha khwotina tsoh," meaning he (or she) brought shame/dishonor on the family (or on us). Obviously the roots of the two meaningful words have nothing to do with "eakh."
>
> Instead of "siy" one can also use the word "Yakh," which means a good, well behaved, respectful, honest, faithful, conscientious, tradition-observing person. It is close to the English concept of "decent" or, simply, "a good man" or "a good woman."

Another concept is guilt. It is called "bekhk." It is used together with the other ones, since bringing shame on the family equals being guilty of a major sin. It is also commonly used in the phrase: "bekhk mobil," which simply means "I am sorry" or "Excuse me, please." It is used in everyday talk both to attract somebody's attention or for asking permission to ask a question or assistance. But "bekhk" is also used in a moral and even legal context.

As I see it, the conceptual tools here shed a bit of light on the Chechen ancient tradition. Of course, a woman can bring dishonor on her family if she does not behave according to the rather strict rules. I did not dare ask, but I am afraid that a rape victim would also be seen as a shame on the whole tribe... That is, thank G-d, beginning to change in the last few years. Some women (their number is increasing) have begun approaching—i.e., my friends with stories of rape during the wars by Russian servicemen—and asking for psychological counseling and legal help. That lifts a bit of the stigma and also the sense of family shame. They begin to understand that they are victims of violence, just like their abducted, tortured, or killed husbands, fathers, and sons.

The first thing my Chechen friends talk about in discussing these concepts is Islam. But then they quickly move on to Chechen tradition. The two overlap to a certain extent, but I tend to believe that the real core set of values comes from their ancient tradition.

The Ingush (Ingushetia is the central region if the Caucasus) have the same traditions and also use the same words. The two languages are closely related and mixed marriages between the two nations are not rare. The Avars have been Moslems a few hundred years longer than the Chechens.

FANTASIES OF SHAME

A lot of valuable cultural and religious information is included in the passage above. I have drawn attention to the incident concerning the bathroom. This gesture of moving away in order not to shame the female who needs to relieve herself is instructive. But how might this then translate into political terrorism if applied to extremist families?

Terrorists, in creating explosive devices, may act out their cultural/religious inhibitions, terrors, and punishments by developing, for example, different kinds of bombs such as anal bombs. Although terrorism is now global and interlocks Chechens with other ethnic groups, still the underlying fantasies about the body in relation to the mother remain. Again, we are more alike as human beings than we are different. We all have the same basic needs, like going to the bathroom. We all have bathroom fantasies. We recall the anal explosive device that a Saudi Al Qaeda terrorist, Ibrahim al Asiri, created for his very own brother to insert into his rectum when approaching the head of Saudi security as a suicide bomber. He died and the target was injured. Asiri is the same terrorist who created the liquid explosive cited above. "During the anal stage, Freud believed that the primary focus of the libido was on controlling bladder and bowel movements. The major conflict at this stage is toilet training—the child has to learn to control his or her bodily needs. Developing this control leads to a sense of accomplishment and *independence* [emphasis mine]."[60] Furthermore, this area of the body and its orifices, which Freud called erotogenic zones, are highly eroticized for the young child. This entire experience links into later sexual experience. In sadomasochistic relationships of dominance and submission in which we know that anality plays a central role. (Putting bombs in the anus is a misuse of the anus, constituting perversion.)

According to Freud, successful attitudes at this stage are dependent on the way parents approach toilet training. Parents who utilize praise and rewards for using the toilet at the appropriate time encourage positive outcomes and help children feel capable and productive. Freud believed that positive experiences during this stage served as the basis for people to become competent, productive, and creative adults.

Thus, a psychological link to shame, which has a major impact on the bathroom fantasies that we have, are associated with shame–honor cultures. In psychological terms, shame and bathroom fantasies are distorted within an internal world of the mind that is filled with bad feelings such as deprivation, hatred, and repression if a child's normal anal fantasies are interrupted. In these countries people are not allowed to express themselves freely, so feelings are felt to be bad and disgusting, whereby affective experience becomes confused with feces.[61]

In these cultures it is common for people to feel shame before going to the bathroom because people will see how bad they are, that they smell (internally). Smell is one the most important senses that we have, especially for trauma-related matters, because it links to the first cranial nerve, which quickly transports us back to trauma. These primitive affects and defenses often get confused with urine and feces as a symbolic representation of repressed feelings. This confusion often arises very early on in the mind of the infant, who cannot distinguish good from bad when the mother's body didn't meet the baby's needs through nursing. In psychological terms this is known as the bad breast mother, one who was depriving and unavailable, as opposed to the good breast mother, one who supplies the baby with nurturance, delicious milk. This frustration is not tolerable and transmits to the baby that he is bad and that having needs is bad, which later leads to failure and humiliation in association with shame. This way of thinking needs to be "demythicized" so a woman does not have to be like a female camel, holding her bladder until she can urinate. Imagine how repressed fantasies play out with regard to their sexual needs. In order to help people caught in the vicious cycle of a shame–honor culture, simple things like demystifying one's bodily needs would be liberating and helpful.

We consider one more tragic example, again in Saudi Arabia, of how this relates to abused children. A well-known religious leader and television personality, Imam Fayhan al-Ghamdi, murdered his five-year-old daughter by torturing and abusing her. Under Sharia law he only had to pay blood money and half the price of what he would have had to pay if he had murdered his son. It was believed that he had raped her, although his reason for killing her is that she had lost her virginity, thus staining the family honor. Notice one gruesome detail in the description concerning her rectum: "Ghamdi confessed to torturing and killing his daughter. The girl's body showed evidence of a fractured skull, brain damage, repeated rapes, burns, beatings with whips and an iron, electrical shocks, a broken back, ribs and arm. *Reportedly, he also had sadistically sought to burn Lama's rectum closed* [emphasis mine]"[62]

The obsession with anal behavior feeds rage. As outlined by Klein, it stems from the inability to control and contain bodily waste, which is terrifying to a little child.[63] Anality, sadism, and cruelty join with uncontrollable rage, yielding a potent, explosive, unconscious mix. According to Klein, since the rage cannot be contained, it is projected outward onto others. That the Saudi father sought to burn this poor little girl's rectum closed signals that it was his obsession and his own inability to contain his own waste/rage that made him turn on his daughter. In my second book, *Penetrating the Terrorist Psyche*, I discuss how anal rape is repeatedly confused with sexual intercourse. Truck, car, and other suicide bombings involving vehicles act out this anal rape trauma in pantomime. Obsession with the anus verifies the perverse behavior and rage.

One other aspect of anality links back to our earlier discussion of ricin, sarin gas, and liquid explosives, which are all inevitable outcomes of a paranoiac's delusion that feces or "shit" is poison. The development of these explosives are a result of this type of obsession.

OTHER CULTURAL PRACTICES COMPOUNDING SHAME

In this section we rethink the meaning of shame in a shame–honor culture from a psychological point of view. We examine some cultural terms that are representative of Chechnya, the North Caucasus and its peoples, and how these terms create a narrative that reinforces shame–honor rather than leading to individual freedom and healthy living that allows a person, and especially a child, to have his needs met.

These terms will be briefly introduced in order to help refract terrorism through a cultural lens. As Matusitz asserts, terrorism is shaped by culture, while Ablow has emphasized that terrorism arises out of the crucible of the dysfunctional family who has lived in denial and paranoia, citing the Tsarnaevs as the prime example.[64] Thus, it is the family's cultural religious frame that gives rise to terrorism, including its shaming practices. Other cultural concepts that exist in the cultures of the Caucasus may not be familiar to the Westerner. However, since all cultures share certain universals, such as the need for food, to be taken care of, shelter etc., we can find approximates to these concepts, which help us to walk in the shoes of the Chechens and the terrorists they have unwittingly produced. Probably only five percent of the Chechen population engages in political terrorism, but the vein of terroristic shaming practices courses through family relations.

Part of the cultural *Erlebnis* of the Chechens involves pre-Islamic spiritual beliefs and practices that were assimilated into its first conquering religion—Christianity—which was then conquered by Islam, forming a kind of syncretism:

As we have mentioned, the eye figures prominently in shaming a person. In pre-Islamic Caucasus, there is the mythical character called the Nart, a one-eyed giant whose image is like that of a cyclops, linking vision and surveillance to terror, hostage taking or fusion and force. The Narts captured and chained hostages. In *Penetrating the Terrorist Psyche*, I discuss at length the quasi fascination and obsession that Muslim cultures, especially in the Middle East, have for the evil eye. The symbolic evil eye is associated with the accusatory eye of the mother. The charismatic draw to a one-eyed being facilitates the projection of its followers' shameful feelings onto the defective charismatic creature.[65] It makes the followers feel more powerful in fantasy than their leader, a kind of sado-masochism replay on fantasy. We may surmise that such is the case with the Nart. "The Chechens have their own versions of the Nart Sagas, common to most peoples in the Caucasus…"[66]

According to Chechen tradition, the mythical tribe of Amazon warrior women originally came from the Caucasus.[67] Themes such as rape and redemption; the outlaw as werewolf or she-wolf; the nameless finest maiden, an Amazon-like warrior who can appear on horseback; the folk motif of a young wife and old husband; Setenaya, a temptress sorceress, vs. the fertile wise mother—all are imbued with the predominant underlying theme of fending off shame while handling aggression and containing these shameful feelings in fantasy. However, with the making of a terrorist beginning in early childhood, the feelings of impotence and the repudiation of the mother become imbricated in such mythology. The scary beings may help to tip the scales of a negative, rageful, persecutory personality whose volcanic iceberg mentality explodes later on in life.

MOTHER'S MILK: A CULTURAL OBSESSION?

We learn from folklore that "mother's milk stands for kinship in the Caucasus as well as in Iran, and the kiss of mother's milk can signify the renunciation of a kinship bond."[68] Colarusso notes about Chwadlazhwiya's folk tale, "This saga…tells the adventure of a youth who sets off to learn the fate of his missing father and by doing so attains heroic manhood. *It offers a vivid example of a smothering mother* [emphasis mine], a well-meaning woman who will not willingly acquiesce in her child's ambitions."[69] In *Penetrating the Terrorist Psyche*, I noted a similar obsession with mother's milk for Somali culture and its terrorists. Somalia means "go milk the camel." Shame–honor cultural environments are rife with deprivation, which Melanie Klein would characterize as the bad breast. This oppression is not only psychological; it is also physical. Dunking one's head into fermented mare's milk is a cultural ritual that underscores the maternal obsession. Putin dunked his head in the milk as well.[70] Quite literally, the unconscious must be immersed in the maternal. We may include this image of head in milk as symbolic of a fusional state with the mother. It is different from dunking your head for apples on Halloween as a child.

THE ABREK: HOW REBELLION AGAINST THE MOTHER IS NEUTRALIZED

In addition to the Narts, the people of the Caucasus have a custom of taking in and harboring the outlaw or wanderer, who is called an abrek. The abreks came to be characterized as outcasts of their clans. Like in the biblical cities of sanctuary, they were able to seek refuge and hospitality. Yet because blood vengeance structures and controls aggression, the most vulnerable are placed at risk. An identification with the aggressor is reinforced within this patriarchal structure. Women are rarely considered to be an abrek.

KIDNAPPING AND HOSTAGE TAKING AS A BUSINESS

Large sums of money were made in Chechnya through ransoming of kidnapped business owners. Kidnapping has a long-standing tradition and practice in the North Caucasus. Politkovskaya links the practice to the abrek, who has been romanticized in the culture as a kind of Robin Hood or a "noble bandit who resists authority."[71]

The Russians also had the custom of taking hostages; they took Jemaluddin and Imam Shamil's son hostage. Alexander II conquered the Caucasus and placed their great Chechen leader, Shamil under house arrest in St. Petersburg, which was perceived as a great humiliation.[72] Hostage taking as a psychological dynamic harkens back to the recreation of the maternal relationship in a state of merger. Hostage taking is also an initial stage of murder–suicide. In order to commit murder–suicide, the murderer must seize the victim as hostage before committing suicide, so that the murderer is victimizer. "Women would snatch at a [Russian Cossack] soldier and throw themselves and the soldiers over the cliff in the mountain passes."[73] This is an underlying template, which female suicide bombers from Chechnya can act out. It is part of the cultural/religious repertoire.

Yet if this image of women snatching soldiers seems passé and not relevant to Islamic suicide terrorism, one needs to consider what happened recently in Moscow at the Duma, its parliament:

> A Russian nationalist party leader and a Duma MP from Chechnya began a brawl after failing to settle an argument over a monument to the 19th-century war in the Caucasus. The fight ended abruptly after the Chechen politician dropped a golden pistol.... The monument, which was opened personally by the head of the Chechen Republic, Ramzan Kadyrov, in September this year, is dedicated to the memory of those who fought against the Tsarist Russian army in 1819. *It especially glorifies the heroism of 46 girls who, according to local chronicles and legends, were taken prisoner, but jumped into a mountain river from a bridge taking several Russian soldiers with them, killing themselves and their enemies* [emphasis mine].
>
> The monument caused a wave of criticism in Russia. Journalists and historians doubted the veracity of the original story and the Officers of Russia NGO insisted on retaliation by installing a monument to General Aleksey Yermolov—the commander of Russian forces in the Caucasus War.
>
> Also in September Aleksey Zhuravlyov addressed Russia's Prosecutor General with an official parliamentary request to study the legality of the Dadi-Yurt monument. He wrote that the wide resonance around the story raised suspicions that the memorial was stirring up ethnic hatred—a criminal offense in Russia. "The attempts to revalue and praise some distant and ambivalent history pages are fertile soil for the seeds of extremism and separatist moods," Zhuravlyov wrote. When the two MPs met in the State Duma elevator hall on Tuesday afternoon, Delimkhanov started shouting threats, saying that Zhuravlev should not have written any request and that "everything

> would now end badly," Zhuravlev told Kommersant. Also, according to the Rodina [the name of the Russian political party, which ironically means "motherland"] head, the Chechen MP attempted to punch him in the head and after this a brawl started between the politicians with involvement of their aides and bodyguards.[74]

The extreme degree to which the Chechen narrative is invested in the females sacrificing themselves while murdering Russians is part and parcel of the fabric of the collective identity. Interlocking conflicts like the one between the Russians and the Chechens fall short in mutually understanding how both sides, which embrace shame–honor in their cultures, use and manipulate the female. The drama here is really about protecting the mother. The little boy who witnesses his mother being abused feels impotent to protect her and himself. The image of fusion runs unconsciously deep. If we were able to read it more thoughtfully, we might be able to deescalate the violence and understand the childhood drivers that carry over into political violence.

BRIDE STEALING–A FUSION WITH THE MOTHER

Bride stealing is a subset of hostage taking or kidnapping. Psychologically, its imagery creates a forced fusion or attachment with the other—bonding through assault. The kidnapper forces himself upon the female. This is an expression of the repetition compulsion of traumatic bonding with the mother, played out later in life with a different female. To the best of my knowledge, I know of no expert on hostage crises who has addressed the underlying unconscious dynamic of hostage taking and how the cultural practice informs terrorist behavior. This lack of attention to unconscious nonverbal behavior hampers effective solutions to cultural practices, which impact negatively on the mind and body. Part of the problem arises in the developmental deficit of lacking empathy and the psychopathology of borderline behavior. We can imagine that hostage taking reenacts a trauma that occurred in the early maternal fusion where the baby felt at the mercy of the mother. Upon moving into adolescence and adulthood, one owns the other and hence controls the object. It is misuse of the person as a support object for a fragile and highly paranoid personality. In its most extreme forms, it can end in murder–suicide.

The cultural practice of bride stealing is used as a threat by parents to regulate a daughter's behavior. In the Kumyk clan in the Caucasus, a daughter was told by her parents, "You had better come home now, otherwise an Avar (opposing clan) man will stop by and take you along with him to the mountains."[75] The Avars took over the land of the Kumyks in Dagestan and have assumed the top jobs. Zubeidat Tsarnaeva, the mother of Tamerlan and Dzhokhar, is an Avar and a member of the Kumyk clan, as was Shamil, the eighteenth century Muslim military hero.

THE TRADITIONAL ROLE OF WOMEN

Mat Ogni is the Chechen term for "keeper of the home fires," or "guardian of the hearth," which is the name given to the traditional Chechen Woman.[76] Another significant expression is that "paradise is at the feet of the mother." Arab Muslims also have this saying Patima Suleimanova, the aunt with whom Tamerlan stayed while in Dagestan, was quoted as saying that Tamerlan "knew that heaven was at the mother's feet, and he would tell that to his sisters."[77]

Baiev, the Chechen surgeon who wrote *The Oath: A Surgeon under Fire*, was also helped by Tamerlan's aunt when he first came to Boston. He claims the following concerning the role of women in Chechen society:

> Some westerners may assume that all Muslim countries are the same, and that women in Chechnya are oppressed, as they were by the Taliban in Afghanistan. That is not true. Chechen women are educated and have professions. Education is a positive legacy from Soviet times. Often women stay at home because we have large families without such conveniences as

> washing machines and dishwashers. Women usually cover their heads with scarves outside in the street—such traditions help preserve our cultures. Without them, we will disappear as a nation, our traditions are the glue that hold us together especially in the chaotic times when everything is falling apart.[78]

According to Ro'i, who writes of the role of women in Islamic Central Asia, although the Caucasus are not part of Central Asia they have a similar attitude. Due to the shortage of men, polygamy was practiced—including leverage marriage, where the widow of the brother who is killed is married off to her brother-in-law.[79] Adolescent girls were married off in Muslim rural society when their school studies ended upon reaching puberty.[80] Ro'i notes that "All these diversions from customary Soviet legal practice demonstrate the *tenacity* [emphasis mine] of social custom and public opinion."[81] Society and clan pressure could be great. Because so many are descendants of those forced into exile in Central Asia, Kazakhstan and Kyrgystan, the Chechens were exposed to these cultural practices of their Muslim brethren.

According to local custom, the husband's word is law in the home,[82] yet often the husband defers to his wife. In the case of those extremists who practice polygamy, better called polygyny, the father is often absent and the husband is ineffective; he is a symptom of the underlying problem of having been a male baby who was the object by which his mother gained her first taste of honor. While preferred as a cultural remedy for the small number of available men for marriage, especially when there has been a war, polygyny has also been the source of conflicts that arise between the more senior and younger wives: "One Soviet writer noted in the late 1960s that presumably senior wives who sought to shift household chores on junior or less favored ones or among intelligentsia …*of their own accord*"[83] [emphasis mine].

In defiance of the entire male population, the women of the Kumyk clan launched a protest defending their men against the Russians.[84] Despite this group protest, it does not signify that Kumyk females have individual psychological power. The group in a shame–honor culture persists to dominate the individual psyche so group actions occur that can falsely give the impression of independence for the female. It still remains a group effort.

According to Chechen physician Baiev, the father does not necessarily attend the birth of the baby. He writes concerning the birth of his first child: "I didn't attend the birth itself on October 31, 1993. Birth in our country is a private matter between women."[85] In fact, Baiev goes on to say that for the birth of his second child, it should have been his *brother* [emphasis added] who accompanied his wife to the hospital as was the custom, not himself. He goes on to note that "war forces people to ignore traditions."[86] While I would assume that some men do in fact attend the birth of their children, generally we can surmise that it is more optimal for both parents to be present at the birth. The baby is cognizant and can smell his or her parents, initiating bonding.

In Central Asia and the Caucasus there has been the long-standing cultural practice of women and young girls who have been victims of domestic violence committing suicide by immolation. Statistics are not kept and obtaining information is further complicated by its being a shame–honor culture, making it a difficult subject to research.[87] "The most flagrant of all violations of Soviet law and order, however, was perhaps the self-immolation of women. Strictly speaking, this custom could not in any way be portrayed as religious, Islam being unequivocal in its condemnation of suicide. The original logic informing this practice was apparently that to avoid compromising her class or family, a woman or girls who had been dishonored had no alternative to taking her own life."[88] A female committing suicide in Chechnya was once rare but "[it] is more common, sometimes because of stress-related spousal abuse."[89] Death by suicide becomes normalized for the sake of shame, not honor. Honor is a pseudo mask to hide deep shame and terror of vulnerability and needs along with inability to express anger in appropriate nonviolent ways.

While Baiev's characterization of women is correct with regard to education, he fails to understand the implication that education does not necessarily guarantee a healthy maternal bond because if it is set within the frame of a shame–honor culture, the female is under unbelievable stress concerning issues of sexuality and control. We know from Western cultural practices concerning domestic violence that educated women can easily become the target of abuse and perhaps are all the more vulnerable, since who would believe that the husband of an educated woman could be an abuser?[90] It is a false assumption that education guarantees there will not be an environment ripe for abuse. The abuser, most often a male, has been "educated" by the clan of the shame–honor culture that it is permissible to hate and abuse females.

Big families also become problematic because, though I speculate based on object relations theory and my own clinical experience, big families generally mean less quality time per baby and more chaos vis à vis object stability in the family. It is as if the mother gives up interest in the baby as the baby begins to assert his or her own autonomy through walking and talking. The mother feels that she is losing control. I have treated a series of women who had numerous siblings, ranging from ten to sixteen, and each poignantly described the chaos in which they grew up. There also tended not to be healthy boundaries in these big families. The mother is exhausted and the older children begin to assume the role of proxy mother at far too young an age, often manipulating and taunting their younger charges. None of this is optimal for maternal attachment. In addition, the child-rearing strategies employed in large families tend to revolve around shaming, which in turn teaches the young child to blame the other. This does not allow the child to learn to assume personal responsibility. It facilitates externalizing aggression and rage. This compromises the maternal attachment. Unfortunately, the psychological impact of shame in a shame–honor culture is that the development of the baby is often minimized.

LONG-STANDING TRADITIONS AND CUSTOMS

Besides shame, Chechens have the custom of parading their sorrow before the family as a gesture of solidarity.[91] Envy is another prevalent notion. It precipitates attacking in a shame–honor environment. Chechens are envious of Dagestan because Chechnya is a landlocked "trapped" country, whereas Dagestan is located on the Caspian Sea.[92]

The Chechens have a long tradition of fighting. Alexander Dumas, who created the legendary tale of *The Three Musketeers*, wrote about the Chechens and their weapons after he visited and traveled through the Caucasus in 1858. This was when they were fighting the Russian Tsar: "All the mountain fighters are fanatically brave and whatever money they acquire is spent on weapons. A Chechen … May be literally in rags, but his swords, dagger and gun are the finest quality."[93] The *kinjal* or dagger is their favorite weapon and it is tied to ch'ia, the blood feud and revenge.

Islam made the Chechens different from the Russians. They are not Christian or Eastern Orthodox. Islam facilitated communal identity by adding another layer so that they were not just Chechen but also Muslim.[94] Jihad means "warring" in Arabic, literally "struggle." It appears 42 times in the Quran.[95] Modern interpretation has tried to give it a more positive spin and has whitewashed it as a "personal struggle." However, if one examines the sacred text of the Quran, its meaning involves violence, slaughter, and killing the infidel in order to spread Islam. It is understood by many scholars, especially Princeton's eminent Professor Emeritus Bernard Lewis, that Islam is not just a religion but also a political movement.

Islam continues to spread in three ways: through the demographics of having large families with many wives, what the neurocriminologist Adrian Raine would identify as spreading the "selfish" gene to reproduce;[96] by the sword or through terrorist attacks to weaken the will of the enemy so that he will submit; and by conversion. Here I would hasten to add "forced" because when there is so much violence, it becomes difficult to subscribe to a notion of "free will." After all, terrorist attacks are used to manipulate and instill terror into the hearts of the infidels to win them over, to force them to convert. Because of Islam's history of conquest and violence, it is hard to ascertain the meaning of conversion by free will when 96 percent of the world terrorist attacks have been perpetrated by Islamic terrorists since 1970.[97]

Ghazawat is an Arabic term meaning military raids and ambushes. It was appropriated during the Islamic conquest of the Caucasus region and is often viewed as the preferred Chechen term for jihad. Psychologically speaking, an attack such as ambushing is a strategic way of bonding through violence.

Taken from Arab culture into Islamic legend is the jinn, the spirit who is summoned to do someone's biding—essentially a proxy. In *The Banality of Suicide Terrorism*, I raise the dynamic of proxy as the epitome of passive-aggressive terrorism. The suicide bomber is essentially a proxy. Suicide bombing allows one not to take responsibility and for the group to manipulate the weak. The proxy purges the group of its rage. The idea of the jinn instills and normalizes the passive-aggressive behavior template to embrace and even venerate other cultural and religious proxies such as Islamic suicide bombers.

Because Chechen culture and tradition have been predicated on shame–honor, Islam has proved a very good fit with this preexisting cultural agenda. It is very difficult to criticize religion because of political correctness. However, political correctness has a psychological function: to inhibit inquiry and shield the object of inquiry from taking a critical look at its psychodynamics.

The mosque, in analytic terms, represents the mother, especially the womb, the safe haven for Muslims. The mosque becomes a maternal holding environment that was absent in the early bonding attachment with the mother. Under the guise of protection, it also represents the paternal sword that will protect them from all evil. However, despite the truth of this symbolism, there is much role/identity confusion between who is the feeding mother to nurture a deprived starving child and who is to protect them from danger and evils—e.g., the infidels. Because a shame–honor culture privileges the group over the individual, one must be in sync with the group. The group manifests itself in the centrality of the mosque, the epicenter for keeping the group fused and intact. The group has a primary attachment to the sacred space of the mosque. It is the consummate maternal object to be protected, though as we have seen in warring among different kinds of Muslims it can be a site of attack, hence repudiating the mother.

Because of identity confusion resulting from the nature of the maternal bond, the males have internalized a feminine side of their own needs, which they must deny as it reminds them of the female. Therefore, their masculinity predominates by ruling the female. However, it is an illusion because their need for the female is so great that the theme of the female and the maternal haunt their lives. This can be seen in the male's relationship to "place." We know from psychogeography[98] that a place represents the maternal. Even though the mosque is almost exclusively dominated by males, the mosque represents the unconscious male wish and need to remain attached to the mother. It is as if the mosque gives the illusion of the paternal because it is always swarming with men. But this image masks the mosque's hidden maternal base. The battle cry "Allahu Akhbar", God is Greater, is a cry for the father but at the site of the mother, revealing a need for both parents. Ironically an Iranian rapper's album cover of a famous mosque elucidates their symbolic understanding of the mosque as a breast with a fledgling, flagging penis. I blogged at Family Security Matters about "The Mosque as Mother."[99] The men are in perpetual need of attaching to objects throughout the day, ranging from being obsessed with their sister's sexual purity, or a hard object like a weapon, or a place like the mosque. They are in constant search of the mother unconsciously because they are wed to her but fear losing her. The relationships in a shame–honor clan are completely enmeshed by Western standards. They are reminiscent of the borderline personality. That is why the themes of freedom and death course through their culture.

IN BRIEF: WHAT WE KNOW ABOUT CHECHEN VIOLENCE

Violence arises out of a combination of genetics, biology, the brain and the maternal attachment early in life. This book seeks to give a kind of CT scan or MRI of the terrorist behavior and his relations with others by examining a series of famous Chechen terrorist attacks and what they symbolize unconsciously about the culture and problems in adaptation, particularly the problem of gaining freedom from the mother, who is experienced as suffocating and smothering in the frame of a shame–honor culture. We can read the jihadis violent behavior in light of early childhood. To do so is to understand the root causes of the problem.

A shame–honor environment entails a unique social configuration in which the female is at the eye of the storm. The male is dominant and yet he is bound to the female, actually his mother. The female has been abused—psychologically, physically, and often sexually—as she is related to as an object, not a real person in her own right. Furthermore, there is a cultural prohibition for the male baby: He is not permitted to separate from his mother and instead is permanently infantilized. The mother, who has already internalized male rage toward the female, gains her honor by giving birth to her first son. This is part of the package of alleged honor. The men have honor by guarding the part object of the females in their families—namely the site of her sex, deeming it pure. If the male loses control over his females that is a loss of honor or brings him shame. For the female, her site of sexuality, the vagina, is unconsciously perceived as terrifying; hence it is dirty or contaminated and thus embodies shame. It is scary to the male, who is terrified of the female body. Terrorists cannot understand how they could be born from a devalued female body. It is a conundrum they defend against through rage and pseudo honor. They experienced traumatic bonding. Their maternal attachment was fraught with unconscious conflict, compounded by physical abuse that included neglect. The cultural and religious sanctions making violence permissible backfire in developmental terms because they do not permit a child to grow up.

A good example of how problematic child-rearing practices and a dysfunctional family yields criminality and jihadis is provided in the observation made in a Denmark Court by a former juvenile delinquent, who is Palestinian Muslim:

> Yahya Hassan, an 18-year-old Palestinian-Danish poet, has attributed high criminality rates among Danish youths with migrant Muslim backgrounds to poor Muslim parenting. Hassan, who entered an institution at age 13 after several years of juvenile delinquency, complained of watching "our fathers passively rot on the couch with the remote in their hands, living off state benefits, accompanied by a disillusioned mother who never put her foot down." Muslim youth "who became criminals and bums…weren't let down by the system, but by our parents." Although Hassan has not faced any Section 266b prosecutions, numerous graphic death threats have appeared at the Facebook page of a television show in which he appeared.[100]

While Hassan is not from Chechnya, he is part of the global Ummah, Muslim community, and his words may help in part to understand how ineffective the fathers are—to wit, Anzor Tsarnaev. Hassan comments on how the mother fails to set limits vis à vis her son. She fears the "little monster" she has created, her own "terrorist" son, because she also falls under his authority. He could murder her if she breaches societal norms. Her own grandiosity and use of her son as her omnipotent narcissistic object has not helped matters either. She felt empowered when he was a baby. She finally had power over a penis.

REVENGE KILLINGS/VENDETTAS AND HONOR KILLINGS

According to neurocriminologist Adrian Raine in *The Anatomy of Violence: The Biological Roots of Crime*, revenge killings can be characterized as reactive murders, differing from more cold-blooded murders. There can, of course, be a mix. Describing revenge killing, he writes: "Someone gets really upset by an insult, and in response they set about carefully getting their own back, they are indeed reacting to a slight but they plan their sweet revenge carefully and thoughtfully, and obtain satisfaction in doing so—a psychological gain. *They are not unlike terrorists who react to a sociopolitical, ideological insult by carefully planning a counterattack* [emphasis mine]."[101]

Earlier in his book Raine cites the Munduruccu Amazon basin tribe, which engages in revenge killings. This culture participates in the *forced appropriation of women* [emphasis mine]. Thirty percent of the males murder. Revenge killing is common and can take place over a series of days. Often the revenge is about *sexual jealousy* [emphasis mine].[102] Does this sound familiar in ways to Western culture's domestic violence or Chechen honor killings? They share commonalities.

Let us take a closer look at Chechen culture. Psychologist A. Speckhard has done forensic analysis of the Black Widows, the female suicide bombers: "All the Chechen suicide bombers that we conducted psychological autopsies on (over half of the total) had lost a family member traumatically to the two wars but the women had lost not only husbands, but brothers and fathers as well—so many were widows, but some were simply traumatically bereaved and seeking revenge. For Chechens this was the first time that women had been involved in *revenge seeking behaviors* [emphasis mine]—a domain in Chechen culture usually reserved only for the men." [103] In addition, Speckhard asserts that the jihadis are suffering from post-traumatic stress.

Baiev also states that Chechens suffer from post-traumatic stress disorder.[104] Generally PTSD is later developmentally and thus overlooks the underlying time-frame for traumatic bonding, the first years of life. Neither Baiev or

Speckhard mention the ramification of child-rearing practices in a shame–honor culture in which you are essentially shamed from birth if you are female. Being brought up in a shame–honor society with revenge killing at its heart places the female under undeniable stress and the projected terrors of the revenge seekers. We can add to that war and an unconscious matricide prominent in shame–honor cultures, which inevitably hampers nursing and maternal attachment. Murphy, in his *Allah's Angels*, makes a significant observation: "Mothers have difficulty lactating. According to Aida Ailarova, the UNICEF psychosocial recovery officer in Chechnya, every third child in 2008 showed pronounced symptoms of post-traumatic stress disorder (PTSD)."[105]

There are several points to be made. First, it is not true that the Black Widows, the female suicide bombers, marked the first time in Chechen history that women sought revenge. As we have already noted, there is a long-standing tradition in Chechen history of women committing suicide by attacking, taking momentary hostage of Russian soldiers, and then jumping over mountain precipices with them to their deaths.

Meier writes in his *Chechnya: To the Heart of the Matter*, "The Russians stopped each car, scoured the occupants' papers and searched the trunk. They feared the suicide bombers who had taken to blowing up their checkpoints and barracks with regularity. The tactic of turning your body into a bomb may have come from the Middle East, but the Chechens made a significant advancement in the technique. Long before Palestinian women and girls joined the bombers' ranks, Chechen women had done so."[106]

A common phrase found in Chechen jihad writings articulates the centrality of the concept of revenge such as "in revenge for our brothers and sisters."[107] Baiev described how a blood vendetta works:

> Blood vendettas are a way of life in Chechnya, a time-honored method of justice practiced for centuries, although during Soviet times the KGB tried to put a stop to them. Vendettas were the community's way of dealing with crime.

> For example, if a drunk driver kills someone it is considered murder. The relatives and clan members of the accused bring him before a large assembly of relatives and people from the clan of the deceased. He wears a black felt cloak, and his head is covered in a white veil symbolizing his readiness to pay for what he did. The family may kill him or forgive him, in which case the veil is removed and he is set free. However, with forgiveness comes the obligation of the acquitted to offer compensation to the victim's family. There are even cases where the accused is taken into the family as their surrogate son. "I have not lost my son; I have found him again," the *mother* says [emphasis mine].
>
> Women play an important role in keeping the peace. Men must stop fighting if a woman removes her scarf and throws it on the ground between the antagonists. This gesture can take place at a specially convened group of the family and elders involved, or spontaneously in the street to break up a brawl.[108]

The mother's proclamation of losing her son underscores the mutual separation anxiety they share in their maternal merger.

Gammer relates that weapons signify Chechen manhood and *freedom* [emphasis mine].[109] They would not disarm in 1925. We know what a weapon means psychoanalytically in Freudian terms—a phallus—while in Kleinian terms it demonstrates an attachment to a hard object that symbolizes a replacement for the mother and the object owner's ambivalent relationship with her. In another shame–honor culture, that of the Kingdom of Jordan, a similar anecdote was related when the Jordanian parliament attempted to pass a bill to disarm men and keep weapons such as a the pistol at home because of high rates of honor killings. The leader of the opposition party to King Abdullah, Dr. Ahmad Uwajdi al Abbadi, a prominent Bedouin, said that he could never surrender his handgun because he slept with it under his pillow at night.[110] This is another image of maternal fusion, where literally a hard, autistic-type object lies at the center of the unconscious, indicating a cognitive deficit in interpersonal relations as well as a trauma in bonding. While children have their teddy bears, men in shame–honor cultures have their hard weapons, an expression of a maternal deficit in attachment.

The president of Chechnya recently came out in favor of honor killing. It is similar to the practice in the Middle East of the woman being a piece of property, with her value residing in her vagina and its purity. The Chechen women were extremely concerned to hear of the president's position on honor killing.[111]

> ACHXOY-MARTAN, Chechnya—Chechnya's government is openly approving of families that kill female relatives who violate their sense of honor, as this Russian republic embraces a fundamentalist interpretation of Islam after decades of religious suppression under Soviet rule. In the past five years, the bodies of dozens of young Chechen women have been found dumped in woods, abandoned in alleys and left along roads in the capital, Grozny, and neighboring villages. Chechen President Ramzan Kadyrov publicly announced that the dead women had "loose morals" and were rightfully shot by male relatives. He went on to describe women as the property of their husbands, and said their main role is to bear children. "If a woman runs around and if a man runs around with her, both of them should be killed," said Mr. Kadyrov, who often has stated his goal of making Chechnya "more Islamic than the Islamists."[112]

BLIND SPOTS IN UNDERSTANDING THE MOTIVATION FOR VIOLENCE

BLIND SPOT #1: DEBUNKING REVENGE AS A PSYCHOLOGICAL MOTIVATION FOR VIOLENCE

A psychologist as researcher who is examining the motivation for a suicide bomber that has been proffered as a revenge killing cannot leave the discussion at this superficial level with the attitude that each culture gets to enforce its own cultural norms. In doing so, does not the Western psychologist show a lack of empathy, and perhaps due to his own sadomasochism even disclose his unconscious, perverse need to identify with the perpetrator—the revenge seeker? Although the world is shrinking more and more, not all cultural practices in Eastern cultures transfer to acceptable human norms in Western culture—like sex trafficking, child marriage, female genital mutilation, or honor killing.

This raises the issue of revenge killing as a "reasonable" motivation and explanation for those suffering from post traumatic stress. The psychologist claim is that it is the psychological motivation for jihadi attacks and the treatment of the female. Just because an interviewee may claim that the motivation is revenge killing does not mean that we should automatically believe what we are told. A dose of skepticism may be in order, as A. Lankford in his *Myth of Martyrdom* has noted.[113] However, not all members of a clan who suffer the loss of relatives resort to revenge killing, which targets innocent individuals. Does not such a skewed justification diminish the standing of those who do not seek revenge by adhering to the code of shame–honor? The cultural demand and expectation that one spill blood can only encourage violence and stunt psychological and developmental growth. Psychologically this shame–honor dynamic infantilizes both the male and female.

Scholars dealing with the problem of terrorism find themselves trapped at a superficial level in unraveling the Gordian knot of political violence when they limit their understanding to this laissez-faire rationale for motivation of a revenge crime. It does not allow one to look beyond the confines of tactical and strategic measures. By and large, experts have been forced to limit their explorations and theories to political motivation. This fails to take into account unconscious behavior. Terrorists are highly dissociated. That means that the characterological problem has arisen early in the development of their personality, before the age of three. Chechnya provides us with a good example. First, the aim was a nationalist separatist movement to free itself from Russia, then the struggle became linked to global jihad.

Strikingly enough, Hanna Segal, a well-known object relations psychoanalyst who was a student of Melanie Klein,[114] reminds us that, similar to the Afghans, the Chechens were our friends in their fight to disengage from the Russians. She writes:

> I think September 11 was highly symbolic. We have been precipitated into a world of fragmentation, and at points total disintegration and *psychotic terror* [emphasis mine]—and also into total confusion: Who are our friends? Who are our enemies? From what quarter do we expect aggression? Old enemies, like Soviet Russia and Northern Alliance fundamentalist groups [once supported by the USSR] are now our friends. Old friends could be enemies—Chechnya, for example. And are there enemies on the inside?
>
> The same confusion can be seen in the Arab world. The spreading fragments of a collapsing empire were felt all over the world and imbued with evil like the plague. This is the most primitive terror in our personal development—not ordinary death, but some vision of personal disintegration imbued with hostility. And the situation is made much worse when God comes into the equation. The fundamentalist Christian longing for Armageddon is now matched by Islamic fundamentalism. Our sanity is threatened by a delusional inner world of omnipotence and absolute evil and sainthood. Unfortunately, we also have to contend with the God Mammon.[115]

My previous books have attempted to deepen the understanding of the limitations for keeping "political violence" sacrosanct, as if its specialness does not have to account for unconscious psychopathology. Violence is violence; it does not care how we label it. Violence is also extremely grandiose, showing its omnipotence. Because a suicide attack is considered a crime, Raine has demonstrated that it then has a psychopathology. Its psychodynamics can be examined, which means problems in early childhood development. As Raine has further shown, the underpinnings of violence are heavily influenced by biology, the brain, genetics, and the mind–body connection. He even acknowledges the importance of the early childhood environment. From the work of Margaret Mahler, we know that the psychological birth of the baby is a process unto itself.[116] When we look at the psychological birth of a baby, it stands to reason cultural practices also inform its development.

A well known lyrical Chechen song "The High Mountains" reveals the infantile deprivation and its accompanying omnipotent despair, which the collective identity feels:

> You are standing high, oh ye mountains!
> You are spreading far and wide, oh ye mountains!
> How many starving orphans have found refuge
> On the cliffs that cut through the clouds...
> Oh, if I could only share the grief of my heart
> With the blue sky, the sky would drop down
> To the sprawling expanses of oceans and deserts–
> So much grief I hold in my breast![117]

I have been noting ramifications of Chechen shame–honor practices, sketching them out briefly to help us understand the psychological underpinnings of Chechen jihadi identity. I suggest some additional blind spots below that complicate and inhibit better understanding of the violence. Of course, there may be many more, and I would welcome hearing from you, the reader, at nhkobrin1@gmail.com.

BLIND SPOT 2: THE COUNTERTRANSFERENCE OF DENIAL MASKING TERROR

In psychoanalysis there is a very important and useful concept called countertransference. It is defined as "redirection of a psychotherapist's feelings toward a client—or, more generally, as a therapist's emotional entanglement with a client."[118] It entails a projection of unconscious feelings into the other. As a result, the therapist may act out what the patient is trying to communicate in a nonverbal manner and by doing so retrospectively understands what the dissociated patient was experiencing. Countertransference may be brought into the field of counterterrorism as a way of examining reactions to terrorist behavior. All too often law enforcement, the targeted enemy and even psychological researchers studying terrorism may develop a countertransference with their subject material without being aware of it, thereby skewing the analysis. Here are some more instances in which a countertransference blind spot may arise. By being aware of the parameters of the problem, one can be more effective in establishing long-lasting and productive interventions. Therefore, it is particularly important for those dealing with terrorism to know the culture and language and factor this into their analysis.

BLIND SPOT 3: RUSSIA AS A SHAME-HONOR CULTURE

The Russians have the saying: "If you live with wolves you must howl with them."[119] There has been considerable bias and unjust treatment of the Chechens by the Russians, who have often portrayed them as mafiosos and criminals, and now as jihadis as the region has become more Islamized. The majority of the Chechens are good people, but it has been easy for Russia to posture against the Chechens, given the history of the tzars and conquest.

Baiev records the relationship between the Russians and the Chechens: "History had taught us to expect attacks from Russia. But now that one actually had happened, we found it hard to accept. For more than seventy years, we had lived under Soviet rule. We were all supposed to be Soviet people, living in harmony, and many of us had good Russian friends. How could Russia bomb its own citizens? How could it bomb Grozny where half the inhabitants were Russian?"[120]

According to a 2013 internet article, "Russia is trying to control a simmering deadly insurgency in its mountainous North Caucasus, and Dagestan has become the most violent region with near daily killings of police, government officials, religious leaders and journalists. However locals and rights activists have also accused the Russian authorities of a heavy-handed approach to counterterrorist operations including of blasting residential houses and extrajudicial arrests."[121]

The Cossacks also hated the Russians. Putin crushed the separatist movement in Chechnya so it just moved next door into Dagestan where, as of this writing, the war still rages. There were two wars during the 1990s that were reminiscent of Somalia. Tens of thousands were killed. It then became Islamized or Palestinized by Al Qaeda, who joined the "insurgency" and went into the forest.

There is long-standing mutual hatred between the Chechens and the Russians. Yemolov is quoted as saying, "The only good Chechen is a dead Chechen."[122] The Russians gave the name Caucasus to the region, meaning mountain of languages.[123] There are more than 55 languages in this one region, in which it was common to go from one village to the next and not be able to speak the language. Pliny quoted Timosthenes, who recorded that the ancient Greeks counted 300 separate languages of the Caucasus. According to a myth, God stumbled while dividing the nationalities and spilled far too many in the mountains. However, it was Arabic that became the linguistic glue for uniting village to village through the holy language of the Quran.[124]

The Russians called the Chechens by an ethnic slur—"the Black Faces."[125] Given the trauma of the forced deportations in the 1940s it is understandable how the cultural V-spot[126] (the area of greatest psychic vulnerability, a concept coined by J. Lachkar) of this now chosen and memorialized wound has hampered reconciliation with the Russians. The Chechens have been locked in war with Russia for over three centuries. It has been characterized as the fight between the Lone Wolf—the Chechens, and the Bear—Mother Russia. The fact that the Russian culture is to a significant degree a shame–honor culture like Chechnya has also exacerbated the intractable conflict since neither side could disengage from violence. The Russians are not the focus of this study, but it should be noted that like in Afghanistan against another Muslim people, the Russians also engaged in brutal retaliatory behaviors and were much less concerned or accountable with regard to human rights issues.

Russia remains a shame–honor, highly authoritarian, militaristic culture. Stalin is still venerated. When the mountaineering division was in Chechnya, they invented Russian roulette.[127] Lieven titled his book *Chechnya: Tombstone of Russian Power*, referring to the no-win situation of the Russians, very similar to when the Russians were in Afghanistan during the war from 1994 to1996. He characterized the social and cultural roots of the Chechen victory through their motto, "We are free and equal like wolves."[128] This imagery also runs deep in their anthem "Freedom or death," which is sung in Russian: "Our mothers pledge us to our people...." The group overrides the individual. It is the mother's family more than the teip or clan itself that "decides whether a youth goes to fight or not—unless he's already decided for himself, of course."[129]This fighting spirit was also immortalized by the legacy of their nineteenth century leader Shamil, who said: "The prayers of slaves are not heard in Heaven."[130] Islam is something that makes them different.

It is interesting that the issue of the mother also surfaced on the Russian side of the war. It was the mothers who went in to look for their sons and sought their release from the abusive conditions of the army serving in Chechnya. They founded the organization The Committee of Soldiers' Mothers of Russia in 1989.[131] Baiev writes how he had contact with them when they found the bodies of Russian soldiers:

> "We wrapped the remains in sheets and buried them. Hasilbek shook his head in disgust. 'What kind of people are the Russians?' he said as we shoveled earth over the remains. 'They don't even bother to collect and bury their dead.' Later, we sent word to the Committee of Soldiers' Mothers, a grassroots

> organization in Moscow, about the dead and urged them to send someone to pick up the remains. to search for their sons or what remained of them."[132]

Many ethnic Russians were indiscriminately killed by the Russians in the bombings of Chechnya as related by Collins in *My Jihad*.[133] An American convert to Islam who was radicalized to fight in Chechnya, his mother was murdered when he was young; his father was absent in his life and had also served in Vietnam.[134] One wonders if the father suffered from combat PTSD.

Baiev relates the incident, which was fairly common in their field hospitals, that the Chechen mothers would also feed injured Russian soldiers just like their own: "The Chechen fighter's mother, there to look after her own son, also fed the young Russian soldier and gave him clean clothes. She then passed his name on to the council of elders, who tried to contact his family in Russia to come and collect him. A few days later, there was a report on Russian television about the cruel way Chechens supposedly treat Russia prisoners… Our women said these boys shouldn't be away from their mothers."[135]

BLIND SPOT 4: COUNTERTERRORISM AS A SHAME-HONOR DISCIPLINE?

With my professional experience and training, I ponder whether counterterrorism as a discipline isn't also an academic shame–honor culture. Whenever women are not given full access in a discipline and have difficulties advancing within it, it can be surmised that the psychodynamics of the discipline might resemble a shame–honor environment.[136] While there has been focus on the female terrorist, there has been considerable resistance in counterterrorism to contemplate the effect of the maternal relationship on the development of a terrorist psyche.

This tells us several things—that, by and large, counterterrorism as a field of inquiry remains male dominated. Many counterterrorism experts come from a law enforcement and military background. It is a challenge for them to raise the issue of early childhood development, gender relations, and sexuality. To a degree, there is also sexual harassment in these professional fields, which are tinged with a shame–honor code that causes a blind spot. Since there has been reticence to identify the link between domestic violence's murder–suicide and the murderous Islamic suicide attack (both variants of violent bonding), the denial reveals an intellectual limitation in developing effective strategies to get to the root problem in the family. Rachel Paine has argued that there are similarities between the two.[137] She has also noted that there has been resistance to this, as I have in my two previous books. The counterterrorists who are supposed to make our world safe fail on their watch if they do not begin to factor in the maternal platform of terrorism. We can see it clearly in the case of the Chechens. It is critical that these connections be made; otherwise the situation for women will be increasingly eroded by violence, which has at its base hatred of the female, especially the mother.

SUMMARY

This chapter gives a brief history of Chechnya and some of the customs and beliefs of its shame–honor culture. The sadomasochistic draw to hatred and violence makes leaving such violent bonding extremely difficult. Modernizing the culture requires giving up shaming, which has precipitated the addiction to violence. The Chechen jihadi embodies an iceberg mentality with a volcanic rage simmering below its surface, the groundwork for which has occurred during early childhood development. In the next chapter we will look at the terrorist groups that have been spawned in an attempt to understand the violence as a distorted intrapsychic adaptation. Like the psychiatric patient on the locked ward who sits frozen like an iceberg, the terrorists communicate to us through their acts of violence what their inner world is like. All human behavior is potentially meaningful. For terrorism, the violence becomes more meaningful in light of the maternal platform.

CHAPTER 2

THE UNCONSCIOUS TERROR OF THE FEMALE AND HER BODY

"If we die, we win"
–*Chechen Saying*

The Caucasus region has spawned a significant number of terrorist groups and jihadis. This chapter takes into account an isolated unconscious, which demonstrates the iceberg mentality and its psychotic thinking. Psychoanalysis is oriented to early childhood development. Hence its analytic tools are extremely helpful in understanding the chaos of the psychotic attacks. While many non-psychoanalytic counterterrorist experts claim that terrorism is just politically motivated violence to gain an advantage, this argument falls short. It does not make terrorist behavior meaningful because it sidesteps the core problem—what went wrong during early childhood development. Understanding terrorist attacks has been further complicated by mass social media, which does not delve into the root cause. If we knew better the motivators of terrorist behavior, we could potentially alleviate a good portion of such violence. By and large, counterterrorist experts are themselves terrified of dealing with the mother and early childhood development. This is based on my personal experience, which I have written about in *Penetrating the Terrorist Psyche.*

The idea of terrorism as an attempt at psychic adaptation allows entry into the mind of terrorists and their "psychic retreats," as Steiner has named it.[138] A forensic psychiatrist highly informed by psychoanalytic thinking, Dr. Keith Ablow characterized the Tsarnaevs as having grown up in a "crucible of denial" and having been formed by such blatant paranoia.[139] This assessment raises interesting questions and an opportunity to examine the family dynamics arising out of a shame–honor culture such as Chechen, Avar and even Central Asian cultures, along with pertinent aspects of their social values vis à vis the religion of Islam.

Some questions come into focus:

- What is the nature of the terrorists' behavior?
- Why do the terrorists lack empathy for their victims?
- How does a shame–honor culture interfere so pervasively with childhood development?
- What is the role of the mother?
- How was she treated as a little girl?
- What is the value of the son?
- How is he mistreated?
- How is terrorist behavior a psychic adaption to their perverse view of the world?
- What can we do to remedy this plight?

The relative isolation of the Caucasus region and its tough mountainous terrain helps to facilitate jihadis, who can "fly below the radar," unseen by government and the military. I associate this with the Arabic word *hashishiyy*,[140] which gave us the word assassin. The assassins were also mountain people and similarly group oriented. Mountains provide out-of-sight areas in which to train, infiltrate, and recruit. Moreover, in today's world it is very hard for these rural people to modernize, and some of them will be prone to jihad because of the level of violence experienced in their shame–honor families and clans. Even though many have moved to more urbanized areas or even to the Pankisi Gorge in Georgia, they remain psychologically attached to this rugged cultural environment. These violent groups are dominated by paranoid thinking, which object relations theoreticians remind us can easily dominate group think.[141] A similar parallel can be drawn to families that are dominated by paranoia. This helps to account for the radicalization of Western and Russian converts to Chechen jihadi. In *The Banality of Suicide Terrorism*, I deal with the example of Christian Ganczarski, the German convert to Al Qaeda. They tend to be isolated because those in power—the father and, by proxy, the mother—seek compliance of the children. It is easier to control and manipulate an isolated family or community.

In the context of discussion on Chechen/Avar jihadis, very little attention has been given to the maternal identification with the child, be it a son or daughter, the devalued female object. The most critical years for brain development and attachment are from birth to age three.[142] The fused identification with the mother is critical not only as it impacts the child's psychological state but also because of its genetic and biological implications—such as how the developing brain of the baby is built during the attachment experience, particularly the important neurons necessary for empathy. Instead of internalizing the good, mirroring mother, the baby incorporates the mother's terror and annihilation anxiety within the context of this unconscious structure, precipitating the psychological birth of a terrorist. Even though this configuration may lay dormant for years, it can lead to radical violence during adolescence and even later.

In subsequent chapters we will look more closely at the Boston Marathon Bombings and a triple homicide in Waltham, Massachusetts, which drew American attention to the problem of a Chechen jihad in a personal, intimate way. What the public may not be aware of is the number of terrorist groups in the northern Caucasus. To give the reader an idea of the different terrorist groups in this area, here is a list, along with a selection of targets and terrorist events, The statistics below form a background against which one can conceptualize the group and family psychodynamics:

Terrorist Groups in the Northern Caucasus Post Soviet Union:

- Caucasus Emirate (Vilayat Dagestan)[143]
- Armed Forces of the Chechen Republic of Ichkeria

- Riyadus-Salikhin Reconnaissance and Sabotage Battalion of Chechen Martyrs
- Dagestani Shari'ah Jamaat
- Islambouli Brigades of al-Qa'ida
- NVF
- Chechen Lone Wolf Group
- Special Purpose Islamic Regiment (SPIR)
- Other[144]

The targeted regions of the attacks were: Chechnya, Dagestan, Ingushetia, Kavardjbo Balkariya, North Ossetia, Stavropol (Krai), Moscow and other miscellaneous in Russia.[145] The types of targets chosen between January 1992 and December 2011 were, in descending order: Police, government, private citizens and private property, military, transportation, business, religious figures and institutions, utilities and journalists/ media, educational institutions, telecommunications, NGOs, airports and airlines.[146]

Attacks by tactic type in descending order were: Bombing/explosion, armed assault, assassination, facility/infrastructure attack, hostage taking, hijacking.[147]

Ranked as major terror attacks,1999–2011:

1999 Vladikavkaz Bombing
1999 Apartment Building Bombing in Dagestan and Moscow
2000 Argun Barracks Bombing
2002 Moscow Theater Attack
2004 Beslan School Siege
2005 Nalchik Assault
2009 Bologoye Train Bombing
2010 Moscow Subway Bombings
2011 Airport Bombing[148]

The terrorist groups cited acquired their violent underpinnings in the shame–honor clan, the first organization after the immediate family that further sets interpersonal skills—that is, how people relate to one another, violently or not. As we saw in Chapter 1, terrorism in the domestic setting of a shame–honor family pulses through the daily lives of Chechen inhabitants, given their cultural repertoire of beliefs, myths, traumatic historical experiences of warring, the value of weapons as hard objects, the low status of the female, and child-rearing practices. While not all will become violent, we can surmise that those who do not experienced a better initial entry into communal life that was not violent and shaming. One can conceptualize the Chechen terrorist as the epitome of the clan's essence—in other words a terrorist's terrorist. He is the brother bully who also grew into a "political" terrorist. A psychological X-ray reveals an inner world of psychotic chaos. Its unconscious "lived experience" and its projection of blood, guts, fire, explosives, and fighting to the death in suicide bombing paints a picture of a violent, iconoclastic breaking of the maternal attachment.

In a fascinating, seemingly unrelated short essay entitled "Crime as an attempt at intrapsychic adaptation,"[149] the late Marti Tuovinen, M.D., a Finnish psychoanalytically trained psychiatrist, explains the point of view of the perpetrators of crime from within their mindset. Tuovinen walks in their shoes, explaining the adaptive value of their seemingly bizarre violent behavior. In doing so, he helps the observer of criminal behavior understand the bizarre violence as having specific meaning to the perpetrators, who are without real thought or empathy for their victims. It is an important explanation precisely because it lays bare the root problem of highly problematic violent behavior so that law enforcement and other officials can develop appropriate and effective interventions. In addition, this perspective on the perpetrator's mind educates the public to the real causes of the violence rather than just societal bandaids. It also explains the force of the criminal's projections onto the victim, as well as the witnessing public's own unconscious.

Elsewhere I have argued that because we all have mothers the early experience of terror in the maternal attachment is tapped into during the outbreak of political violence. The mother is the global communicative circuit that we all share. Maternal attachment is our first experience in life, determining how we relate to and trust others. If the bonding is traumatic, it may turn violent later on. The maternal bond casts a life-long shadow over every being, even if they are high functioning and do not become criminals or terrorists. We can all live a kind of half-life embedded in very early terrors without ever really having to recognize our anxieties. This is very often the problem for people who suffer from personality disorders. Only when a crisis happens are they forced to confront their terrors.

In a nutshell, if one understands the bound relationship of the terrified child to his terrified mother in a shame–honor culture, it becomes possible to factor in this crucial element to explain the lack of empathy and the violent behavior of the terrorist. The violence created by the terrorist, who was once a terrified child, becomes his attempt to flee from the excruciatingly shameful life experience of having been abused through his bond with his abused mother. We can enter the terrorists' mind and walk in their shoes, although not to the extent that we have empathy for them. On the contrary, a deep level of understanding of the flawed maternal bond provides insights into how to deal with the jihadis. The maternal platform is the launching pad for this violence. This is NOT meant to blame the female, for that would be to buy into the countertransference of a shame–honor society and to say it is okay to harass and abuse little girls. But understanding the early dynamics between mother and child at an unconscious level has been successfully avoided by most counterterrorist experts, as well as the media and the general public.

The Chechen proverb cited at the beginning of this chapter, that dying is winning, shows that the fatality of life is valued in their mindset. The child becomes trapped in a culture belief that is split between winning and losing. This splitting, a hallmark of a shame–honor culture is internalized very early on. Saving face may entail dying. Importing Tuovinen's idea of violence as a psychological adaptation, particularly with regard to the Chechens, allows for exploring how the terrorist fends off the excruciating pain of shame from within his perverse, fragile, and violent psychotic world of fantasies. Below I offer a brief sketch of the crime scene of a suicide attack, which offers clues to decoding the psychotic behavior of a jihadi.

Clue #1: Snapshot of an Islamic suicide attack site

In this case a Chechen suicide bombing—an image of traumatic, disorganized attachment. In this generic depiction of a suicide bombing, there is no hierarchy of destruction. The pieces include:

- The dead
- The suicide bomber, who is often decapitated by the blast, a type of beheading
- Wounded victims with various kinds of injuries that often lead to amputation, which produces body parts
- Conjoint murder–suicide
- The murder of one's own—that is, the suicide bomber
- The crime scene covered in blood, body parts, and burnt carcasses of people, buildings, vehicles, etc.

In *The Banality of Suicide Terrorism*, I explain that this graphic crime scene represents psychotic thinking involved in traumatic bonding and disorganized maternal attachment similar to that found in serial killing; hence, I call suicide bombing a form of serial killing by proxy.

Clue #2: The psychological meaning of body parts

As I stated in *The Banality of Suicide Terrorism*, body parts at a crime scene, especially in a serial killing, are a psychic representation of an unintegrated picture of the mother's body—the mother as part object. Serial killers experience a rage that exceeds murder itself. This, too, is an indicator of traumatic bonding with the mother.

Clue #3: The killing of one's own—the suicide bomber as an alleged martyr

Murder of someone within one's own group or family is domestic violence. The terrorist group creates a suicidal zone and kills off one of its own, as in the Muslim world of honor killing. While it is true that honor killing also occurs in non-Muslim communities, such as Hindu communities, it shares a bond even in the West with delusional jealousy and domestic violence that can culminate in murder. This is also a form of traumatic bonding.

Clue #4: A "Wedding" of Violence

The suicide bomber and his victims are wedded through violence while manipulating the underlying template of murder–suicide found in Western-style domestic violence and often rampage shooter violence, wherein the shooter commits suicide after he has murdered.

Clue #5: The Black Widow, also called Shahidka, suicide bomber

Chechen terrorists have been particularly skillful in "branding" a type of female suicide bomber whom the Russians dubbed The Black Widow. An English speaker immediately associates the phrase with the kiss of death of the black widow spider, even though it does not hold this meaning in Chechen or in Russian. The semiotician counterterrorist expert Matusitz also notes that the English term black widow spider magnifies the power to communicate the terror.[150] The term was coined to describe women who were bereaved and then avenged the loss of their husbands or brothers, allegedly redeeming family honor by murdering the enemy under the Chechen vendetta code intertwined with jihad. Dressed in black hijab and veiled, the appearance of the Black Widow is meant to strike terror, yet there are many substantiated reports that these women were manipulated, drugged, and controlled. Matusitz in his *Symbolism in Terrorism* textbook offers an interesting chapter on brand management with a discussion on dress code as a means to create terror:

> Brand management through style of dress becomes a type of cultural knowledge that can fit a specific agenda (e.g., militarization of the rural poor, anti-Western hatred, anti-capitalism, revival of ancient values and practices, and so forth). In this respect, dress code is synonymous with social code. A social code bestows the terrorist group the symbolic resources for making statements about itself and for controlling interpersonal activities among members. A social code also drives the symbolically-guided social behaviors that characterize daily interactions in a specific terrorist culture. Social codes create an all-encompassing set of regulations based on a symbolic system.[151]

In brief, the internalized rage of the female turns into self-hatred. Killing themselves under the guise of kamikaze-style suicide alleviates the borderline pain of unspeakable terror. The Black Widow image also encapsulates the buried image of a prenatal female outfitted with bombs—a Mom bomb. The devalued female finds an outlet for her rage, which can be paralleled to the bathroom needs we have seen earlier. If a male is near the bathroom, she has no outlet for her bodily needs; in suicide bombing she has found one. Because she has had to stifle her rage for so long as the devalued female, she becomes a ticking time bomb.

Throughout the demonstrations in the Arab world, especially in Egypt during the Arab spring, you frequently saw women demonstrating, screaming, and protesting along with their men. They were willing to fight the men's battles because it offered them a socially sanctioned outlet for their rage, even though they may have been abused behind closed doors. Now it is reported that women's condition in post-Arab spring Egypt is even worse.[152] There is no adequate internal psychological infrastructure to support a fully functioning citizenry because of the abuse of the female. Egyptian sociologist Halim Barakat has noted that the family is a microcosm of society.[153] The same can be said of women and Chechen society, which, like Egypt's, is evolving but is held back by both the Chechen jihadis and the Russians, who are too heavy handed.

Often the clan's males will characterize the wife or mother as "ruling the roost," but this pseudo strength merely masks the fact that the female lacks power. Women are made out to be powerful, but in a shame–honor culture the men make the ultimate decisions. A commonality is found in the concept of the Black Widows as token terrorists. Mia Bloom, a professor of terrorism describes: "One example I made in my book *Bombshell* is how in the 2002 Dubrovka Theater siege, there were several Chechen black widows wearing suicide belts, but they were not in control of the mechanism that detonated those suicide belts. So, while the women may be used, in essence, as the shells for bombs, they're not making the decisions, they're not writing the ideologies, and they're not performing a leadership role that they did in previous generations when women held positions of power and influence."[154]

Clue #6: Understanding the unconscious communication about the use of chemical weapons, especially liquid explosives

The theme of chemical weapons has taken center stage with Syria's Assad and his use of gas against his own people in Damascus. As noted in Chapter 1, the long-standing hatred between Russia and Chechnya has involved chemicals as well. Russians used gas at the Chechen theater hostage take-over in Moscow as a means of ending the standoff. Russians overreacted and did not supply information to medical rescue teams and hospitals as to what gas they had used, and many people died because no antidote could be administered.

> A second observation derives from the Russian use of a chemical agent in 2002 when Chechen terrorists held more than 700 Russian hostages in a Moscow theater. The Russians used a crowd suppression agent that killed 116 people, but enabled 650 to be rescued. The agent is not banned by the Geneva convention on chemical warfare. If the Syrians used such an agent, which can be delivered by mortars and artillery as well as aircraft, there would be no international legal justification for attacking Syria based on the Geneva convention. It would not have been violated. The possibility that a non-banned substance was used makes it all the more urgent that competent investigators inspect the sites to identify the agent as well as the culprit.[155]

Nonetheless, Chechen jihadis also used chemicals and poisons for their attacks:

> A 2003 plot involving ricin, a virulent and deadly toxin, demonstrated the Islamist co-option of the Chechen nationalist conflict and its transformation into a global jihadist training ground. According to U.S. intelligence sources cited in the Italian indictment, Abu Mussab al-Zarqawi, the Jordanian terrorist alleged to mastermind much of the Iraqi insurgency, dispatched Adnan Muhammad Sadiq (Abu Atiya), a former Al-Qaeda instructor at a Herat, Afghanistan training camp, to Pankisi. In the gorge, Abu Atiya, a Palestinian who had lost a leg during the Chechen war, trained terrorists in the use of toxic gases. He also was behind a 2002 scheme to stage biological and chemical attacks against Russian or American interests in Turkey.[156]

It is known that the author of the "Jihadi Mein Kampf," Mustafa Setmariam Nasar, known as Abu Musab al Suri (the Syrian), a consummate explosives engineer, trained with Al Qaeda in Afghanistan: "While in Afghanistan, al Suri fought with the embryonic Al Qaeda force against the

Russians. This fact may be of particular interest to disaffected American Muslims who identify with Chechen rebels. Tamerlan Tsarnaev also shared al Suri's disgust for Shiite Muslims. He attacked a former friend who converted from Sunni to Shiite Islam as having 'betrayed yourself.'"[157] The crossover to other jihadi arenas is well known through personal contact as well as the Internet.

Abu Musab Zarqawi, whom Brisard called the new face of Al Qaeda[158] and who engaged in the brutal rampage of beheadings, was also involved in the Caucasus. He had two close friends operating in the Caucasus—Abu Atiyya and Abu Taysir—who were implicated in a foiled terrorist attack in Ankara, Turkey, intending to use an envelope containing a biological poison in 2002.[159] Abu Atiyya, Jordanian like Zarqawi, was married to a Chechen. He had a jihadi specialty, using toxic gases.[160] The ethnic affiliations are significant. The early deportations of Chechens to the Ottoman Empire have given the Turks a unique raison d'être for fighting in Chechnya and for seeking to bolster a Chechen identification, as Tamerlan sought to do. A. Schutzenberger has written about the impact of the ancestor syndrome on the descendants and the psychotic nature of the trauma that is transmitted across the generations.[161]

It is against this backdrop of Chechen involvement in explosives that we take a look at the development of a liquid explosive that currently is not detectable by standard counterterrorism equipment. The reason the jihadis decided unconsciously to develop such an atrocious weapon reveals another level of terrorist behavior and its unconscious communication. While it is true that liquid explosives provide a unique strategic and tactical advantage because they are undetectable, I argue that something else much more important *can* be detected in the choice to create such a lethal weapon—the disturbing aspect of maternal attachment gone wrong.

In a blog at the *Times of Israel* called "Fire—Detecting the 'Undetectable' in Liquid Explosives,"[162] I wrote that one of the main reasons reported for shutting down U.S. embassies has been the fear of these liquid explosives. Immolation is key to explosives and also the suicide attack. While necessity is generally the mother of invention, this time it takes on a nefarious twist of hatred, aggression, and rage. To quote my colleague, Joan Jutta Lachkar, Ph.D., "Their hatred for us is so out of bounds that the drive and passion become nearly unstoppable." This addition to the terrorist's wardrobe involves clothes dipped in a liquid explosive. Think about it: a reversal of flame retardant material for children's clothing, developed in the United States in the 1970s, has been turned on its head. The liquid explosive has an obvious tactical advantage, since it is hard for security to identify and intercept.

What is the psychological meaning of this new terrorist tactic? What else are the terrorists communicating about themselves that even they are not aware of? What is the significance of their unconscious, dissociated behavior? And why might it be important for the lay public to understand? Fire signifies unconscious rage but in an autistic-like manner, as if the terrorist themselves do not understand what burning means and what it translates into. They send others to be immolated, not themselves, these engineers of jihad. It is very schizoid behavior. Also, clothing is a second "skin" for us. Clothing acts as an envelope for the human body. The Japanese designer Yuima Nakazato views clothes as an extension of the body.[163] Skin is the body's porous barrier, taking in from the environment but also keeping out and protecting—titrating the interaction with what is outside one's self.

Terrorists are terrified of people and intimacy. Yet terrorists have "velcro" personalities. They want to stick to you because they lack psychological infrastructure. They need to hate you and bond through violence in order to momentarily stabilize their fragile personalities. They have no boundaries. This reveals a major problem in their personality development. Terrorists have a split similar to what Hervey Cleckley described years ago for serial killers in his *Mask of Sanity*.[164] They may look normal but they are not normal. They speak to us through a kind of pantomime, in this case via liquid explosive-saturated clothing and its fire and immolation. By studying this pantomime, which has been likened to the terrorist Rosetta Stone,[165] we can better understand the terrors of the terrorists in order to create more effective law enforcement and counterterrorism interventions, thereby protecting the public without reinventing the wheel.

Like patients on a psychotic ward who sit stiffly in a chair, shivering and mute, terrorists cannot tell us in so many words that they are emotionally freezing to death. Rather, they become an iceberg and communicate nonverbally. They cannot contemplate the origins of their own rage or why they are the way they are. Instead they force us to participate in their high drama. Terrorist groups send their own suicide bombers to literally become the rage by bursting into flames, but it is never enough as they must take out innocent others. I wrote about this bizarre, unconscious pantomime in *The Banality of Suicide Terrorism*, in which I explore the importance of decoding the nonverbal behavior with the verbal messages and ideologies.

Terrorists have a fundamental developmental problem in conjunction with genetics and neurobiology. This problem has been further complicated by early child-rearing practices in shame–honor cultures in which the female is devalued. It becomes a treacherous, vicious cycle because the devalued female molds the brain of the future terrorist in utero as well as during the first years of life, when the brain quadruples in size. Maternal attachment includes the development of the psychological birth of the infant. When this attachment is optimal, it provides a psychological envelope for the body, a feeling of safety. The cutaneous stimulation of skin is extremely important as it is an early sensory perception, how the baby experiences the mother in the maternal attachment, which carries over to how terrorists bond with objects. Terrorism is, then, very much about sensory perception of the body.[166] Terrorists fail to develop empathy during these earliest years. (Currently there is a debate that terrorists have empathy but the switch in the brain that turns it on is broken.

It is not within the scope of this text to deal with this issue or its potential for being a minimizing, politically correct excuse for such aberrant behavior.)

The wardrobe of liquid explosive-dipped clothes reminded me, too, of the fence that Israel built to keep out suicide bombers. A line in the sand was drawn. A fence concretely communicates nonverbally to the terrorists, in their own unconscious language, that since they have no boundaries (no functional "envelope") a barrier had to be created for them. Suicide bombings dropped drastically after the fence was erected. However, the fence is only a temporary solution. A more realistic, far-reaching solution demands that the public be educated about the unconscious psychological meaning of terrorist behavior in order to demand extensive changes to child-rearing practices at the international level. Granted, it is a tall order, but the intervention must factor in maternal attachment, as outlandish as it may sound to many. Only then will we be more effective at detecting violence before it becomes reality. Meanwhile, we will just keep reinventing the wheel at tremendous cost.

In short, the problem points to the maternal attachment in the early life of the terrorist, which gets played out under the guise of political violence. It is a two-for-one kind of thing—killing the other and their own because they harbor a rage that exceeds murder itself as in serial killing. Murdering one is never enough.

While the Boston Bombings were not strictly speaking suicide bombings, they do fit within the frame of these psychodynamics and perverse adaptation. In order to understand this violent "adaptation," what it must be like to feel suffocated by an inescapable bond to one's mother, we need to work backwards and move from the terrorist crime scene and speculate about the terrorist's early childhood development, focusing on the issue of maternal attachment. It is commonly held in neuroscience as well as psychoanalysis that the maternal relationship plays a crucial developmental role in forming the personality by age two.[167] A baby is not simply born physically; the baby undergoes a psychological birth, to recall Margaret Mahler's impressive work. Alessandra Piontelli, taking clues and cues from Esther Bick, the psychoanalyst who developed the field of infant observation, has added breadth and depth to the complexity of the personality and its attachment to the mother. To be sure, there are many others who have contributed to and expanded our knowledge of treatment, diagnosis, and concepts concerning borderline psychopathology, violence, murder, suicide, and disorganized attachment disorders.

We may not be able to understand everything about a terrorist attack, but by understanding some of its behavior we can seek to be more effective. Neurocriminologist Adriane Raine, in commenting about hardcore criminal offenders said that "Once we find out more about the etiology and causes of behavior, it gives us a more benign and humane perspective."[168] He noted that we used to burn witches, implying that we have come to understand our own ignorance and fears. Witch burning links back to immolation, the unconscious rage that cycled through the witch hunt, the vilification of the other, who could be eradicated. From a psychoanalytic perspective, the witch has been known to be a stand-in for the repudiated mother.[169] There is a similar need to overcome our own ignorance and fears regarding terrorism, too. Kathleen Taylor, a neurologist, claims that religious fundamentalism and radical Islam may one day be classified as a treatable mental illness.[170]

SUMMARY

Terrorists relate to people as objects, not as human beings, because they have been dehumanized when they were growing up. That is their template, their model for how to relate to people. They do not know any other way. Hence, terrorists seek to dehumanize us through their violent behavior. They project their terrors into us. They become their terrors, rather than being in touch with their own internal terrorist and learning that it is wrong to project.

They blame the other because they were raised in a shame–honor culture and have learned only how to blame. It is the shame–blame game writ large and communicated through the suicide bombing. If we are willing to examine the early mother–terrorist relationship as the prologue to violence,[171] we can make sense out of their aberrant behavior, predict, profile, and fashion more effective interventions at an earlier stage.

CHAPTER 3

THE MATERNAL CAMEO: AN ICON OF FUSION AND VIOLENT ATTACHMENT

The maternal relationship is the launching pad for jihad. Its graphic representation can be seen in images of fusion—by which is meant, primarily, the mother holding the infant or the mother with child. The maternal platform is the crucible that molds the minds of these terrorists. It may seem far-fetched to many to link the inseparable bonding of a first-born son to his mother in families with a psychologically ineffective or absent father with the equally unconscious behavior of launching suicide attacks. Why is this so? A lot has to do with having a Titanic mentality in responding to terrorism. The volcanic iceberg mentality that creates these kinds of atrocities precipitates in us a numbing response to the horror of terrorism.

THE FUNCTION OF THE MATERNAL CAMEO[172]

I created the term "maternal cameo" as a psychoanalytic tool to help facilitate reading the iconoclastic behavior of the Chechens. The maternal cameo can be thought of as psychoanalytic "ammo" that targets the problematic behavior in a non-violent, explanatory way. Knowledge is power. The maternal cameo is an articulation of a maternal life fusion at one end of the spectrum, and of the maternal death fusion at the other end. The maternal cameo gives concrete form to the experience of the maternal symbiosis. It replicates the terrorists' habit of engaging in imitative behavior because of their inability both to separate psychologically from the maternal fusion and to mourn the loss of the Early Mother.

The maternal cameo plays an important role in decoding the violent behavior because the issue of maternal attachment is always unconsciously in the terrorist mind, buried like a palimpsest beneath the disorganized, psychotic thinking that underlies their iconoclastic behavior.[173] It helps us read the unconscious, dissociated levels of terrorist behavior. The jihadis do not bother to think about their unconscious rage at being fused with the mother. They are blinded by their own hatred, which is self-hatred. They cannot tolerate not being perfect. The shame–honor culture imbues the little boy with chronic devaluation of the female. It makes the male feel better about his inadequate self. The maternal cameo distills the violent imagery down to the basics.

Suicide attacks are understandable if we are willing to return to the psychodynamics of the family and understand the kind of environment in which the volcanic iceberg mentality is created in shame–honor cultures such as that of the Chechens. Due to the lack of individuality and healthy boundaries, the suicide attack encapsulates and reflects a psychotic reality by which the embattled "child" seeks to extricate himself from the maternal fusion. This is his jihad. He is filled with shame because of being bonded to the mother. This is the consummate maternal drama. This unconscious intra-familial drama occurs in a crucible of denial. The mother in shame–honor cultures is larger than life, meaning that she really doesn't have any power at all. The heroics mask denial of her lowly position as female.

"In all the cultures in which the mother is venerated, ironically the female is the most oppressed." This observation was made by Bronwen Clune in her opinion piece entitled "I am not a good mother." Clune continued: "Religion also plays a critical role here; I was raised as a Roman Catholic and Mary—mythically virginal or historically not—has a lot to answer for."[174] The same can be said for both Judaism and Islam when the ideologies are taken to an extreme. However, the imagery differs somewhat between the two with regard to the female.

Judaism has its *eshet khayil*, woman of valor, the ideal woman, the honorable one cited in Proverbs 31:10-31. Judaism has no Virgin Mary or Madonna and Child. Instead the dominant image of fusion is the Torah scroll and the person holding it. In ultraorthodox communities it is almost exclusively the male who cradles the Torah in his arms. The Torah scroll becomes a replacement for the female as a hard object to be venerated. She is dressed in gold or silver embroidered velvet and kissed and held tight to the breast when being paraded throughout the synagogue. The Torah is the female/mother in unconscious terms. The Torah as a positive hard object reminds its believers of ethics and boundaries to be maintained. Death is not venerated. Thus, how we attach to objects is critical to understanding the unconscious. How objects may be a substitute for the mother is key to understanding terrorism and its violence.

Among the key figures of fusion in Christianity is the Virgin Mary and the Madonna and Child. These are life-giving images that express maternal nurturing over deprivation. Even the Pietà—Mother Mary holding the warm, just-murdered body of Christ taken down from the Cross—communicates love, compassion, and loss. The female, the mother, lives on while the son has been martyred alone.

Islam borrowed the imagery of the Madonna and Child through its cooptation of the New Testament. Since the image is borrowed and there is no belief in Jesus as the Son of God, it has no psychological fit with Islam's ideologies. What does "fit" for Islam's believers is the life of the Prophet Muhammad. Everything that he did is venerated. Hence, the most outstanding image of fusion is the death of the Prophet Muhammad. Echoing the Pietà, he died in the arms of his favorite wife, Aisha, who, at nine years old, was his only virgin wife when the marriage was consummated. Muhammad was buried in her room, where she continued to live and receive alms from those on pilgrimage to see where the Prophet died.[175] But since Aisha was never a mother, there is no sense of life giving or nurturing. I was once told by an

Israeli taxi cab driver that when he was serving in the army an Arab told him that they did not believe that the Prophet Muhammad was born from the body of a female. It goes beyond Christianity's Virgin Birth. The denial of being born from the female is psychotic thinking, a way in which to repudiate the need for the mother and her life-giving attributes.

The negation of the female in Islam has been dealt with in detail by Dr. Abdelwahab Bouhdiba, a Tunisian sociologist extensively trained in psychoanalysis. Another noted Muslim psychoanalyst, Fethi Benslama, has raised the issue of the highly ambivalent relationship to the female as one of the greatest challenges to the religion of Islam.[176] Judaism is a self-standing religion whose identity is not predicated on any other religion, unlike Christianity and Islam, which both have Judaic roots. Hence the treatment of the female is different, even though in ultra-orthodox sects such as the sikrikim the female is also devalued. However, there is no martyr imagery of murder–suicide. The extreme ideologies act as a girdle for a fragile personality. If someone wants to commit murder–suicide, they will find a way.

MATERNAL FUSION, CHILD-REARING, AND TERRORIST BEHAVIOR

The political violence of jihadi terrorism does not occur in a vacuum. It is real-time global violence that spreads like wildfire, inflaming the aggression as violent fantasies are acted out and inciting others to violence. Suicide attacks degrade cultures and children's lives. Terrorists are particularly drawn to attacking children, who are most vulnerable because they are identified with the mothers. This vicious cycle can only be stopped if the root problem is treated with adequate intervention for the young, brutalized females who grow up to be mothers in these shame–honor cultures, misusing their male sons and, by extension, their daughters. The intergenerational transmission of trauma further compounds these interlocking links of violence and hatred. There has been no opportunity to mourn loss. In fact there is a lack of genuine mourning, which may be a cultural prohibition in shame–honor cultures, thus locking in the revenge killing and warring.

In *The Banality of Suicide Terrorism*, I discussed problematic child-rearing practices in Islamic shame–honor cultures and how such abuse brutalizes the concept of connection to others, first in the infant and later in the toddler who begins to explore the world and learns whether it is a safe place. When abuse happens, it threatens the very connectedness within a family. Abuse causes violent attachment, or what is called traumatic bonding.

When you are afraid of connecting with others, or have what some may note as a problem with intimacy, it is a red flag that you have been misused/ abused in early childhood and have become the unwitting object of chronic hatred. Terrorists are actually terrified because they themselves have been abused very early on This abuse is dissociated and projected onto others. However, this does not justify their turning the tables and abusing others or mean that we should have empathy for terrorists.

One of the ways I seek to describe terrorists' emotional problems is by looking at how they connect to other people and by examining how they use objects. Terrorists relate to people not as people but as objects. What is an object? It is "A material thing that can be seen and touched" or " A person or thing to which a specific action or feeling is directed."[177] A person is merely an object to terrorists, who also misuse physical objects, such as using pressure cookers for bombs. How the terrorist concretely connects to objects is revealing. I began looking at the Islamic suicide attack and saw murder–suicide as its distilled template. It seemed to me to be so obvious. Like the fairy tale *The Emperor's New Clothes*, people were initially very resistant to look at the murder–suicide crime scene from this new perspective. In my mind that meant that they were terrified of the unconscious psychodynamics.

While the scene of a terrorist massacre is much more graphic, nonetheless it remains helpful to distill its chaos to murder–suicide as a starting point to explain the terrorists' volcanic iceberg mentality. Whenever I spoke about this connection, everyone balked and said I was wrong, which put me in mind of Shakespeare's famous line: "She doth protest too much." Certainly Tamerlan's mother, Zubeidat, protests too much. Her protests reveal her defense mechanism of denial.

My research on murder–suicide led me to the term "death fusion," where two people become a psychological or physical one. I found the term in an essay on suicide written by psychoanalyst Shelley Orgel.[178] Orgel argued that suicide is always a return to the mother, a psychotic regression fusing the maternal object. I also found that it was shame–honor cultures, in which the female is devalued, that were spawning suicide attacks—e.g., the Tamil Tigers. In Japanese Kamikaze culture, pilots were instructed not to fear death because as they approached their targets the face of their mother would appear and they would return to her: "You are two or three metres from the target. You can see clearly the muzzles of the enemy's guns. You feel that you are suddenly floating in the air. At that moment, you see your mother's face. She is not smiling or crying. It is her usual face." [179]

Hence, the collective shame–honor culture embraces the unconscious fantasy of fusion with the mother as rebirth. But why do they become one? Why must they reunite with their mothers? Simply put, they are not psychologically individuated and cannot function alone. They must always seek out objects to recreate the deprived maternal bond. Think of the time when an infant is totally dependent upon its mother. We speak of this unique relationship as maternal attachment, in psychological terms as the maternal symbiosis or the maternal fusion.

> An infant is intimately dependent on its mother at birth and is compelled to fuse with her, not realizing that the mother is a separate person. The Early Mother is only known as "part object"—the warm breast, the nipple, eyes, mouth, lips, cradling

> arms, and warm, maternal lap. The infant's desire for fusion is an early, erotic, and physical love that is experienced along with inevitable failures on attunement and causes both pleasure and pain. It is a two-way street as the mother is also fused with the baby out of a need to care for the child as well as its attendant pain and pleasure.[180]

This twosome, or dyad, of mother plus infant is a merged state that gives life to the baby. The mother is the baby's power supply. Their relationship is a life-giving fusion. The prenatal or pregnant mother represents the earliest fusional image. "In psychoanalytic parlance an object may be further defined as referring to the object of one's sexual desire: Freud, for example, refers to one's 'object-choice,' the earliest one being the mother (and before her the mother's breast)."[181]

Terrorists are obsessed with re-creating the dyadic experience through their use of objects, both animate and inanimate. This behavior concretely expresses their helplessness, which is experienced as terror. Those feelings then yield to murderous rage against the mother, which is displaced onto innocent victims. The murderer confuses his target with his unconscious fantasy of early life with his mother. He harbors extreme hatred and rage and feelings of inadequacy overwhelm him. He cannot live without her or a substitute for her—a wife or partner in an abusive domestic violence situation. In the case of political violence, such as the Islamic suicide attack, the prey is maternal. This is also true of the Chechen version of the Islamic suicide attack. Think of the image of the female suicide bomber, who is often depicted as pregnant. Terrorists cannot control this unconscious aspect of their behavior and its message. The body does not lie.

NONVERBAL COMMUNICATION IN TERRORISM

With the concept of the maternal cameo in place, I had a "concrete" image and format against which I could begin to decode behaviors in this maternal drama. The maternal cameo serves as a kind of lowest common denominator to hone and distill the chaotic, disorganizing psychotic imagery of terrorism to its basics. Prior to my conception of the maternal cameo, there had not existed a term that graphically represented the maternal symbiosis of early childhood—the mother and infant dyad—along with its psychological, interpersonal, and intra-psychic implications for jihadi terrorism. We rarely talk about terrorists having their own terrors, but obviously they do. That is what they project into us. They cannot process and understand their terrors. Insight does not exist for them. With their volcanic iceberg mentality, they are cold as ice, relating to people as objects; yet they are extremely volatile.

FIRE, SELF-IMMOLATION, EXPLOSIVES, RAGE

Fire is the essence of the volcano. Death by fire is perhaps one of the most threatening deaths possible, with its absolute disfiguration and near erasure of identity.[182] Al Qaeda's ezine, *Inspire,* has given directions for creating firebombs for the purpose of setting forests on fire to terrorize the population and destroy Mother Nature [183] Immolation plays a central role in bomb making and suicide bombing. Firecrackers in pressure cookers were used in the explosives made by the Brothers Tsarnaev. Firecrackers are commonly used for celebrating, particularly on the Fourth of July, and pressure cookers for cooking which "contains" the symbolic taste of maternal nurturing. This is a misuse of the object. Besides being a tactical weapon for killing, these objects have a snug fit with the terrorists' violent, lethal unconscious. The pressure cooker embodies their perversity and a tendency to explode from the pressure that builds up in them like a volcano. Yet it is not a symbol or metaphor; it is a concrete object. The Tsarnaevs wanted to attack on the Fourth of July,[184] which is celebrated with firecrackers and fireworks, but had built their bombs ahead of schedule and decided to deploy them on Patriot's Day. The Fourth of July is America's Independence Day; thus, the Tsarnaev's were seeking to attack those whom they perceived to be free and independent because they themselves psychologically lacked freedom. People are not really free in a shame–honor based culture, society or household. Hence, there is a constant struggle for freedom.

BODY PARTS AND BLOOD

What about body parts in suicide bombing and beheadings? They, too, represent the mother's body, which is dismembered by explosive rage, an attack on aspects of the maternal cameo. The body parts express the infant's part-object perception of the mother. For terrorists, the infant's unintegrated image of the mother—her mouth, breast, smell, skin, eyes, etc.—persists in adulthood in seeking to fuse with the mother in death. The mother is not perceived as a whole person separate from the terrorist. Rattling around in the terrorist's mind are images of bodily experiences with the early mother. Body parts are found in serial killing; the serial killer makes a tableau of these parts, communicating his rage to the police, taunting them to find him. Body parts are a concrete representation of the mother's body.[185] Here is one report from Chechnya that appeared in a 2000 *Chicago Tribune* article: "We walked into a minefield …you didn't know where to step. We walked through blood and pieces of flesh."[186]

In a shame–honor culture, blood plays an important role. In Arab Muslim culture, honor can only be redeemed through the willful spilling of blood. Later on, *diya*, or payment, was devised as a kind of compensation for having been wronged. Blood is delusionally associated with cleansing the psychological defect of shame.

BEHEADING AND MUTILATING THE BODY

The battlefield code of honor covers over the terrorists' own unconscious shame:

> Chechen fighters commonly killed, decapitated, and mutilated their Russian prisons. Videotapes from the first war once sold in Grozny's market show Arab and Chechen fighters

> holding up the severed heads of Russian soldiers and shouting "Allah Akhbar!" Aukai Collins, an America who converted to Islam and became radicalized, became a mujahideen who fought in the Chechen side in the first war and writes about one of these grotesque executions in his book My Jihad: "He [the Chechen fighter] pulled the [Russian] soldier's head back by his filthy hair and ran the knife back and forth over his neck in a ghastly sawing motion. Bright red blood squirted out as the…throat was severed....A noise came from his throat as his last breath escaped through his gaping neck. Then the Chechen simply let the soldier's head flop onto the ground. It was tilted so far back that it was almost completely severed."[187]

Sometimes heads of Russian soldiers would be put on stakes outside villages, booby trapped to kill anyone trying to remove them. Russian soldiers found their comrades nailed to crosses, with honey smeared across their bodies to attract flies, their torsos riddled with bullet holes, or their testicles cut off. In his book *Ya byl an etoi ovine* (*I Was in That War*), Vyacheskav Mironov tells about the nailing of a Russia soldier to a rooftop cross and the mutilation of his body: "A dead soldier's body was up there, just like Jesus, his own penis cut off and stuffed in his mouth."[188] The Russians in retaliation also castrated Chechen men or made human trophies of sliced-off ears of Chechens.[189] The castration is the concrete expression of their own projected impotence. Since the rage cannot be assuaged by killing, they must dismantle the body. Cutting off ears concretely reflects their not having been heard in early childhood.

In both of my preceding books, I wrote about beheadings as a form of jihad but, what is more important is that unconsciously they communicate that the jihadis cannot tolerate ideas different from theirs. Ideas are located in the head and metaphorically the unconscious. Hence, they must destroy the other's thoughts, which links to the disrupted maternal bond. In Saudi Arabia where beheading is a common punishment, it is an Islamic version of *Alice in Wonderland* where the queen says "Off with your head." But *Alice in Wonderland* is a fantasy narrative. The jihadis do not distinguish the difference between fantasy and reality. They have no filter and act on their psychotic thoughts. In shame–honor cultures such as the Chechens, child-rearing practices are different and children do not have the opportunity to develop a sense of play, which facilitates the ability to distinguish between fantasy and reality.[190] Matusitz notes the semiotics of beheading in jihadi videos of ritualized sacrifice.[191] I add to this the idea that it also constitutes a pornographic perversion.

KIDNAPPING, HOSTAGE TAKING AND BRIDE STEALING

Chechnya has a "rich culture of kidnapping for ransom."[192] Kidnapping, hostage taking, and bride stealing are variants of the same psychological behavior, taking someone against their will in order to assume control, and in many instances reaping financial benefits. It is again a fusion with another person, becoming one unit as in suicide bombing. The fusion reenacts a return to the mother at an unconscious level. It asserts power and control over the other. It is not just about money and financial gain.

The suicide bomber also takes a person hostage prior to detonating. Unlike Christ's martyrdom on the Cross or Joan of Arc being burned at the stake, suicide bombers do not die alone. Lachkar's profile of the suicide bomber characterizes it as borderline personality disorder.[193] Such malignant, adhesive behavior is a derivative of the closed circle of the clan or *teip* in Chechen culture. Living in the Middle East, I have witnessed some Arabs who sit next to other men and constantly have to touch them, similar to patients who seek to touch the therapist. It is as if there is a lack of boundaries and fear of identity dissolution—i.e., falling into the black hole of nothingness, which is like death. They need to remain in physical contact with the other, in a state of fusion. Touching makes certain that there is someone at the other end of the touch.

Touching is further concretized in this description of kidnapping: "Kidnappers [in Chechnya and Chechens in Russia] singled out Jewish children because they brought more money. The tips of Alla Geifman's fingers were cut off and a videotape made of the act to hasten ransom payment. Alla, the thirteen-year-old daughter of banker Grigory Geifman, didn't even live in Chechnya. She was abducted in May 1999 near her home in Saratov, Russia, and taken to Chechnya."[194] Why were her fingertips cut off, you may ask? Not only to instill terror in the parents of this poor child hostage but also because of the brutality underlying this unconscious nonverbal communication. Understanding the shame–honor culture helps to clarify why these hostage takers did this. They literally projected their shameful, "touchy" fingers and the need for contact into the other and were compelled to cut off her fingers. It is similar to an enraged husband cutting off the nose of a female in Afghanistan in an attempt to "save face" in his paranoid shame–honor world.[195]

It has been very difficult to know who is doing the kidnapping in Chechnya because the Russians, Chechen gangs, and the Mujahedin all wear the same camouflage and carry the same weapons. Nonetheless, hostage taking is more central to Chechen culture because of the history and custom of bride stealing, a variant of hostage taking, beginning with holding the female (the mother) hostage.

Bride Stealing, kidnapping, hostage taking, suicide bombing are all variations on the unconscious theme of the maternal fusion, which is acted out in a concrete way and propelled by terror. The behavior of terrorists is not so much about their targets as it is about themselves and their terrors, by which they literally inject themselves into their victims. They lack the psychological infrastructure to be free, independent thinking and feeling human beings. This incapacity carries a deep burden of shame, which they mask with the bravado of alleged honor.

WOMEN AS MARTYRS

One Chechen woman reported that she had taped a grenade to her body, which would detonate if a Russian soldier tried to rape her. She was told to do this by her brother, that it would alleviate her worrying about losing her honor.[196] This harkens back to the image of the female suicide bomber strapping bombs on herself. It is also an image of fusion of an individual with a hard object weapon—a grenade. The suicide preserves the shamed group's alleged honor. It is the female's return to her mother, who cannot protect her in life.

The maternal cameo functions as the hidden image of the annihilation of mother and child. The use of vest-bombs, or breast bombs as they have been called, focuses on an overt, unconscious attack on the nursing mother.[197] Counterterrorist experts do not address this issue of the destruction of the life-giving body, tending to ignore the obvious because it is so terrifying and distressing to them. They are uncomfortable, perhaps because they also have their own fantasies of rage and wish to control the female. Since the development of suicide vest bombs, there has been the abhorrent innovation of breast implant bombs, signaling how the unconscious rage must find a deeper outlet for its expressed rage because the vest bomb is not sufficient. These surgically implanted breast bombs are much more difficult to detect.[198]

FERROR: TERROR OF THE FEMALE AND HER BODY

A Russian immigrant to Israel, artist Galina Bleich, and her colleague Lilia Chak invented a special word to describe terror of the female—Ferror. Bleich and Chak created a series of Madonna and child paintings that were exhibited at the Beit Sokolov Journalist Center in Tel Aviv in 2009. Bleich portrayed the terrorist mother as a Madonna and the infants as terrorists in the making. To a large extent, she was dealing with the Palestinian conflict, but as a Russian Jew she was well informed of the terrorist acts committed in Russia after 9/11. The exhibition caused such an uproar among families of victims of terrorist attacks that the show was immediately cancelled.[199] It seems that these families had a very poor understanding of what Bleich and Chak intuitively understood concerning jihad and the suicide bombings. Bleich was trying to communicate that the child was endangered. The public misunderstood and was outraged by the manipulation of this iconic maternal symbol.

> The artists defended their work...with Bleich telling Ynet that she didn't understand how the exhibit was misconstrued as glorifying suicide bombers. "I don't understand how this turned into an insult to bereaved families. We came actually to emphasize the exact opposite. The baby in Madonna's hands is in danger. This really needs to disturb people. It isn't just an Israeli problem, but a global one. Therefore, we chose Madonna, who is a symbol of Christianity. This issue came up for me after I personally experienced a trauma when I was next to a terror attack on French Hill in Jerusalem. Ever since, I couldn't stop thinking about it. It isn't at all a political issue, but a personal issue. We are trying to ask how a woman, who is meant to love and give birth, became a source of hatred and murder. I don't at all go into politics. But because we are such a political country, everyone is trying to figure out if we are left-wing or not," explained Bleich.
>
> "If it impacts people so much, this means that the message is getting across. We wanted to think together with the audience about what is happening, and, apparently, now they are reflecting on it. Modern art can speak in a free language without a framework. Modern art is actually a language that shakes up the subjects that are painful to us. It's not only flowers in a vase. Art asks questions and doesn't provide answers," said Bleich.[200]

That the painting exhibit was forced to close showed that Bleich had touched the "third rail" of terror, the forbidden topic of the maternal relationship. Bleich and Chak had unconsciously stumbled upon the semiotic code of terrorism when they created their fusional image of mother and child and proved the existence of my abstract concept of the maternal cameo. The Israeli public experienced a "negative countertransference" to the artists' aesthetic expression of the devalued female in Palestinian Muslim shame–honor culture. It struck a profound nerve, which proved to be too painful for Israelis to tolerate. This is partly because Israeli Jewish culture venerates "imah" (Hebrew for mother) and the fused group, although to a lesser degree. The exhibit was perceived as being shaming Israeli Jewish culture, which felt vulnerable in its inability to control suicide bombings.

Some important maternal cameos bespeak death, sacrifice, heroism. It has been noted that perhaps the most famous image seared into our minds from the Oklahoma City bombing of the Alfred P. Murrah Federal Building on April 19, 1995, was that of the fireman carrying the bloodied baby. It is reminiscent of Michelangelo's Pieta, the sculpture of Mary holding the lifeless body of her son, Jesus. What is so striking about this image is the deep, universal meaning of the life-giving mother not being able to protect her child from death. The father is not linked to death in this way. The French playwright Genet, who was a PLO aficionado and friend of Yasar Arafat, used and manipulated this maternal image in order to elevate the sense of drama and martyrdom in Palestinian attacks when he described the relationship between a widowed mother and her son Hamza, as noted by Zulaika, a Basque counterterrorist expert.[201] Yet Zulaika as well as Genet remain clueless about the underlying nature of the maternal attachment and its critical role in the creation of empathy, which terrorists lack. It's easier to romanticize terrorism than to deal with its reality.

SEEKING FUSION

When I was a psychoanalyst candidate in training, I was sent to interview my first child patient, a six-year-old boy, on a locked ward in a psychiatric hospital at the University of Minnesota. No sooner had we sat down together at a children's table in a psychotherapy playroom than I felt something on top of my foot and realized it was his foot. Within a split second, this child had forcefully placed his foot on top of mine. After being momentarily taken aback, I associated his behavior to that of an alpha male dog, which seeks dominance by putting his paw on top of you. The terrors oozed out of this little boy onto me. He had been hospitalized for setting fires, among other things. In that split second he communicated more to me through his gesture than any words could have. His nonverbal behavior fused him to me in a physical sense, and in his mind the two of us became one. He sought to recreate the maternal attachment and thus communicated to me the disrupted attachment he had felt as a baby. I was thrown back into the position of being a maternal object to him, the object that had disappointed him, abandoned him, neglected him, frustrated him, and deprived him of emotional well-being—an object that he learned to hate.

His putting his foot on top of mine did not just signal dominance and a wish to seek control in predatory terms; more significantly, he concretely connected to me and communicated his dependency needs, the mothering he may have experienced, and his unconscious terrors about trusting others. He "fused" to me. He could not maintain boundaries as he was developmentally arrested; he had never psychologically separated from his mother. The fires told us that he was full of rage over this developmental arrest. He sought fusion with his mother in order to experience the trust, power, and security he needed.

Through acting out his terror, he gave me a glimpse into how the mind works to defend itself. He was grappling with his rage in a concrete way and burning with pain. He was not yet setting himself on fire in a suicide bombing, but this could have been a prodrome to psychotic behavior. In addition, I came to understand through others who have worked with autistic children that they also have a difficult time understanding the concept and the concrete nature of fire. This little boy could not put his pain into words. Instead he communicated his rage nonverbally by setting fires and by trying to dominate the interviewer. Learning how to use verbal language in a meaningful way by identifying feelings and emotions and mourning loss would be a long-term task during ensuing therapy. Did this little boy become a political terrorist, a jihadi? I believe it is quite possible because the jihadis are developmentally arrested children, even infants, trapped in an adult body.

SUMMARY

The above clinical experience and the image it left helped me investigate the idea of fusion—touching or sticking to someone as if the other were a maternal object. This led me to investigate sacred images of fusion, which drive the three Abrahamic faiths, with a particular focus on the Islamic suicide attack. Inscribed into the maternal cameo for those who embrace Chechen suicide terrorism is a hint of necrophilia, worship of death. In cultures, as well as with individuals, magical thinking predominates where and when there is a great deal of shame and humiliation. It is a compensatory force of omnipotence and grandiosity to mask extreme vulnerability. Magical thinking serves as a protective defense against dealing maturely with the pain of one's shame. Everything becomes Inshallah, Allah's will. It facilitates splitting at an unconscious level and helps to maintain it by providing an opportunity to project one's bad parts and feelings onto others by attacking them.[202]

The next chapter discusses how the choice of the terrorist attack site relates to the maternal cameo and its fragmentation—the conflicting wish to remain fused and to split apart the maternal bond through bloodshed. It is a psychotic adaptation to the terrorist's shame-filled world.

CHAPTER 4

UNCONSCIOUS CHECHEN ATTACKS ON THE "MOTHER"

"The Mother of the Hero Doesn't Cry"

—*Chechen Proverb*

This chapter explores and analyzes three of the most famous Chechen terrorist attacks committed by Shamil Basayev. Shamil's volcanic iceberg mentality can be viewed more readily through his unconscious choice of targets, mainly the attacks directly upon the maternal cameo. Shamil was so heavy handed in his psychotic behavior that it is as if he took a sledgehammer to a crystal figurine of a mother and child (our maternal cameo) in order to set the child free from the maternal fusion. The resulting bits and pieces are the body parts, beheadings, blood, corpses. Shamil attacks his mother, their failed relationship and others in various ways and aspects. The three attacks are his maternal drama writ large.

BACKGROUND

Many Chechens continue to venerate violence as an accomplishment. It is about honor, an identification with the charismatic, aggressive leaders who offer some kind of messianic group fantasy bonding through terror brought about by identification with the mother. As terrifying as rage is to experience in the home, abused children become compliant and learn to live with it. This creates psychic confusion in the child's mind. Sometimes they get fed and sometimes they don't. Sometimes they are "loved" and sometimes they are raged at, especially the little girl, who may also be passive-aggressively manipulated by her father. This projected, unconscious rage creates confusion, ambivalence, and an inner chaos. Where does such rage go? "How does one get rid of these unwanted parts?"

We speculate that Shamil must not have had a stable childhood but one that was manipulated by his overinvested, devalued mother. Children experience their mothers as an extension of themselves. It is terrifying for children to see their mother abused because they are completely dependent upon her and see her as an extension of themselves. Shamil's unconscious targets were a maternity hospital, a theater, and a school. These thinly veiled targets were repeated attacks on the mother, who must be repudiated because of his unmet dependency needs and terrors. All these targets were united as attacks on different aspects of his unconscious image of the maternal cameo. This begins to make more sense of Shamil's atrocious behavior. These attacks build on the theme of splitting between the mother and son, the in-group and the other—good and evil within the context of the paranoid mind. The Chechen jihadi's volcanic iceberg mentality acts out the maternal fusion–fission. The terrorists are conflicted. They have a desperate need to connect; at the same time they feel stifled and want desperately to break free, which they try to accomplish with their violent acts. Just as object relations centers around splitting between the good and the bad breast, I have extended the meaning of splitting between the mother and child to the hot and cold behavior of the volcanic iceberg mentality.

Splitting is a key psychological defense that the terrorist psyche utilizes along with projective identification. Matusitz, referencing the works of Manfield and Lifton, succinctly explains the terrorist dynamic of splitting the world. It involves totalizing and constructing binary oppositions of an us-vs.-them mentality:

> Totalism and exemplary dualism symbolize, to true believers, a perfect, flawless system led by exemplary leaders and overflowing with values; everything in the outside world, of

> course, is diametrically opposed. Because totalism is absolute, there is a profound intolerance for ambiguity. Totalism, then, is a polarized self-construct that creates "divided selves." Now, young terrorists or recruits can identify with heroic leaders and the idealized values they embody. At the same time, prior feelings of weakness, failure, low self-esteem, irreverence, shame, and guilt can be rejected more easily and projected onto chosen enemies considered fundamentally inferior and abhorrent. Through the dynamics of such projective identification, the self-image of in-group terrorists becomes, in part, psychologically dependent on the out-group scapegoat and the contrast symbols that were projected onto people of the out-group and that are antithetical to the in-group.
>
> Projective identification is a psychological defense mechanism associated with splitting. Splitting reflects the notion that the enemy is totally different, morally weak, and worthy of extermination. Consequently, everything about the enemy is totally shuffled off to the "evil" category. Splitting is fundamental to totalitarian thinking and involves a strategy to divide all world nations into good and evil, saved and doomed, human and subhuman, etc., and to switch back and forth rapidly between these polarized categories.[203]

To help develop a sense of the unconscious communication and terror of these terrorists, I show the primitive and often quite literal nature of their nonverbal communication. Their communication is so startlingly blunt that it nearly blinds one from seeing what they are doing and what they cannot feel. We have difficulty believing that the communication could be that simple. Often the analysis of terrorists' unconscious behavior in light of the maternal bond is dismissed or minimized by many counterterrorist experts because they themselves are so terrified of the significance of the maternal bond that they defend against it, and hence against their own terror and vulnerability.

The North Caucasus people are depressed and have been so for generations. Living in a shame–honor environment is exhausting, difficult, and terror ridden. In *An Anthology Of Chechen-Ingush Verse*, Chechen poet Mamakayev wrote: "These manifestations of the oral tradition are reflective of the life of the Chechens and the Ingushis, their hopes and dreams, and all their joys and sorrows. There is nothing *sadder* [emphasis mine] than old Chechen songs: the autumn wind rustling in a mountain canyon, tears shed for the people who seemed to have no future."[204]

The Chechens are characterized by their own writers as a depressed people. Depression is anger turned inward. However, jihadi attacks are precipitated by rage turned outward and projected. The jihadis bear the hallmark of severe characterological psychopathology on the order of a hybrid of sociopathic and psychopathic—a socio-psychopath. The sociopath is the neighbor who lives next door and is always described as so nice. His or her psychopathology is rarely detected by the neighbors. The psychopath, on the other hand, is more overtly unstable in his aggression.

One of the leading problems in counterterrorism studies is the poor level of training in psychology. The experts are not trained to detect characterological pathology—that is, problems in the development of the personality or "character armor" itself. Even though criminologists look at violence all the time, many have not been able to factor in the roots of violence in terms of genetics, neuroscience of the brain, and early childhood history. This early time frame is when the personality is built. Its underpinning is the maternal attachment. When this attachment is flawed, it allows the potential for terrorist behavior, which can lay dormant until it is mobilized to violence. To quote Matthew Levitt, a leading counterterrorism expert at the Washington Institute for Middle East Studies, there is also a conceptual problem within the field [of counterterrorism, my addition], which lacks the capacity to deal with violent extremism's *early* roots:

> When it comes to countering violent extremism (CVE), there are two problems, one conceptual and the other structural. The conceptual problem involves figuring out who—comfortably within the law—will be able to move the needle so that violent extremists can be countered earlier in the process, instead of when they have already been radicalized and are thinking about committing a violent act. The FBI and other federal law enforcement agencies, for their part, are not set up to engage in such earlier participation. A federal agency does not want to be seen as the thought police, *nor are its officials trained to be social workers* [emphasis mine]. In addition, a central challenge involves determining how to identify the ideas that drive people to violent extremism rather than focusing on a particular religion. This type of reckoning must also include consideration of the sociocultural factors that may affect a person's susceptibility to radical ideas.[205]

One can begin to understand how and why it is so difficult to put the issue of early maternal attachment and the idea of the maternal drama of the volcanic iceberg mentality on the table for discussion concerning the creation of jihadis. Such aberrant behavior does not arise de novo. It has its own history rooted in a mix of genetics-neurobiology-maternal attachment set within a cultural frame of shame–honor. In the case of Shamil Basayev, a disrupted maternal attachment is glaringly obvious in the chaos, bedlam and massacres he deliberately caused. The topical layer of political violence's rage against the enemy masks the underlying unconscious layer of rage against the mother. Rage is a layered emotional matter.

Chechen Islam used to be a tolerant form of Sufi Islam, not so strict and fundamentalist. Yet Sufi Islam also has a history of violence woven into its more pacifistic, lodge-oriented worship. The Chechens came under the influence of Wahhabi Salafi's Islam spread by the Saudis. Salafi's ideologies are more prone to violence. Prior to Al Qaeda's involvement in Central

Asia, including Afghanistan, Chechens practiced a rather moderate Islam unaffiliated with Wahhabi Salafi Islam. I witnessed a moderate Islam when I was in Uzbekistan in 1977, though there were tensions percolating beneath the surface because they were also dominated by the Soviets, as the Chechens were. With Shamil Baseyev's training in Afghanistan against the Russians, he came under the influence of Wahhabi Salafi Islam and imported his experience of jihad to Chechnya. As the former Soviet Union fell apart, Chechnya became a fertile training ground for jihadis returning from Afghanistan. Just as today there are concerns that Chechens fighting in Syria will return home and further radicalize others to fight jihad.[206]

Others who spread radical Islam included foreign Arab Mujahedins such as Zawahiri, Osama bin Laden's second in command, who was arrested by the Russians in 1996. When Zawahiri attempted to cross into Chechnya, no one recognized him. They had little idea who he was. He was jailed for six months and then let go. There was also the case of Ibn Khattab, whom the Russians wanted to assassinate:

> In early March 2002, the FSB [Russian Federal Security Service] learned that Magomedov [an aide of Khattab] was going to Saudi Arabia to pick up a package for Khattab from his *mother* [emphasis mine] (including letters, a Sony video camera, and a wristwatch). The FSB intercepted the package while Magomedov was in Baku and laced the letter with poison—a neurotoxin that was absorbed through the skin, rapidly causing a heart attack or suffocation. On March 19, Magomedov delivered the package to Khattab. Half an hour later, Khattab emerged from his bunker where he was reading the letters, white and disoriented He fainted predictably, but regained enough clarity to have Magomedov, who was immediately grabbed by Khattab's bodyguards, released. Minutes later, Khattab was dead.
>
> Moscow needed proof of Khattab's death to present to the public, and when they received a tip that Khattab's chief

> bodyguard Ilyas Isayev (a.k.a. Elsi the Red) was arranging to have a videotape of Khattab's burial sent to Khattab's family, Russian special forces tracked him down. "We waited for Elsi and ambushed him in the mountains," an FSB officer recounted. "We killed him and retrieved the tape." The tape was soon broadcast on Russian TV.[207]

Tracking the mother has often led to finding the terrorist. The maternal relationship is the Achilles heel of terrorists because they are emotionally unable to separate from her. Yet even here counterterrorists fail to realize the significance of the maternal drama and its intrapsychic dynamics of creating the volcanic iceberg mentality. This limited understanding causes a blind spot that inhibits long-term solutions. Basically, the strategy is cutting off one of the heads of the hydra but not getting to the root. For example, the famous Palestinian bomb maker/serial killer Yahya Ayash, "The Engineer," was found through his contacts with his mother. The Israel security forces tracked him and developed a bomb in a cell phone, which was given to Ayash. When he went to call "home," his head was blown off.[208] Blowing off his head is also a nonverbal communication of Israeli security forces' attempt to get rid of his hatred and lethal negativity, but this does not ultimate solve the problem of ongoing terrorism. Another incident of tracking was that of Osama bin Laden's messenger in Abbottabad as portrayed in the movie, *Zero Dark Thirty*. Bin Laden's messenger called his mother nearly on a daily basis, which allowed tracking of his hiding place.

Frequently Chechen families are collectively held responsible for their jihadi relatives.[209] This police tactic underscores the nature of the enmeshed clan families in which there is a lack of individuality. The group acts as if it were one undifferentiated body, with someone being perpetually scapegoated as the safety valve for relieving the group's swirling, unconscious rage. In a shame–honor culture the centrality of its "uber-mother" actually masks the extreme hatred of the female. It is a defensive measure. That is why we can see more clearly that Basayev's attacks were really meant for his mother. It is a displacement in which the male seeks to free himself from the grip of mother, who is experienced as emasculating because of her smothering environment. The psychological emasculation manifests itself through a macho façade of bravado. Terrorists do not work through this early developmental problem of the maternal fusion. Resorting to violence signifies that they are developmentally arrested.

THE THREE MAJOR ATTACKS

- A maternity hospital—an attack on the mother
- A theater—an attack on the maternal cameo, representing the darkness of death
- A school—an attack on the school child, the envied object

These three attacks, which made Basayev internationally notorious, were hostage-taking events that ended in the wounding and deaths of innocent victims, including women and children. Two of the attacks took place in provincial areas, while the middle event was in Moscow. How might we understand these nonverbal messages about Chechen terrorist psychological development and their volcanic iceberg mentality?

The first thing to note is the conflict over Basayev's own death. This dispute gives us pause, considering the many thousands of innocent victims he murdered and injured. Yet, in his own death there is disavowal or denial of what really happened. The Chechen terrorists claim that he was not assassinated by the Russians in July 2006.[210] They claimed that his death was due to an accidental explosion. Why? Because if they were to grant victory to the Russians, it would bring shame on the group.

The second aspect of these three attacks is their absolute grandiosity and flagrant disregard for the civilian population. Basayev justified his actions by claiming that the Russians also attack the collective, the Chechen people. This is what I characterize as the you-do-it-too syndrome, the tit-for-tat argument that shifts the focus away from the grossly inappropriate killing of children. It is also the kind of claim one hears from those who suffer from borderline personality disorder. Lachkar analyzed the terrorist personality as borderline in "The Psychological Make-Up of the Suicide Bomber."[211] Borderline behavior shows adhesive personalities. They stick to you like glue. They take you hostage. They seek to velcro themselves to others through hostage taking, both physical and mental.

From a psychological perspective, an unconscious thread runs through all three of these attacks, linking them in sequence like a serialized nightmare. As in serial killing, attacks are read functionally to detect meaningful clues concerning the killer in order to prevent future attacks. These attacks are interrelated, thereby facilitating an unearthing of their unconscious destructive forces—e.g., death instincts as opposed to life. They bolster support for a volcanic (eruption of an unquenchable rage) iceberg (lacking empathy) mentality that is out of touch with reality. Read together, these three attacks compose a psychotic constellation. Terrorists have no feelings, no understanding, and, worst of all, act with no empathy toward their victims, who are objects to be repudiated—objects connected in fantasy to the mother.

Basayev equated his psychotic fantasies with reality. Imagine little boys in pre-school building a tower out of blocks and then taking another block and knocking the tower down. These children are learning how to master their aggression and rage. But even more important is that they are playing and discovering the difference between play and reality. Basayev never played, we can surmise, because he took his fantasies to be real. The internal object of the maternal cameo becomes projected outward onto innocent targets, basically mothers and children. The violence escalated from attacks on a maternity hospital to a theater and then to a school. The locations and targets reveal the nature of the object whose fragmented parts temporarily re-create a fusion with the maternal cameo, which is then shattered by the attacks.

The attacks are like splitting the atom by fission. One attack is not sufficient because Basayev's rage was so psychotically excessive.

THE BUDENNOVSK MATERNITY HOSPITAL HOSTAGE CRISIS: A TRANSPARENT ATTACK ON THE MOTHER

Terrorists' inability to mourn loss, show sadness, and deal with loss brings up the demeanor of the Chechen mother of a terrorist. She doesn't cry, or is not supposed to cry, and must not show any sign of remorse. In Chechen culture the mother is considered a "hero." According to Melanie Klein, this is what occurs in the paranoid-schizoid position, which is a very fragmented primitive state in which one does not have the capacity to mourn and is dominated by persecutory anxiety and other primitive defenses, as my colleague Joan Lachkar has articulated.

> Budennovsk Hospital Hostage Crisis took place from 14 June to 19 June 1995, when a group of 80 to 200 Chechen separatists led by Shamil Basayev attacked the southern Russian city of Budyonnovsk...some 70 miles (110 km) north of the border with the de facto independent Chechen Republic of Ichkeria. The incident resulted in a ceasefire between Russia and Chechen rebels, and peace talks (which later failed) between Russia and the Chechens. It caused a major political crisis in Russia.[212]

Shamil Basayev, the leader of the plot, had lost his mother and then launched the three attacks before he was finally killed.[213] The loss of his mother and her unmourned death acted like a tripwire, precipitating his violence. We can surmise that Basayev became psychologically unglued. His fragile personality could not sustain such a loss. Even his assassination can be understood as a return to his mother. Through his anti-social behavior he sought out death, almost begging to be killed in order to return to his mother in fantasy. The loss is repeated rather than mourned.

Numerous terrorists attacked the hospital. Initially, the attack's aim was Chechen independence from "Mother" Russia. It began as a hostage-taking crisis, which extended over a five-day period. Basayev could not let go of his "symbolic mother." He wanted the impact of this hostage event to increase the momentum of his movement.[214] He turned the hospital into a battlefield. In addition to his mother, two children, and a sister died during the Russian bombing of his uncle's home on June 3, 1995. His brother also was killed in another incident.

Since it is not permissible to mourn loss in the Western sense, in less than eleven days after his mother's death, Basayev retaliated by taking the Budennovsk maternity hospital hostage. His mother was no longer alive to protect him, to maintain the fused state from which he derived limited stability. We have seen this before with other terrorists such as Zarqawi, who went on a beheading rampage in Iraq the day after he finished the requisite Islamic mourning period of forty days for his mother. Bouyeri, who butchered Theo Van Gogh to death in Amsterdam, nearly decapitating him, also acted out his rage after the death of his mother. His own sister pointed to maternal loss as a means to explain his violent behavior. I wrote about this in *The Banality of Suicide Terrorism*.[215] Such violent behavior indicates that these terrorists are confused by the emotions they experience with the loss of their mother. Their feelings are contaminated regarding the body and its functions, including giving birth. This ties in directly to Basayev's choice of a maternity hospital as a target.

I have heard male experts declare that an attack on a maternity hospital shows the depravity of the terrorists. Such an anecdotal comment is indicative of the uneasiness of experts who lack training in child development. By dismissing the unconscious aspect, they can temporarily alleviate their own anxieties. Budennovsk as a target raised the ante. It extended Chechen terrorism beyond an ethnic nationalist separatist movement as the Chechens began to capture the attention of the world. Since terrorists have never developed empathy, they lack the cognitive capacity to understand the relationship with their mother. Instead they lash out at the mother under the banner of political violence. The attack on the maternity hospital reveals the unconsciously motivated obsession not only with the prenatal and postpartum mother but with birth itself. This attack became emblazoned in the mind of the Russian public. It was a precursor of the ruthlessness with which the Chechen jihadis sought to terrorize the public because it was an unconscious attack on everyone's mother, including "Mother Russia."

Shamil Basayev went on to pledge alliance to Osama bin Laden. We can speculate that Basayev's disturbed omnipotence and grandiosity was on the same order of psychological magnitude as that of bin Laden—"twins" of violence.

There has been only one other attack on a hospital maternity ward as of this writing. It occurred during the Mumbai attacks in November 27, 2008. Lashkar-e-Taiba, a Pakistan Islamist terrorist organization, launched a maritime attack against the Cama and Albless Hospital, a women's and children hospital, at times referred to as a maternity hospital.[216] While it remains unclear if the Budennovsk Hospital attack served as a model for this segment of the Mumbai attack, the Chechen jihadis had established a precedence in cruelty, exceeding the bounds of human morality. We can further extract from this attack on maternity a transparent disregard for the sanctity of the female. It articulates the "ferror" of the terrorists.

Basayev also revealed the limited way in which he engaged the world. His was an autistic, insular world in the sense that he (as are all terrorists) was completely removed or disconnected from what it means to have a stable, nonviolent relationship. "Maternity hospital" became an unconscious metaphor. According to Basque cultural anthropologist Joseba Zulaika's research and writing on violence and metaphor, the terrorist does not have an elaborated sense of symbol and metaphor.[217] The lack of empathy inhibits the development of such a sense. Instead the behavior and dependency upon the mother and the terror of the female are so great that they cannot be hidden from sight. The use of this nonverbal language is concrete and transparent, yet they themselves do not see this tragic irony.

I see this initial attack as a glaring example of the disconnected, volcanic iceberg brutality of Basayev's terror as related to the Lost Mother Syndrome.[218] The attack on the maternity hospital allows us to see a fragment of the Chechen terrorist's psychotic, immature mind communicated through the unconscious choice of a place that embodies the essence of the mother-infant relationship—birth and life.

MOSCOW THEATER HOSTAGE MASSACRE: AN ATTACK ON THE MATERNAL CAMEO

Why would a terrorist want to attack a theater? What psychological function or symbolic meaning might a theater serve the terrorist? A theater is a place for spectacle and entertainment and also healing of the human spirit. J. Shay, an internationally renowned expert on Post Traumatic Stress Disorder, has brilliantly argued that ancient Greek theatre's concept of the chorus was created in order to facilitate the return and transitioning of struggling Greek warriors to civilian life, helping them with their war trauma. This was theatre's positive communal endeavor.[219] The attack on the Moscow Theatre is in direct opposition to the ancient Greek function. In terrorism studies there is also discussion of terrorism as "theater" in a metaphorical and symbolic sense. That terrorism creates a kind of theater setting has been discussed by a series of scholars, most recently Brigitte Nacos and Gabriel Weissman.[220] Mass murders have often taken place on the "public stage before an audience," with victims who are largely strangers "chosen for their symbolic significance or targeted at random."[221]

Yet there is an important oversight in this discussion—namely, the unconscious choice of the target and its accompanying unconscious dynamics, which are literally "played out" on the hidden aspect of this theater's stage. While we may never know what was going on in the disturbed volcanic iceberg mind of Basayev,[222] it is certain that the choice of target and murderous attack on a Moscow theater embody a troubled history of relations for Basayev in his primary familial dyad of mother–infant and in the triad that included his absent father. The theater goers become triangulated and targets of his violence.

With Basayev's misuse of the theater as object, he destroyed the socially accepted code for entertainment and manipulated the use of mass media as well, which also held the potential for entertainment. Instead his is "jihadi entertainment," constituting a perversion and sado-masochism. The Moscow Dubrovka Theater attack by Basayev inverted the normal use of the theater to a destructive end. Thus, we see the difference between the normal mind and the autistic-like mind. To commit these heinous crimes against humanity requires a volcanic iceberg mentality that acts out the terrorists' grievances, which they cannot articulate. They become enraged and attacking, justifying under the banner of jihad what they cannot express emotionally. Geifman zeros in on this aspect of the Moscow attack. "The as-if quality of terrorism had reached the point of refined dramatization: the audience was forced to play a part in the real-life performance, in which it was being killed by both the terrorists and the state."[223] The same can be said for rampage shootings that have taken place in movie theaters, as in the case of the 2012 Aurora theater shooting in Colorado. The thread of the theater and its misuse runs throughout different types of violence, but the underlying connection and interlocking links concern the enactment of the maternal drama.

A hallmark of terrorism is that terrorists work against socially accepted norms and seek to destroy them. The Moscow theater attack concretized the notion of attacking a group that was enjoying itself. Bion's concept of a working group is helpful here.[224] He wrote about group dynamics that could either be positive or negative. The audience represented a positive assembly of people working toward the social goal of having a night out and enjoying their culture without violence and aggression. A healthy group sublimates its aggression through art. Bion also noted that a regressed destructive group, like the terrorists, envies and destroys.

Stephen L. Carter, a Yale professor of law, commented intuitively about the theater of terrorism with regard to the Boston Marathon attacks. Even though he does not mention the Moscow Theater attack, his words are applicable:

> The notion that terror is theater was popularized by the British novelist John le Carré in his masterpiece "The Little Drummer Girl," published in 1983. Years later, le Carré traced the genesis of the phrase to a conversation with a "Palestinian firebrand" in Beirut: "He was talking about the murder of Israeli athletes at the Munich Olympics, but he might as well have been talking about the twin towers and the Pentagon." The late Michael Bakunin, evangelist of anarchism, liked to speak of the Propaganda of the Act. It's hard to imagine more theatrical, more potent acts of propaganda than these.
>
> Thus terror is also theater because it is intended to send a message. Contrary to common understanding, the message isn't in the first instance political or ideological. It is psychological. Terrorism, writes Leo Braudy in his fascinating book "From Chivalry to Terrorism," is "primarily symbolic and propagandistic," signaling "that all the high technology in the world cannot stop a determined enemy, even one armed only with primitive weapons."[225]

I added to this idea the notion of a maternal communicative circuit in my first book, *The Banality of Suicide Terrorism*. We are all plugged in globally since we all have mothers. This circuit is dependent upon tapping into our earliest nonverbal terrors linked to the maternal relationship and concerning dependency needs and abandonment. It is through this maternal network that terrorists play out their fantasies as we watch it through the media as if we were sitting in a global theater.

Dolnik details the strategy and tactics of the spectacular Chechen attack on the theater, which dominated the media. It raised great criticism and wide debate concerning Russia's response. Dolnik notes the difficulty in reconstructing the hostage-taking event. Eyewitness reports were often conflicting. Thus, he used three witnesses in order to corroborate details of the terrorist attack. No two Chechen terrorist groups are alike.[226]

The Russians used chemical weapons to bring the hostage-taking crisis to an end. The issue of chemical weapons has recently come into focus in Syria, where Assad allegedly used them against his own people, although it is not clear if it was Assad himself or the anti-Assad force, Nusrah. Nightwatch, a reputable counterterrorism daily news update, raised the issue of the Chechens and the Russians in conjunction with what was going on in Syria on 27 August 2013. Ironically, Putin seeks to intervene in the Syrian chaos, despite the known history of Russians using poison.

THE BLACK WIDOWS IN THE THEATER ATTACK

We must note the importance of Basayev "weaponizing" females in suicide bombing, which denotes his attempt to kill off his prenatal mother. Many of the females that Basayev armed had been abandoned because of the jihadi deaths of their husbands or brothers. In a normal society, if you lose a husband or brother in war you do not engage in revenge killing. In the Chechen shame–honor culture, the female can be easily manipulated in this regard. In addition, a further element is revealed through the attack because of the death fusion. The Black Widows, female suicide bombers who join in death with their targeted victim/object, illustrate the misuse of the female as a lethal object. A. Berko has referred to the suicide bomber as both victim of her own terrorist group and victimizer.[227] I have written in *The Banality of Suicide Terrorism* that suicide bombing is group-assisted mass murder by proxy—the suicide bomber.

Between 2002 and 2004, generally young female and often widows of the Chechen jihadis gave a new face to the war effort, recasting terrorism in a spinoff from the Palestinian arena of the female suicide bomber, but with a new twist. There was an uptick in attacks. Bodansky claims "It was a final, and desperate, symbol of the Islamist influence on segments of Chechen society."[228] He writes, "These women, particularly the wives of the mujahedin who are martyred, are being threatened in their homes. Their honor and everything are being threatened," Abu-al-Walid told Al-Jazeerah TV. "They do not accept being humiliated and living under occupation. They say that they want to serve the cause of almighty God and avenge the death of their husbands and persecuted people."[229]

The latter quote encapsulates the shame–honor culture that has become radicalized, and, in this particular instance, Islamized. Bodansky notes the differing background of the Black Widows. Yet the underlying psychological mechanism is traumatic bonding and seeking a death fusion. "While the Black Widows themselves came from a diverse array of backgrounds—some widows and others not, some well off, some poor, some claiming having been raped, tortured, some depressed, some social outcasts—they had one thing in common...they all ended up in the hands of the Islamist terrorist cells, submitting themselves to training for suicide missions."[230]

The Moscow theater attack seared the image of the Chechen Black Widow—a scary, caricaturish image of this special brand of female suicide bomber—into global consciousness. However, these female terrorists did not run the Chechen jihadi groups. They were nothing more than dressed up terrorist "dolls" who were expendable. The Black Widows are reminiscent of disposable, abused children. These black-shrouded female suicide bombers appear pregnant because of the vests or girdles they wear to carry the bombs. They become a concrete visual representation of the prenatal mother, whom the terrorists cannot stand because the mother holds the potential to arouse their needs. Thus, the terrorists target their unconscious rage against the prenatal mother.

As impending perpetrators, the female suicide bombers are manipulated by their male handlers. They, too, are victimized from within the terrorist group. They are murdered by one of their own, but it is not called murder. The Black Widow brand becomes a strategic means of terrifying victims and the global audience by subverting the norm of the female as the embodiment of all life-giving forces. Again, this shows us how jihadis misuse objects, specifically the female.

Not all female fighters are Black Widows, women who seek to avenge the death of their male relatives, thus fitting with the shame–honor code of cleansing shame and restoring honor by willfully spilling blood. From an email exchange with Anonymous, we learn more about these female jihadis from the Chechens:

> The "Black Widows" term seems to have been coined by the Russians. These were widows of Chechen men tortured and killed by the Russian servicemen. Some of them had also lost their fathers, brothers, or sons to the same barbarians... There is no evidence that these men took part in the armed conflict. They were tortured and killed because they were Chechen. Of course, there were those who took to arms to counter the Russian invasion of 1994 and then (much more forceful and much more brutal) in 1999. And with a very few exceptions they were Chechen first and Moslem second. They fought for their country and people, not for Islam... It makes sense that their widows having lost everything sought closure by giving their own lives in blind revenge. BTW: the most famous "Black Widows" took part at the Moscow Theater Hostage Tragedy in 2002. All of them were killed while unconscious and harmless by the Russian "security" services. Many people believe that they were killed because the regime did not want to leave witnesses alive. One was executed by a bullet in the back of her neck while lying unconscious on the pavement—on camera for all the world to see. And the authorities eventually recognized that the suicide belts they wore were fake. (Anna Politkovskaya's book provides ample evidence of the foul play...)
>
> I have met many Chechen women, who had lost their husbands, or brothers, or sons, due to Russian war crimes. A small percentage wore a scarf, none of them wore niqab, let alone hijab. They were trying to get back to a normal life, mostly for the sake of their children. Jihad was not a movement in Chechnya. No mother or wife of tortured and killed men seemed to take pride in their men's paying the ultimate price for

> their cause. They were just plain mourning and in pain. This is not what we hear from e.g. Arab women in Yehuda, Shomron, and Gaza.
>
> I understand there is a small number of men from the North Caucasus fighting these days alongside Salafis and Jihadis in Syria. Nobody knows how many or from which of the numerous nations in the North Caucasus. I must assume that some of these men are Chechen. Their radicalization is relatively recent and can be ascribed to the sense of despair felt by many, who now see their country run by a brutal, Tamer-Lan type tyrant, protected and financed by Putin. I am sure that their childhood was formed by over-protective mothers and that they were spoiled and deprived of sincere motherly love and adult guidance. Yet, these people are few in numbers compared with those (also rather few) who wage a guerrilla warfare against the Russian forces and their local henchmen at home. Apparently, this year there were 76 killed Russian servicemen in the North Caucasus...
>
> Chechens are about independence. They have never accepted Russian bondage. As a good friend of mine remarked: "Every generation of Chechens fights its own war for independence." And, that began long before the revival of the Jihad against the Kufr...[231]

Paul J. Murphy in his *Allah's Angels* claims that death continues to haunt the Chechen woman, with peace and sanity remaining elusive for her.[232] He also argues, and I agree, that there is a tradition among Chechen women of taking up arms. Those who claim that there isn't a tradition, disregard "the heroines of the nineteenth century Caucasus wars who fought at Dadi-Yurt, Akhulgo, and other Chechen villages attacked by Russian forces, not to mention the legendary Taimaskhw Molova, who for ten years eluded Tsaritsyn armies until she was finally captured."[233]

Here is a snapshot of the best-known Black Widows:

- Hawa (Khava) Barayeva: 2000 July. Niece of Arbi Barayev, the terrorist senior leader in Basayev's retinue. She drove a bomb-laden truck into a military post, reminiscent of the Syrian Socialist National Party's (SSNP) Sana'a Mehaidli, who attacked an Israeli convoy in Jezzin, South Lebanon on April 9, 1985. Mehaidli is often referred to the first female suicide bomber and the "Bride of the South."[234]
- Khava Barayeva: said to be the first Shahidka or Black Widow; attacked a Russian Army base in Chechnya in June 2000.[235]
- Lyuba, Black Fatima: real name was Lida or Lyuba. She was a kind of evil den mother handler, who drugged and manipulated other Black Widows, preparing them for their suicide attacks and even escorting them to their attack sites.[236]
- Luiza Asmayeba: This 22-year-old was raped by mujahedin and felt martyrdom was the only way to purify herself, which she related to security authorities. A postmortem examination confirmed that she was pregnant.[237]
- Zulikhan Yelikhadzhiyeva: abducted and taken hostage at age 20 on the orders of one of her half brothers. She had fallen in love with another half brother and had consummated the relationship. If the family had found out about it, she would have been honor murdered. She was forced into becoming a female suicide bomber, carrying out an attack at a rock concert in Moscow in 2003.[238]
- Amanta Nagayeva: 27 years old, and Satsita Dzhebirkhana: 37 and divorced, took part in the suicide bombing of two Russian commuter planes attacks by Black Widows in the fall of 2004.[239]
- Yassira Vataliyeva: 42 years old. A veteran female fighter of Basayev's.[240]

Bodansky stresses that at best these women had a very superficial ideological motivation in Islam to become martyrs, as Anonymous also notes. The majority felt deep shame. However, Bodansky, like so many other researchers, did not mention the significance of shame on early childhood development.

While the Chechen Black Widows have had a profound effect on global jihad, what is not so well known is the impact the Chechens had on the Palestinian arena, particularly Hamas, the Islamist terrorist organization that had taken over Gaza after the Israeli unilateral withdrawal. In 2004, Hamas debated the use of female suicide bombers, inspired by the Chechen Black Widows.

> The immediate impetus was Reem al-Riyashi's successful January 2004 suicide bombing at the highly secured Erez crossing in Gaza. After several attempts by male mujahedin to reach the crossing had failed—Riyashi, the mother of two young children—had "volunteered" to commit martyrdom rather than face an inevitable honor killing for adultery. Her success captured the attention of Hamas, leading the group to establish its own Black Widows unit in the summer of 2005.[241]

We note a crossover effect. The Chechen fatwa or legal ruling on the permissibility of using female suicide bombers was written by Muhammad bin-Abdallah al-Seifert, the mufti of the Chechen mujahedin. Interestingly enough, after the Moscow Dubrovka Theater hostage event with the Black Widows, Basayev escalated the use of suicide bombing, as was being done in the Palestinian arena.

> Dubrovka was a watershed event, creating a new dynamic, with two fundamental and qualitative changes taking place on the Chechen side. First, terror became the strategic weapon of choice. Second, Shamil Basayev escalated the war by adopting the Palestinian model of suicide terror against civilians." [242]

Thus the two arenas of jihad fed off of each other. Their imitative behavior is formative of the borderline personality disorder.[243]

Even though President Kadyrov, sarcastically called Little Stalin, created a national holiday known as Chechen Women's Day "in honor of Dadi-Yurt's forty-six women and today's Chechen women,"[244] it is reminiscent of the Arabs' claim that they love their children like jewels, yet nonetheless they would not hesitate to slaughter their daughters in honor killings or send their children as suicide bombers. The splitting between being venerated and hated is simply masked by a heroine's day. The shame–honor culture is predicated on the abuse of the female and growing up under a death threat.

BESLAN SCHOOL HOSTAGE MASSACRE: THE ANNIHILATION OF THE CHILD IN THE MATERNAL CAMEO

Why would one want to attack children, the most vulnerable persons in a society, and a school? Children are an extension of and dependent on the mother. To attack them is to attack the mother indirectly by causing her great pain.

The Beslan School attack in September 2004 involved 1,100 hostages, including 770 children, and 385 deaths. Geifman describes the carnage at Beslan as having recreated a mini-concentration camp à la the Nazis:

> These are not familiar scenes from the Holocaust. Nor is it a replay of *Sophie's Choice*, when the captors allowed *11 women to leave with their babies* [here we have an example of a buried image of the maternal cameo, emphasis mine] but did not permit them to take their other children to safety. This happened only several years ago, when Beslan School No.1 became a mini-replica of a concentration camp. The Nazis, devoted clergymen of a death cult, kept excellent records of their abundant sacrifices—on paper and in photographs. The death-worshippers inside the school shot a video to commemorate death's triumphant entrance into postmodernity.
>
> For a while after all captives had been herded into the gym, the children could not calm down, recalled teacher Alik

> Tsagolov: "There was horrible screaming and yelling around. The bandits came up to me, pointed an automatic rifle, and threatened to shoot me, if children did not shut up. And thus they repeatedly 'hushed' the kids—by threatening to kill." The older kids soaked their shirts in water in the toilet and wrung a few drops into the small children's open palms. "I will shoot you all with such great pleasure!" screamed one terrorist, as the kids cried, hugged one another, and said their last goodbyes.... They [the terrorists] ordered, "Sit down and if you make any noise, we will kill 20 children," 10-year-old Georgy Farniyev later told a BBC correspondent. The journalist noted that the boy kept repeating a phrase that he had said to himself for three days of captivity again and again, like a mantra: "Stay as quiet as a mouse.... As quiet as a mouse." "Lord, help me!" whispered a 10th-grader, but a terrorist heard him: "The Lord has nothing to do with this. Pray to Allah!" he screamed.... Other hostage-holders tore off the children's baptismal crosses and laughed: "Pray to whoever you want. Those who will get out of here alive are beloved by Allah." "I will personally kill you," said a captor to Islam Hadikov, a Muslim boy who thought he would not be harmed by a coreligionist. A witness said that it might have been the same terrorist who shot a 15-year-old in the back as he tried to help a girl wounded in the explosion. The only terrorist who survived and was captured "was the most sadistic," testified a former hostage, Kazbek Dzarasov. "I saw him come to the gym just to beat children. He punched a 10-year-old in the stomach with a foot."[245]

Geifman also quoted the first doctor who entered the school:

> Professor Tazret Gatagov was the first doctor to enter the building. In his diary he described what he saw inside: "The entire floor is covered with burnt bodies, body parts, debris—a meter-and-a-half-tall mound. My eyes grasp pictures from hell. Here is *a woman in her last convulsion holding onto her toddler* [once again we encounter the maternal cameo, emphasis mine] ...

> Next to this, a child's hand and leg. There lays on a smoldering board the head of another child ... Half of the head of a woman, whose right hand is holding her hair—all black from the ashes.... Everywhere there are bits and pieces of children's holiday clothes, kids' shoes, aprons, ribbons, school supplies. Every inch of the gym—fragments of ripped and charred bodies of children and adults ... I walked the roads of the Second World War as a reconnaissance unit commander, but never had I seen such a horrifying picture of mass destruction of women and children."[246]

Geifman adds an important insight to the massacre at Beslan—that in essence it was an attack on the entire family network of the town:

> What happened in Beslan, however, was essentially different from past terrorist attacks against children; there, the death-worshippers took their sacrificial destruction to a new level. Beslan is a town of relatives; everyone has familial ties to everyone else. Even distant family members are very close, so much more the siblings, little ones are frequently left in the care of their older brothers and sisters. In this traditional community, for decades people live on the same street or in the same house and are more than neighbors: they spend a great deal of time socializing, celebrating birthdays and holidays together; they have common troubles and memories; their children grow up as playmates and "share moms".... There are no children of "others," felt the Beslan massacre survivors who risked their lives and evacuated little hostages, hoping that someone else would help their sons and daughters to get away from under the terrorists' fire....Prisoners inside the school constituted approximately 3.3 percent of Beslan's 35,500 inhabitants, but by orchestrating the holdup, the extremists aimed at every household and the locality as a whole: by murdering and maiming hundreds of children, they mutilated the town.[247]

I take the argument one step further, in keeping with Melanie Klein's theory of paranoia and envy—that Basayev could not tolerate that a town, which was essentially one big family, could exist and function harmoniously without violence. Therefore, his attack on Beslan can be read as an envious projection and destruction of his own disturbed clan. Unfortunately, we do not have a lot of details about Basayev's early childhood, but we may speculate that it was not a healthy, happy one. An X-ray of the problem reveals an attack and annihilation of the entire maternal cameo, the serialized terror beginning with the Budennovsk Maternity Hospital, moving into the Moscow Theater Hostage attack and culminating with Beslan. With the massacre of the children who had been sacrificed on the sacred altar of the school, there was virtually nothing left. There was no legacy.

In the United States we have had a number of attacks involving children and teenagers. Memorable among them are Columbine, Colorado, where on April 20, 1999 a pair of antisocial, malignant students attacked and murdered in cold blood twelve students and one teacher, injuring another twenty four students; and Sandy Hook Elementary School, where on December 14, 2012, Adam Lanza murdered his mother, who worked at Sandy Hook, as well as twenty-six school children and six adult staff members. Like Columbine it ended in murder–suicide.[248] Lanza shows that there is a link between domestic violence and the relationship to the mother as it spread outward once his volcanic iceberg mentality snapped. Both American school attackers had a paramilitary appearance; the killers were dressed in black and used assault weapons. Often the jihadis dress this way as well. There was also the issue of the killers having been aficionados of violent computer video games. In the last part of this book, I go into greater detail about the crossover effect of murder–suicide found in domestic violence, rampage massacres, and jihadi attacks. Beslan falls into the last category. This attack was drawn out over a series of days like the Budennovsk Maternity Hospital and the Moscow Theatre attacks, as well as the Boston Marathon Bombings.

To attack a school is to attack a special kind of sacred space. Perlmutter applied the concept of sacred space—a holy place generally associated with houses of worship—to the school:

> Sacred spaces are usually associated with churches, synagogues and mosques and are characterized as areas in which members of a community congregate to worship in a shared belief system. It is qualitatively different than profane space. School yards are also sacred grounds where members of a community congregate, engage in highly ritualized activities and have a shared belief system. When students choose to kill on school grounds their actions go beyond random acts of violence to embody qualities of sacrilege, blasphemy and desecration. They are iconoclastic actions. By viewing school yard murders in the context of aesthetic and ritual theory I will demonstrate that these acts of violence are neither random, inexplicable or illogical. They are contemporary manifestations of iconoclasm.[249]

Perlmutter then goes on to underscore the role of shame in these tragic events:

> "The central role of *shame* [emphasis mine] in the causation of violence has been overlooked for two inextricable reasons. First, because the magnitude of the resulting violence is so far out of proportion to the triviality of the precipitating cause that it becomes almost impossible for any normal, rational person who operates by the criteria of common sense to recognize that the cause could in fact precipitate it. And, second, because an essential but seldom noticed characteristic of the psychology of shame is this: If we want to understand the nature of the incident that typically provokes the most intense shame, and hence the most extreme violence, we need to recognize that it is precisely the triviality of the incident that makes the incident so shameful. And it is the intensity of the shame, as I have said, that makes the incident so powerfully productive of violence."[250]

Perlmutter cites James Gilligan's book on violence[251] and ends eloquently: "From the perspective of contemporary iconoclasm it is not surprising that the sacred grounds of the school yard have become the altars for sacrificial acts of righteous slaughter."[252] The shocking nature of the attack underscores the terrorist's volcanic iceberg mentality, which could never admit that he or she has experienced shame.

DOMESTIC VIOLENCE JUSTIFIED

In *The Banality of Suicide Terrorism*, I put forth the underlying template of murder–suicide found in Western domestic violence and manifested by the maternal cameo. *Penetrating the Terrorist Psyche* elaborated on the interlocking links between domestic violence and terrorism. Violence begins in the home and flows out to the larger world, especially political violence of jihadi terrorists, in this case the Chechens. Certainly the Black Widows were abused before they were recruited or forced into jihad.

> On March 10, 2011, Human Rights Watch reported that since Chechenization, the government has advocated for an enforced Islamic dress code and other practices that violently oppress women. Wikipedia reports that the president of Chechnya, Ramzan Kadyrov, is quoted as saying, "I have the right to criticize my wife. She doesn't. With us [in Chechen society], a wife is a housewife. A woman should know her place. A woman should give her love to us [men] .... She would be [man's] property and the man is the owner. Here if a woman does not behave properly, her husband, her father, and brother are responsible. According to our tradition, if a woman fools around, her family members kill her … that's how it happens, a brother kills his sister or husband kills his wife .... As president, I cannot allow for them to kill. So let women not wear shorts." He has also openly defended honor killings on several occasions.[253]

Basayev's triad of attacks—the maternity hospital, the theater and the school—read together, constituted different aspects of repudiating the needed mother in the maternal cameo of his shame–honor culture and religion. This was his drama. The transparency of these attacks point to the volcanic iceberg mentality of this nefarious Chechen jihadi. His brittle personality could not contain his murderous rage, played out under the guise of political violence of jihad and its terrorism.

SUMMARY

All of us hold global season theater tickets to terrorism, like it or not. Media hype of terrorism makes us a temporarily fused group. Our anticipated enjoyment is attacked because the terrorists cannot partake in joy and entertainment. They are envious and extremely grandiose and omnipotent because of the poor quality of their early maternal attachment. They are like the nascent borderline children in a family who must destroy the family outing because of rage and inability to express the emotional turmoil they are experiencing. These tantrum-throwing children are completely terrified and their terrors are projected outward onto their victims. Basayev was located at the far end of the spectrum in envying and attacking.

The next chapter takes a closer look at the internal dynamics of a Chechen/Avar family, the Tsarnaevs. In their cauldron of psychosis, the Tsarnaev brothers and their family were completely out of touch with reality, which led to the triple homicide at Waltham and the Boston Marathon Bombings.

CHAPTER 5

THE FAMILY TSARNAEV AND THE TWINSHIP OF TERROR

Delving further into the volcanic iceberg mentality, we turn to the immigrant Chechen/Avar family, the Tsarnaevs. The two Tsarnaev sons committed the Boston Marathon Bombings and allegedly the triple homicides in Waltham, a Boston suburb, in 2011. The deeds of the Tsarnaev Brothers went global. Yosef Bodansky, one of the leading experts on Chechen jihad, predicted the globalization of Chechen jihad three years before the Boston Marathon Bombings:

> … the growing importance of the Chechen jihadists to the worldwide movement, regardless of their failure at home makes Chechnya a *mythological* [emphasis mine] symbol for the Islamist-Jihadist movement—a symbol they still dream of reclaiming from the Russians. And so the global jihadist movement will continue to invest in the Caucasus, deploying quality fighters and launching new terrorist strikes.[254]

It is painful for a shame–honor culture such as that of the Chechens to acknowledge what went wrong, to wash their dirty linen in public. They experience even more shame with their violent reaction to defend themselves and to blame, as well as their conspiracy thinking. It is not surprising then that the Tsarnaev parents deny that their sons committed these crimes. While their mother is Avar, a clan from Dagestan, she and her sons self-identified as Chechens.[255] This chapter sorts through their disturbed and troubled identifications with the warrior culture of Chechnya and Dagestan, as well as the warrior culture of Islamic jihad, showing how the brothers used this cultural and religious background to structure and justify their actions.

THE MALIGNANT TWINSHIP OF TERROR

I am importing a concept known as twinship to studies on terrorism. The theme of twinning occurs repeatedly in jihad. Psychologically one wonders if this isn't a kind of repetition compulsion from a failed attempt to work through trauma. The malignant twinship helps facilitate an understanding of terrorists' gruesome behavior. The sociopathic twinship is represented by a recurring theme of twoness, such as 9/11's simultaneous attacks on the Twin Towers. There is an even more interesting aspect of twinning, which occurs through the pairing of jihadi brothers or "pretend" brothers.

This nefarious twinning serves several psychological defensive functions. It condones violence when acting in tandem. If someone else commits murder, then it is okay if I do it, too. So goes the cognitive deficit of imitative borderline behavior. Twinship is a psychological way of dealing with one's infantile grandiosity and feelings of isolation and abandonment. It wards off states of loneliness and bolsters the desire to bond and feel needed by the other in order to function. While going to their respective deaths in a suicide bombing, twins are not psychologically alone. Even before the rebirth fantasy of fusing with the mother in death, they have to be led down the path, psychologically holding the hand of either a brother or their handler. In fantasy they are never alone because they are terrified, a fact that we in our own profound terror don't acknowledge or bother to analyze.

Heinz Kohut, a pioneer in the theory of self psychology, described the need for twinship as a normal developmental state, but also as a defense operative in narcissistic personality disorders to maintain parasitic bonding for a defective sense of self.

> The idea of a twinship transference developed out of Kohut's reconceptualization of Freud's construct of narcissism and his discovery of the narcissistic transferences (Kohut, 1971, 1977, 1984). He saw a person's twinship experience, along with

> others, as a means of transforming a self's archaic grandiosity into the human qualities of empathy, humor, wisdom, acceptance of death, and creativity (Kohut, 1966). He discovered this twinship transference through a patient with a fantasy of a genie[256] in a bottle. This genie was conceived as an essential likeness to whom the patient could relate whenever she felt unsupported and alone. At first, Kohut thought such a twinship experience was an expression of a mirror transference but later recognized that twinship was a transference with its own line of development from archaic to mature forms.
>
> Within the context of the transference, an outline will gradually come to light of a person for whom the patient's early existence and actions were a source of genuine joy; the significance of this person as a silent presence, as an alter ego or twin next to whom the child felt alive (the little girl doing chores in the kitchen next to her mother or grandmother; the little boy working in the basement next to his father or grandfather) will gradually become clear.[257]

Kohut also formulated the malignant twinship but did not relate it to political terrorism, to the best of my knowledge.[258] A nefarious twinship fails to promote development. There is no progression because the internal psychological infrastructure of the terrorists is nonfunctional. Instead they become more flagrantly grandiose and omnipotent in their destruction. An added irony is that this malignant twinship allows for jihadi brothers to use each other as mirroring and idealizing objects, which enlivens them to the point that they can then murder and kill themselves in terrorist attacks. They are not able to develop empathy; the other has to be destroyed. That is why in jihadi twinships one often will be killed off by the other as in the case of the Al-Asiri brothers.

Ibrahim Al-Asiri, at present the world's most wanted terrorist, has a special connection to Chechen jihad. Al-Asiri used the as yet undetectable liquid explosive he invented in a suppository bomb that he implanted in his own brother's rectum. His brother Abdullah died, but the intended victim, Saudi Arabia's chief of counterterrorism security Prince Muhammad bin Nayef, survived. Nayef directed a program to de-radicalize jihadis, something that Al-Asiri couldn't tolerate.[259] Al-Asiri also created the underpants bomb for Umar Farouk Abdulmutallib. Obviously fixated on a perverse, sadomasochistic, erotic way to destroy the other's body, Al-Asiri also created the love handles bomb. His sister was interviewed and noted that Al-Asiri became radicalized when listening to mujahedin tapes. Where did the tapes come from? Chechnya.

> After one of the brothers was killed in a car accident, family members say, Ibrahim and his younger brother Abdullah became more religious. "They started swapping videotapes and cassettes on the mujahedin in Chechnya and Afghanistan, and they became at times distant," one of the sisters told al-Watan.[260]

In their shame–honor culture, Abdullah and Ibrahim could not mourn the death of their brother in an appropriate manner that allowed for the expression of genuine, nonhysterical emotions. That they became more religious is an understatement. They became radicalized and resorted to jihad, the standard outlet for the volcanic iceberg mentality. The Tsarnaev brothers, who were also twinned, did the same thing. They listened to Chechen jihadi tapes. Since they were half Chechen, it was even easier for them to self-identify with the Chechen cause. They had a jihadi "jacket" tailor made for them.

This twinning, in my thinking, has to be traceable back to the mother since the maternal bond is the first bonding experience in life. Ideally the twinship can be seen as a normal state of development in which the child can separate from the maternal fusion and move on. This is similar to moving into the stage of parallel play for toddlers, where a sense of separateness between the self and other exists. However, this is not the case when the maternal bond is defective because of cultural prohibitions.

Twinning is routine in Islamic groups. They create brothers left and right as in the Muslim Brotherhood. Synchronized suicide bombings are a hallmark of Al Qaeda. It is a way of psychologically strengthening a fused and regressed group that works to perpetrate violence. It indicates a level of developmental arrest at the age of eighteen months to two years when children engage in parallel play more than genuinely engaging the other.

MU'AKHAT, THE QURAN-BASED CONCEPT OF ISLAMIC BROTHERING

Twinning is inscribed in Islam's ideological practices with the concept of brothering known as *mu'akhat.* It also exists in the Arab social concept of *asabiya*, group solidarity and loyalty, which informs a strong sense of Arab honor.[261] *Mu'akhat* is a practice founded in the early days of Islam by which two men become "brothers."[262] This ideological concept reinforces the potential for misuse of the concept of brother in an antisocial way, as expressed by the malignant twinships that course through the Chechen terrorist attacks.

> The best-known example is the "brothering" by Muḥammad of the Emigrants from Mecca with Muslims from Medina. This may have happened soon after he reached Medina, but is placed by Ibn Isḥāḳ just before the battle of Badr, accompanied by a list of thirteen such pairs (Ibn Hishām, 344-6). It is clear, however, from Ibn Ḥabīb (Muḥabbar, 70 f.) that there had previously been some "brothering" at Mecca, and he gives a list of nine pairs. This is confirmed partly by Ibn Isḥāḳ…[263]

We see the brothering butchery clearly in the pairing of jihadis. The attack on British drummer Lee Rigby by Michael Adebolajo and Michael Adebowale, two radicalized Nigerian converts to Islam, gives us a violent snapshot of such a gruesome twosome. Both were converts, both shared the same first name, and even the first part of their surnames. They worked in tandem and supported each other in perpetrating and acting out their violent thoughts and fantasies under the guise of jihad, hacking to death the 25-year-old Rigby in London's Woolwich district on May 28, 2013. They, too, were influenced by global jihad and Chechnya.

We even encounter the idea of the brother as a microcosm in Israeli slang when kids address one another as *achi*, which sounds close to the Arabic pronunciation of *ochi*, meaning "my brother," even though they are unrelated by blood. Let us not forget the notion of the "Band of Brothers" that occurred during the American Civil War. Like any kind of behavior, brothering has a spectrum, at the far end of which is brutal butchery. In the Middle East and in non-Arab shame–honor Muslim cultures such as that of the Chechens, it runs the risk of taking on an ominous, perverse twist, leading to senseless brutality if not held in check by communal forces. The family looms in the background of all social relationships in the Middle East as well as in Arab and non-Arab Muslim cultures, including the Chechen culture, fueling the flames and inciting the "brothers" to jihadi violence.

From a self psychology viewpoint, Kohut's malignant twinship expands an already embattled alter ego that violently engages the external world in order to bolster a fragile sense of self, experiencing a lack of in empathy because the shame–honor culture creates conditions for a flawed maternal bond. Twinship facilitates the volcanic iceberg mentality.

In his 1919 essay The Uncanny, Freud wrote about the double or *doppelganger*, a fantasy by which to rein in one's grandiosity. In shame–honor cultures, the self is not individuated as much as it is in Western culture (although we, too, have patriarchal shame–honor families; hence, the converts to Islam who become radicalized). Thus, the use of the other as an object plays a critical role in a personality that is inherently fragile and rife with narcissistic, borderline, sociopathic psychology.

My colleague Dr. Joan Lachkar has shown that narcissistic and borderline psychopathology can be conceptualized in eight different ways, meaning that there is a whole array ranging from pathological, antisocial, obsessive-compulsive, passive-aggressive, etc.[264] Each draws on the other for support, which I link to the twinship.

In Chechen culture the pairing of brothers leads to a concrete enactment of violent fantasies. More often than not they are indeed blood brothers, who bond through violence to others. The Chechen child-rearing practice of encouraging warring instills the twinship with an aggressive face. The Tsarnaev brothers formed only one of a number of preexisting Chechen twinships that served as depraved role models. These included Shamil and Shirvan Basayev, the Akhmadov brothers, Akhyad and Alikhan Mezhieve, the Sadayev brothers, and the Magomedov brothers

Shamil Baseyev's brother Shirvani worked with him.[265] Bodansky relates that in 2002 and 2003 the Supreme Islamist jihadists' leaders began to plan attacks from London to Paris to Moscow. The planning involved a diverse group of Egyptians and Chechens, including the brothers Akhmadov and others from Sweden, Great Britain, and Germany. A martyrdom battalion was established by Basayev, the leader of the Chechen jihadis, called the Riyadh-us-Salikhin, meaning the Fields of Righteousness. "In stark contrast deviation from comparable entities in the Middle East and Asia, nearly half the would-be martyrs in Basayev's battalion were young women."[266] The inclusion of women may have titrated the intensity of brotherly sadomasochism. In order to facilitate the desired attacks, sleeper agents were activated and they "approached Akhyad and Alikhan Mezhieve, a pair of Chechen brothers living in Moscow, asking for their help in establishing a clandestine support system in Moscow. The brothers were to rent three apartments to be used as safe houses and to acquire vehicles for their travel and cargo transport, they were given money, including $2,500 in cash, and told to start immediately."[267]

One wonders if the FBI and domestic law enforcement understood the deeper unconscious implications of brothers working in tandem before the Boston Marathon Bombings or the triple homicide in Waltham on

September 11. All three victims had their throats slashed, à la the proscribed slaughter in the Quran,[268] *qital fil sabil Allah*, "fighting in the path of Allah." A Muslim never would butcher for the Prophet Muhammad or any other Islamic leader, for that matter; only for Allah. Yet initially law enforcement did not link these murders to jihad, showing that they underestimated the meaning of two brothers working in tandem.

Brother twinning creates a global connection for Muslims. A Somali Woolwich Boy, a gang member, spoke about "brotherly love" after the butchery of Lee Rigby: "It is easy for preachers to pick off boys. They offer them a way out of violence when they are at their weakest. Many of us, though, like the warmth we get from Islam, the brotherly love. People might find that strange as I've led a bad life."[269]

Keeping the malignant twinship in mind, we now meet the Tsarnaev family

TAMERLAN, THE BROTHER AS BULLY AND INTIMATE TERRORIST

> If you bleat, the wolf will carry you away;
> if you keep quiet, the shepherd will cut your throat.
> –*Chechen Proverb*

The Chechen proverb above forms part of the collective unconscious concerning fantasies of violence and slaughter. Fantasies inform what is ultimately acted out by terrorists in the real world, in real time. How might we understand the unconscious dimension of tactical terrorist operations? If we look at some of the patterns in the triple homicide of Waltham and the Boston Marathon Bombings, we see that they combined classic weapons of jihad, slaughter, hostage taking, and explosives.

The Waltham murders occurred on September 11, 2011 marking the tenth anniversary of 9/11. Three young men were found with slit throats, nearly beheaded. This is classic *qital*, in Arabic meaning slaughter of the infidel in jihad.[270] Despite this message communicated at the crime scene, the police and other law enforcement were reluctant to establish these murders as an Islamic terrorist assassination of infidel Christians and Jews. The murderer was known to the three victims since there was no forced entry. One of the murder victims, Brendon Mess, was considered to be Tamerlan Tsarnaev's closest friend. Tsarnaev never attended his funeral, raising further suspicion. Mess was thought to be Christian. Erik Weissman and Raphael Teken were Jewish. Teken was an Israeli Jew and subsequently was buried in Israel. Both were suspected of being involved in the sale of marijuana. Law enforcement preferred to treat the crime scene as drug related. Could it have been that law enforcement officials were so terrified by the nature of the crime scene that they unconsciously were compelled to deny it was Islamic, let alone Chechen terrorism? Terror creates a dissonance further complicated when it involves Islamic practices.[271]

Only after the Boston Marathon Bombings did law enforcement return to connect the dots. Ibragim Todashev, a friend of Tamerlan, was shot dead when he allegedly attacked an FBI agent while being questioned about his involvement in both the Waltham Murders and the Boston Marathon Bombings. He had also been picked up for an incident of road rage and intimidated his neighbors in Boston.[272] His father claimed that he was a good boy.[273] The father demonstrates a similar denial to that of Tamerlan's parents. Generally, people who come from shame–honor cultures can never admit in public that their children did anything wrong because that would bring shame on the family. The level of denial runs deep.

Initially, the brothers had "Jewish" friends. Paradoxically, the younger brother, Dzhokhar, had thought of attending Brandeis, the first secular Jewish university in America, located in Waltham.[274] In addition to all of this, there is a history and custom of Muslims who radicalized to murder their former Jewish friends.[275] Such was the tragic murder of Ariel Sellouk by his former Saudi friend Mohammed Ali Alayed in Houston.[276] Cold-blood murders speak to the instability of the volcanic iceberg mentality. The splitting of love and hatred, hot and cold, gets easily shifted into a murderous mode when loss is experienced. We speculate that Tamerlan's defensive veneer was shattered when his boxing career stalled, and he unleashed his murderous violence. The ideologies of Islam's jihad as articulated in the Quran and its surrounding schools of interpretation fit hand in glove with a polarized split personality.

A telling sign the police missed prior to the triple homicides and the Boston Marathon Bombings involved motor vehicle violations. While seemingly minor, these violations show a flagrant disrespect for authority. Tamerlan had been pulled over by the police nine times in four years, some stops related to speeding and one for not wearing a seat belt.[277] Timothy McVeigh, responsible for the bombing of Oklahoma City's Alfred P. Murrah Federal Building on April 19, 1995, was apprehended because he was speeding. Some of the 9/11 hijackers also had incurred speeding violations. The inability to read the meaning of such aberrant behavior is part of the projection and countertransference unconsciously inflicted upon law enforcement, to which they may remain oblivious. Motor violations show the tip of the iceberg; they are an indicator that someone is on the verge of losing control and feeling superior to the law.

Another red flag was documented domestic violence. Tamerlan was reported to have a violent temper and overbearing personality. Even Dzhokhar complained about it. Tamerlan's father, Anzor, minimized the domestic violence attack.[278] Elsewhere I have argued that the police should have taken the domestic violence as a precursor of jihadi behavior because of the murder-suicide template in intimate partner violence and the Islamic suicide attack. Had the police also factored in the motor vehicle violations and the triple homicide, they may have been able to put together the pieces of the Jihadi puzzle sooner.

Tamerlan was reported by the New York Times as being overbearing in demanding religious practice from his brother. If the other brother or sisters had gone to the police, the behavior could have been tagged as an escalating precursor to committing jihad. However, since Tamerlan was the eldest of the four Tsarnaev children, he was charged with monitoring the honor of the family and hence was the most powerful. It would be very hard to go against the eldest brother. In these paranoid family dynamics, it is the elder son who is tasked with guarding and putting under surveillance the sexual purity of his sisters. Brothers develop obsessions with their devalued sisters, females who lack agency.[279]

The pressure cooker bombs were modeled on the Al Qaeda e-zine *Inspire's* article "How to make a bomb in the kitchen of your Mom." The volcanic iceberg mentality of Tamerlan had a psychological fit with that of a pressure cooker waiting to explode. I blogged along with my colleague Dr. Joan Lachkar about this particular article. We described how the rage and aggression is "in your face" and masks the impending murder meant for their own mothers, whom they hate but still venerate as a defense against their need for and inability to separate from her. They harbor severe terror of the female body. In the shame–honor Chechen code, a woman's body is supposed to be pure, yet she is a devalued female; hence, by definition this oxymoron shows that mother in the jihadi's mind is contaminated and polluted, thus repudiated.

Reading material on hypnosis was found in Tamerlan's apartment. Hypnosis is used to control others through a psychological regression and temporary bonding. Even Tamerlan's career in boxing should have been a red flag, as well, as his warrior name. Tamerlane or Timur the Lame, who called himself the Sword of Islam, was the fierce Turko-Mongol military leader who conquered west, south and central Asia, ruling from 1370-1405.[280]

Edwin Rodriguez, who boxed Tamerlan, described him as a coward. He had the reputation at the gym of being an exhibitionist exerciser. When Tamerlan traveled to Dagestan, the ancestral home of his mother, to try to meet up with jihadis, they rejected him. Men in the community described him as a dandy, flamboyant, reminiscent of Liberace.[281] It was another "maternal" rejection, a narcissistic blow. His mother could never accept him for himself as he was her narcissistic object in fusion. Through him she could fantasize that she had power.

Tamerlan did not speak English well. He hounded his future wife, Kathleen, into marrying him. We can speculate that she had poor self-esteem, which is an indicator of poor interpersonal skills. It would have been difficult for her to work her way out of the relationship. She was "captured" by him, held hostage as in Chechen bride taking. It does not sound as if Kathleen's affluent physician father and nurse mother helped her get out of the relationship or even understood the psychological risk in which their daughter found herself. Perhaps they were too terrified as well? Here we have the classic story of a young, isolated, beautiful, abused wife who has no family to go back to. She most likely was threatened with murder, verbally or nonverbally, if she crossed her intimidating iceberg volcanic husband. We marry the psychopathology learned in our family of origin. Tamerlan no doubt would have killed her. After all, he did commit murder in Waltham and the Boston Marathon Bombings. His younger brother, Dzhokhar, drove over him while he was bleeding to death from the gunshot wounds. What brother in his right mind would murder his own? But then again Dzhokhar had his own murderous rage and was manipulated, bullied, and controlled by his brother. Why not murder him? Turnabout is fair play in this psychotic world. The volcanic iceberg behavior of Tamerlan and Dzhokhar is further confirmation of the malignant twinship, with one of the brothers being killed off by the other.

In January 2013, Tamerlan disrupted a speech in the mosque and was told to leave. He was already perceived by his own as having been radicalized, but nothing was really done to curb or censor his behavior. The FBI dropped the ball upon his return to Boston. From my experience working with police and the military, there is a tendency to minimize the connection between breaking the law in other seemingly non-related misdemeanor type matters of terrorism, such as speeding violations and even more serious criminal charges of domestic violence. Even the Centre for Social Cohesion in the United Kingdom, which did geo-mapping of jihadis, discovered that where there were elevated incidents of domestic violence, there were jihadis. However, they never connected the dots.[282]

Chechenologist Professor Goltz wrote in an article in *The Nation*: "I did not know Tsarnaev's motivations. But if he is guilty of the bombings—and I have little doubt at this point that he is—there must be a link to the deeply troubled history of Chechnya, and to the generations of anger, despair and trauma experienced by his people."[283] Goltz notes how the Chechens resettled in Boston, including the well-known surgeon Khassan Baiev who wrote *The Oath*, a memoir about the wars in Chechnya and his experience as a field surgeon. In the first pages of the book, Baiev describes a woman by the name of Maret Tsarnaeva as being both a friend and interpreter when he found himself a patient in a New Jersey hospital. This is Tamerlan's aunt, who accused the U.S. government of framing her nephews. According to the aunt, they were completely innocent, a refrain hauntingly similar to the intense denial of their culpability by their mother, Zubeidat.

TAMERLAN IN THE CHECHEN DIASPORA

Tamerlan was steeped in conspiracies. He also developed a relationship with a 67-year-old mentally disabled man, Donald Larking, who believed in conspiracy thinking. According to A. Cullison of the *Wall Street Journal*, Tamerlan did engage in Dawa, the Islamic pillar of faith demanding that every Muslim must seek to convert other people. Tamerlan ultimately converted Larking to Islam.[284]

Professor Brian Glyn Williams, a professor of Islamic studies at the University of Massachusetts, Dartmouth, and an expert on terrorism and the politics of Chechnya, believes that Tamerlan's journey—which he calls "jihadification"—was less a young man's quest to join Al Qaeda than to discover his own identity. "To me, this is classic diasporic reconstruction of identity: 'I'm a Chechen, and we're fighting for jihad, and what am I doing? Nothing.' It's not unlike the way some Irish-Americans used to link Ireland and the IRA—they'd never been to Northern Ireland in their lives, but you'd go to certain parts of Southie in Boston, and all you see are donation cans for the IRA."[285] However, Williams minimizes not only the significance and history of jihad in Chechnya and throughout the global Ummah but more importantly the psychological significance of the volcanic iceberg mentality.

Little brother Dzhokhar was also on a personal quest, as we will examine more closely. But suffice it to say that the search for a stable identity eludes the jihadis. That is in part why they become violent. The volcanic iceberg mentality is by definition unstable. For Dzhokhar, identity likely played into the mix as well, says Williams, who, though he never met him at the University of Massachusetts, Dartmouth, coincidentally corresponded with him during his senior year of high school. One of Williams' friends, who taught English at Rindge "…told me he had this Chechen kid in his class who wanted to do his research paper on Chechnya, a country he'd never lived in." Williams agreed to help Dzhokhar. "The thing that struck me was how little he actually knew," he says. "He didn't know anything about Chechnya, and he wanted to know everything."[286]

While partly agreeing with Williams, I hasten to add that when the search for one's roots becomes violent, it is an indicator of a severe problem in early childhood development that has lain dormant for years and is rekindled in the teen years. Jihad can be thought of as a "malignant journey" to discover one's roots. In my previous books, I discuss how radicalization is a conversion process linked to the maternal deficit. It is a compensatory strategy to right a sinking ship—that is, a troubled conflicted identity.

The Chechens have been dispersed before in history. We have already mentioned the forced expulsion to Central Asia, especially Kazkhstan, during the time of Stalin and in World War II. However, as early as during the Ottoman Empire the Chechens wound up in Jordan, particularly in Zarqa and Amman.[287] During this time another Caucasus people, the Circassians, also went to Ottoman Palestine (before the creation of the State of Israel). It is debated if they were expelled by the Ottoman Empire or immigrated to join their Muslim brethren after they had found themselves living in a predominantly Christian environment now controlled by Russia.[288] With the Sochi Olympics and Chechen Jihad, their Circassian ethnic Muslim identity and grievances have been rekindled.[289] Zarqa also has a large Palestinian population that came to settle there after the 1948 War of Independence with Israel. Zarqa was made famous by the Palestinian Al Qaeda in Iraq. Recall that Abu Musab Zarqawi (his surname means "from Zarqa"), who, incidentally, grew up across the street from a graveyard, went on a beheading rampage the day after completing the forty-day mourning period after his mother's death.[290] She regretted that he didn't get his high school diploma. He was described as ill tempered and provoking fights. He also sent letters decorated with flowers to his mother while he was in prison. There was a question that he had raped a woman.[291] Yet another volcanic iceberg personality.

The Tsarnaev brothers venerated the "martyr" Zarqawi, who was assassinated by U.S. special forces. He had been called at first a "lone wolf" and then the "sheikh of killers."[292] The term lone wolf is used in counterterrorism to describe a self-radicalizing individual. The Tsarnaev Brothers have been labeled lone wolves. Yet Brian Michael Jenkins, a leading counterterrorism expert, prefers the term the Italians use, which is "stray dog," in order to de-romanticize the terrorism and more aptly describe the behavior. Lone wolf terror attacks are a leading concern in the United States. [293]

Zarqawi had two close friends operating in the Caucasus—Abu Atiyya and Abu Taysir—who were implicated in a foiled terrorist attack in Ankara, Turkey, in 2002, intending to use an envelope containing a biological poison.[294]

Abu Atiyya was a Jordanian like Zarqawi. He was married to a Chechen. He had a jihadi specialty, using toxic gases.[295] The ethnic affiliations are significant. Due to the early deportations of Chechens to the Ottoman Empire, these ancestors have given the Turks a unique raison d'être for fighting in Chechnya and for a Chechen identification. Many Turks went to fight. Schussenberg, founder of the field of psychodrama, has written about the impact of the Ancestor Syndrome on the descendants.[296] In the case of Chechnya we see violence normalized as a reflection of transgenerational trauma embedded in their shame–honor society.[297]

TAMERLAN AND THE QUESTION OF AN EMERGING MENTAL ILLNESS

Tamerlan was the favorite of the family. He represented honor to his mother. The first-born son is even more important than the husband. Tamerlan's mother finally had her "penis."

Zubeidat was a doting mother who would "never take any advice about her kids," says Anna, a neighbor. "She thought they were the smartest, the most beautiful children in the world"—Tamerlan most of all. "He was the biggest deal in the family. In a way, he was like the father. Whatever he said, they had to do."[298]

> The mother sought to have her son become more religious in order to stabilize his personality, she had confided to her friend that he felt like there were two persons living inside him, thus suggesting a deep split in his personality, perhaps even bi-polar. His mother would not hear of taking him to a psychiatrist because that would bring severe shame to the family especially to her.[299]

But Anna suspected there was something else that should be factored into the situation. She recalls that once Zubeidat hinted that something might be wrong. "Tamerlan told me he feels like there's two people living in him," she confided to her friend. "It's weird, right?" Anna, who wondered if Tamerlan might be developing a mental illness, suggested Zubeidat take him to a "doctor," because "If I said 'psychiatrist,' she'd just flip." Such a reaction would indicate perception of the suggestion as shaming. But Zubeidat seemed to believe that Islam would help calm Tamerlan's demons. This is an example of primitive thinking. The defense against seeing a psychiatrist is an indicator of her own mental instability and grandiosity, that she alone could solve the problem by keeping it within the paranoid bubble of the hermetically sealed family unit. According to Zubeidat, she and Tamerlan began reading the Koran, encouraged by a friend of Tamerlan's named Mikhail Allakhverdov, or "Misha," a thirty-something Armenian convert to Islam.[300] This joint activity manifests the maternal fusion, which temporarily contained his volcanic iceberg mentality.

In this mixed profile of Tamerlan, we can detect an unhealthy relationship of bondage between mother and son. A perverse way of separating from the mother would be to shift into a malevolent, lopsided twinship with his little brother. He would fight to the end, with his brother driving over him as he fled the scene of the shoot-out. In killing himself through jihad Tamerlan's death was a combination of " suicide by cop" a la Filipinio Moro (Moor, or Muslim), fighting to the death. Yet even in death Tamerlan would be reunited with his mother.

DZHOKHAR, THE "MINI-ME" LITTLE BROTHER IN THE BOSTON MARATHON BOMBINGS

> A brother without a brother is like a falcon without a wing
>
> —*Chechen Proverb*

In the movie Austin Powers, Dr. Evil creates a clone whom he names Mini-Me. The two work in tandem to create destruction. This is the type of duo that applies to the Tsarnaev brothers. Dzhokhar Anzorovich Tsarnaev, the younger brother, whose friends called him Jahar, was born on July 22,

1993 in Kyrgyzstan. Kyrgyzstan and Kazhakstan were the home of the Chechen people deported during Stalin's time. Dzhokhar was a prop for the destructive, controlling Tamerlan. While Tamerlan is said to have greatly influenced and held sway over Dzhokhar and is portrayed as the mastermind of the Boston Marathon attacks, we know more about Dzhokhar because he survived—although we still do not know the details of the triple homicide in Waltham. As of this writing, Dzhokhar has not yet gone to trial, but we do know that the prosecution will seek the death penalty for his part in the bombings.

To a degree, Dzhokhar fits the category of active shooter who survives a rampage under the ideological cover of jihad. He resembles Nidal Hassan and the Fort Hood Massacre, which took place on November 5, 2009. Hassan is a known jihadi terrorist who yelled "Allahu Akbar," the Islamic battle cry. Yet his crime was classified as workplace violence.[301] There was also the attack on the Little Rock Arkansas army recruiting center where two soldiers were killed by Carlos Leon Bledsoe on June 1, 2009. Bledsoe fled the scene and was later arrested.

Lankford did a comparative analysis of mass shooters in the United States from 1966 to 2010 and examined the differences between those who lived and those who died.[302] Could Dzhokhar and Hassan have found it more difficult to carry out a Filipino Moro tradition of Islamic jihadis who fight to the death because they were a bit more Westernized than others involved in jihad? And perhaps because they were actually afraid of dying? I don't know, but it is a question to be considered. Lankford's study does not address jihad per se, yet indirectly much can be transferred and applied to the realm of jihad since suicide attacks have become the hallmark of jihadi attacks and often the rampage shooters are dressed in combat clothing. Lankford cites Malphurs and Cohen's work on murder-suicide, noting that in the United States 70% of murder–suicide involved the spouse or significant other.[303] In *The Banality of Suicide Terrorism*, I argue that the media's effectiveness at hyping terrorism is found in the commonality of the template of murder–suicide, which is more prevalent in the Western population than, let us say, honor killing. Islamic suicide bombing benefits from this underlying Western template because it functions as an unconscious common denominator for political violence.

Dzhokhar did give us his alleged motive for the Boston Marathon Bombings—to avenge perceived slights against Islam and to protest America's involvement in wars in Iraq and Afghanistan. Yet as Landsford is quick to point out, should we believe everything a rampage killer tells us? Some have claimed that, psychologically, Dzhokhar fell sway to his big brother. In many ways Tamerlan (and the mother) recruited the brother into jihad. Together the brothers functioned psychologically as a nefarious duo. They are reminiscent of Dr. Evil and Mini-Me. Mini-me has almost no dialogue but acts in tandem with Dr. Evil. This antisocial narcissism gets played out in the twinship of Tamerlan and Dzhokhar. However, with Tamerlan's death Dzhokhar is not so much abandoned by his own brother, since he participated in killing him off, as he is left alone to stand trial for both his and Tamerlan's part in the Boston Marathon Bombings.

A good example of the ingrained belief that a fused group is superior can be found in Dzhokhar Tsarnaev's justification for jihad and the terrorist attack in Boston:

> When investigators finally gained access to the boat, they discovered a jihadist screed scrawled on its walls. In it, according to a 30-count indictment handed down in late June, Jahar appeared to take responsibility for the bombing, though he admitted he did not like killing innocent people. But "the U.S. government is killing our innocent civilians," he wrote, presumably referring to Muslims in Iraq and Afghanistan. "I can't stand to see such evil go unpunished.... *We Muslims are one body, you hurt one, you hurt us all," he continued, echoing a sentiment that is cited so frequently by Islamic militants that it has become almost cliché.* [emphasis mine] .Then he veered slightly from the standard script, writing a statement that left no doubt as to his loyalties: "Fuck America."[304]

There is a long-standing tradition in Islam to write, as Dzhokhar did, using one's own blood—for example the Quran or posters of protest. This is another example of the misuse of the object. Blood gets confused with ink and even water as honor is "cleansed" through willfully spilling blood. This is delusional thinking. Also, their idea of "one body" of the Ummah, the Muslim community, is experienced intrapsychically as a fusion, as if it were their own body because there is no psychological differentiation within the group, the Ummah. The concept of a fused, regressed group has rarely been explained from a psychological point of view in counter terrorism. This is a dysfunctional, destructive group. It is not a working group for the good of global society, although jihadis may try to justify that through world domination and submission to Islam the world will be better because the world will be like them. The narcissism speaks for itself.

Dzhokhar is described by a Chechen friend in Boston, whose mother had taken them under her wing when the family immigrated, as being compliant to his mother: "He was always like, 'Mommy, Mommy, yes, Mommy'—even if his mom was yelling at him," says Anna's son Baudy Mazaev, who is a year and a half younger than Jahar. "He was just, like, this nice, calm, compliant, pillow-soft kid. My mom would always say, 'Why can't you talk to me the way Dzhokhar talks to his mother?'"[305] On the surface the maternal relationship appeared to others as "positive." People were blind to the volcanic iceberg rage that lay lurking below the surface. The extremes are a manifestation of the psychological splitting.

The tactical choice of attacking at the Boston Marathon also has an unconscious dimension driving it. Chechen culture is oriented to the sports of fighting, boxing, and wrestling, not running marathons. Baiev in his autobiography, *The Oath: Surgeon under Fire,* writes about his training and competing in judo.[306] In the cover story of Dzhokhar in *Rolling Stone*, a Chechen friend encapsulated the cultural aspect of the fight: "Jahar idolized his older brother, Tamerlan—all the children appeared to—and as a child followed his brother's example and learned to box. But it was wrestling that became his primary sport, as was also true for Baudy, a squarely built kid who competed in a higher weight class than the slender, 130-pound Jahar. 'It's a Chechen thing,' says Baudy. 'When I went to Chechnya to see my cousins, the first thing they ask is, You want to wrestle?'"[307]

Wrestling speaks volumes about the way in which Chechens engage and attach to one another. It entails close body contact, yet elicits a feeling of false intimacy, of raging against the other and an inability to extricate one's self from the grip of the opposing wrestler. There is even a picture of the entire Tsarnaev family dressed in judo gear. However, it was their uncle, Ruslan, who tapped into the code of sports vis à vis the tragedy of the Boston Marathon, calling his nephews "losers." Like an extreme sport, the attack was linked to winning or losing. It was dependent upon the imagery of a spectacle. The image-oriented massacre went global in the media. Nacos has termed such events as mass-mediated terrorism.[308] The Marathon attack began to resemble the Mumbai attack of November 2008 as it spread across three days and was called "… the worst mass-casualty attack on US soil since September 11, 2001, a crime that could bring the death penalty."[309]

While speculative, it is thought that the Caucasus Emirate, a Chechen terrorist group, may have provided support or at the very least influenced the mindset of the brothers.[310] The emblematic photo of this group has them seated against their jihadi banner, which contains a horizontal sword that appears to skewer their heads. It is an unconscious communication that jihad is projected outwards to the beheading of the infidels. One might claim that there is no connection between the terrorist's head and the sword or scimitar, but another image, published and circulated by the *Wall Street Journal* on 12 July 2013 as photo of the day, shows a protestor in Cairo running a fake sword-like dagger through his head,[311] intimating that he is committing suicide if he cannot protest. The cultural unconscious communicates nonverbally the self-infliction of pain, like the malignant borderline who cuts himself in order to feel alive. They target their own unconscious in a concrete manner through the sword.

I surmise that those in the Chechen Caucasus Emirate Organization are unaware of this deeper level of nonverbal communication because they are highly dissociated from the meaning of their own behavior. How does this relate to the maternal cameo of the mother–infant attachment? The iceberg portion of the volcanic iceberg mentality bonds to hard objects like weapons such as the sword, which becomes a replacement for the repudiated mother. The sword cuts through their own "unmentalized thoughts," the fantasy life that they do not understand. They have what Bion characterized as "thoughts without a thinker."[312] They take their thoughts to equal reality.

In contrast, the protestor in the Cairo photo mocks the Egyptian Muslim Brotherhood, which is a cover for Muslim terrorists, protesting the fact that he does not want to run a sword through his head. The sword is an unhealthy image to display before children. It is terrifying, and the children are flooded with anxiety, confused, disoriented, and helpless. It is a negative developmental process that helps to create the volcanic iceberg mentality.

The black battle flag of jihad, called *Al-raya*, with the sword underneath the Shahada, the Islamic proclamation of faith, was said to have been carried into battle by the Prophet Muhammad and his companions. It was taken global by Al Qaeda. Many terrorist groups use it as their banner, such as is the case in Chechnya and Dagestan. How might this black flag relate to the female body? It is said that it was made from a square piece of black velvet from Aisha, the Prophet's most beloved wife, his child bride.[313] Think of it as a negative transitional object, like Linus' blanket in the Peanuts' cartoon gone wrong, since rather than calming it stimulates and is linked to violence.

The sword is intimately linked to honor, valor, purity and pride. It is a key element for imposing the honor code, but fundamentally it triggers terror and embraces the violence of the sword piercing and skewering the head, the locus of thought with its linkage to feeling, like a piece of meat, a kabob.[314] The frequently appearing crescent moon, which is linked to the Islamic religious calendar, coincides with the commonly occurring form of the sword or scimitar used for beheading. This string of images further embeds terror into the heart of its branding and communication. "The sword, a pre-modern weapon, symbolizes violent struggle…"[315] The sword is also a linking device to early Islamic history of the Prophet Muhammad's battles and victories, which are to be venerated because they spread Islam.

Following the Boston Marathon Bombings, the celeb magazine *Rolling Stone* glamorized Dzhokhar on its cover, which caused a brouhaha. Many stores reported that they would not carry the magazine. Yet lawyer and family therapist J. Kaufman has been one of the few who has critiqued the accompanying article as weak and failing to understand the psychiatric concept of the mask of sanity, that a perpetrator can look normal but is not normal.[316] The mask, as developed by Cleckley, is an effective way to understand the deep split in the personality of a sociopath. The title of the article was "The Bomber. How a popular, promising student was failed by his family, fell into radical Islam and became a monster."[317] Dzhokhar's wrestling coach was quoted as saying: "I felt like a bullet went through my heart...To think that a kid we mentored and *loved like a son* [emphasis mine] could have been responsible for all this death. It was beyond shocking. It was like an alternative reality."[318]

The Associated Press critique of the *Rolling Stone* cover began with, "Sultry eyes burn into the camera lens from behind tousled curls. A scruff of sexy beard and loose T-shirt are bathed in soft, yellow light."[319] This media treatment articulates a facet of the mechanism that propels terrorism and is nearly impossible to stop because it has to do with a democracy's quest for freedom of expression. It is further complicated because the target audience is in the same age group as the terrorist himself. Droves of young girls called Dzhokhar "hot, and wear T-shirts with his image." This comes at a time when Internet recruitment of terrorists, and lone wolves in particular, is rampant. Yet the real victims of terrorist acts do not receive appropriate treatment, and they have to struggle with their losses. One Boston Marathon participant felt that the cover tricks one into thinking at first that Dzhokhar is an up-and-coming celeb, a rock star.[320] Said Kathleen Hall Jamieson, a communications professor and the director of the Annenberg Public Policy Center at the University of Pennsylvania, "I can't think of another instance in which one has glamorized the image of an alleged terrorist. This is the image of a rock star. This is the image of someone who is admired, of someone who has a fan base, of someone we are critiquing as art."[321]

This romanticization of a terrorist harkens back to other controversies such as that involving O.J. Simpson, who was ultimately acquitted of murdering his wife. There was a documented history of domestic violence, which links back to my argument that it has to do with a problem that occurs very early in attachment patterns. This romanticizing of violence acts as a defense against seeing criminality for what it is. Instead it hypes and taps into the sadomasochism of terrorism, which is sexual in nature and which masks the traumatic bonding to the mother.

Rolling Stone defended the cover, recalling that it provoked similar controversy when it published the cover of Charles Manson and the serial killing by proxy of his Creepy Crawlers. Manson's murders fit with the theory of traumatic bonding in targeting and murdering Sharon Tata, who was pregnant. "*Rolling Stone* earlier told *USA Today* that the outcry is reminiscent of another polarizing cover, more than 40 years ago, on cult leader and mass murderer Charles Manson. That cover, in June 1970, including a prison interview with Manson, became one of *Rolling Stone*'s biggest selling issues and won a National Magazine award."[322]

In an emotional response to the magazine cover, Massachusetts State Police Swat team photographer Sean Murphy, in an unauthorized move, released a set of photos to *Boston Magazine* showing the other face of Dzhokhar.[323] On August 27 more photos of Dzhokhar being arrested were leaked to the press.[324] Murphy, who was immediately relieved of his duties, said he was insulted by what *Rolling Stone* had done: "The truth is that glamorizing the fact of terror is not just insulting to the family members of those killed in the line of duty, it could also be an incentive to those who may be unstable to do something to get their face on the cover of *Rolling Stone* magazine."[325] Murphy also wrote something revealing about his perspective on photography: "Photography is very simple, it's very basic. It brings us back to the cave. An image like this on the cover of *Rolling Stone*, we see it instantly as being wrong. What *Rolling Stone* did was wrong. This guy is evil. This is the real Boston bomber. Not someone fluffed and buffed for the cover of *Rolling Stone* magazine."[326]

Two years before the bombing, within the time frame of his going away to college, Dzhokhar was described as being homesick. Homesickness is an indicator of not having separated psychologically from the family, albeit a dysfunctional one:

> Much of what is known about the two years of Jahar's life leading up to the bombing comes from random press interviews with students at UMass Dartmouth, none of whom seemed to have been particularly close with Jahar; and from Jahar's tweets, which, like many 18- or 19-year-olds', were a mishmash of sophomoric jokes, complaints about his roommate, his perpetual lateness, some rap lyrics, the occasional deep thought ("Find your place and your purpose and make a plan for the future") and, increasingly, some genuinely revealing statements. He was homesick. He suffered from insomnia. He had repeated zombie dreams. And he missed his dad. "I can see my face in my dad's pictures as a youngin, he even had a ridiculous amount of hair like me," he tweeted in June 2012.[327]

Dzhokhar regressed further and found his social niche with rich students from Kazakstan at the university, a place he found boring. He became more identified with these Central Asians and could speak Russian with them. Before he was captured, Dzhokhar tweeted, "I am a stress free kind of guy."[328] Thus speaks his denial. Anxiety is one of the hardest emotions for beginning therapists to detect, to say nothing of those who are experiencing it. Often they are so dissociated that they are not even aware of what they are feeling. Dzhokhar's tweet demonstrates how utterly oblivious he is to his volcanic iceberg life.

DZHOKHAR'S PSEUDO EMPATHY

What is pseudo empathy? Borderlines have what Winnicott refers to as the false self. They are unable to walk in the shoes of the other and understand the other's predicament and life experience. Paradoxically, borderlines often claim that they have great empathy for the other. What we notice is that borderlines do not have a well-grounded personality. They tend to camouflage their limited capacities by making this claim. It is part of their imitative personality, their "you-do-it-too" syndrome, which is a verbal maneuver to distract the victim from what has been perpetrated on them and to justify their vicious aggression. Consider Dhzokhar's claim that the entire Umma is a victim, which he uses to justify his murdering innocent others.[329]

A female friend of Dzhokhar, who was quoted in *Rolling Stone*'s cover story, claimed that he had empathy. But she, too, was misled by his phony demeanor, just like serial killer Ted Bundy seduced numerous others into thinking that he was a good guy:

> Cara, a vivacious, pretty blonde whom some believe Jahar had a secret crush on, insists they were just friends. "He was so sweet. He was too sweet, you know?" she says sadly. The two had driver's ed together, which led to lots of time getting high and hanging out. Jahar, she says, had a talent for moving between social groups and always seemed able to empathize with just

> about anyone's problems. "He is a golden person, really just a genuine good guy who was cool with everyone," she says. "It's hard to really explain Jahar. He was a Cambridge kid."[330]

The untrained lay public confuses empathy with pseudo-empathy. He murdered in cold blood by ambush. This is another feature of the volcanic iceberg mentality. Borderline antisocials like Dzhokhar only have "empathy" for their own group. That they do not show or understand empathy for others is evident in their choosing indiscriminate violence. There is one quoted instance of Dzhokhar affirming that terrorist attacks were justifiable:

> In retrospect, Jahar's comment about 9/11 could be seen in the context of what criminal profilers call "leakage": a tiny crack in an otherwise carefully crafted facade that, if recognized—it's often not—provides a key into the person's interior world. "On cases where I've interviewed these types of people, the key is looking past their exterior and getting access to that interior, which is very hard," says Tom Neer, a retired agent from the FBI's Behavioral Analysis Unit and now a senior associate with the Soufan Group, which advises the government on counterterrorism. "Most people have a public persona as well as a private persona, but for many people, there's a secret side, too. And the secret side is something that they labor really hard to protect."[331]

Following is a characterization of a malignant split self:

> There were many things about Jahar that his friends and teachers didn't know–something not altogether unusual for immigrant children, who can live highly bifurcated lives, toggling back and forth between their ethnic and American selves. "I never saw the parents, and didn't even know he had a brother," says Payack, who wondered why Jahar never had his family rooting for him on the sidelines, as his teammates did. "If you're a big brother and you love your little brother, why don't you come and watch him in sports."[332]

Dzhokhar was probably ashamed of his family.

In short, Dzhokhar was Tamerlan's mini-me narcissistic self-object. His elder brother misused him as his own psychological prop. Together they constituted a malignant twinship, murdering the innocent. Their mother was fused to both, and the brothers learned to misuse each other as they had been misused. People were objects to them, not human beings. The volcanic iceberg mentality, which lacks empathy, does not distinguish between the appropriate and the inappropriate use of an object.

DHZOKHAR'S KAZAKHSTAN "TWINS"

Dzhokhar may have shared a special camaraderie with his two Central Asian Muslim schoolmates, Dias Kadyrbayev, and Azamat Tazhayakov. Both were 19, on student visas, and hailed from Kazakhstan, where the Chechens were deported during Stalinist times Charges have been brought against Dias and Azamat, who have pleaded guilty to destroying evidence implicating Dzhokhar in the Boston Marathon Bombings.

> Two friends accused of trying to hinder the probe into alleged Boston Marathon bomber Dzhokhar Tsarnaev were indicted Thursday for obstruction of justice—a more serious charge than they originally faced.[333]
>
> Dias Kadyrbayev and Azamat Tazhayakov were charged with conspiracy to obstruct justice and obstructing justice with the intent to impede the bombing investigation.[334]
>
> The indictment alleges that Kadyrbayev and Tazhayakov removed a laptop and backpack from Tsarnaev's dormitory room after they learned he was a suspect in the April 15 bombings, which killed three people and injured more than 200. The two are accused of discarding the backpack in a garbage bin outside their New Bedford, Mass., apartment.[335]
>
> The FBI claims that the two students threw away a rucksack belonging to Tsarnaev with fireworks and a laptop inside. Police found the rucksack and its contents inside a dumpster. [336]

> If convicted of both counts, the men could face up to 25 years in prison and deportation."[337]

The license plate on Dias' car read "Terrorista." He claims that it was a gift from a Latina friend who used this name on Facebook. In retrospect, he says it was a stupid thing to do.[338] This is transparent behavior along the lines of hiding in plain sight concerning their real intentions—a facet of the volcanic iceberg mentality

There is another interesting aspect of Dhzokhar's relationship with the Central Asia "twins" besides the Chechen deportation history to Kazakhstan and Kyrgyzstan as persecuted Muslims. Could Dhzokhar's exposure to a Muslim Asian culture through his cronies have influenced the Tsarnaev brothers' limited empathy for the Chinese American hostage named Danny taken in the car hijacking that occurred after the bombings? The pseudo empathy that Tamerlan and Dzhokhar showed may have facilitated a kind of temporary identification with Danny via the relationship with Diaz and Azamat. I speculate that this pseudo empathy could have saved Danny's life.[339] The Tsarnaevs released Danny unharmed. However, one of the murder victims at the Boston Marathon site was a Chinese foreign student, Lu Lingzi, who did not have such luck, thus underscoring the superficial nature of their "empathy" for the other.

There is one other friend of Dzhokhar's, Robel Phillipos, an Ethiopian American citizen whose religion remains unknown. Phillipos, also 19 years old "… was charged May 1 in a criminal complaint with lying to federal investigators. He appeared in court for a probable cause hearing on Aug. 12."[340]

What has been overlooked is the political conflict between Christian Ethiopia and Muslim Somalia, which have been locked in conflict for years. It is unclear as to where Phillipos held his allegiance but for the Muslims this is the global jihad. Somali American refugee youths have been recruited by the Somali terrorist group Al Shabab for the jihad. Chechen terrorists have also been fighting in Somalia.[341] Could Dhzokhar's friendship with Kadrybayev, Tazhayakov and Phillipos be an example of pseudo empathy?

The latest neuroscience research on empathy suggests that killers have empathy but claim that the switch in their brain to turn empathy on and off is broken. In the case of psychopaths, they can be extremely charming.[342] Could their switch only work under certain conditions, such as empathy for their in-group? Still in the early stages of understanding the neuroscience and with a paucity of research concerning the nexus between this "alleged" switch, maternal attachment, and neurobiology, the idea of an empathy switch raises more questions than it answers.

An op-ed by a retired Los Angeles Times journalist who is currently an associate professor of Communication at Nazarbayev University Kazakhstan raises the question of cultural differences with regard to empathy and violence concerning Kadyrbayev and Taxhayakov's behavior. Writes Professor Foster: "Boston arrests show that the 'help your buddy' mentality doesn't play well in some countries." He relates an episode in which an American colleague walked into the bathroom of the college where a student was being brutally beaten by another student. The professor tried to intervene, and two cronies of the bully in turn attacked him. Helping your buddy Kazakh style encompasses the sociopathic aspect of brothering to which I draw attention. Ethics do not come into play. What Foster does not point to is the role and function of a shame–honor culture, which protects the aggressor. Nonetheless, Foster argues effectively that the Kazakh "twins" completely underestimated how their intervention on their buddy's behalf as Muslim brothers will be prosecuted under U.S. law as terrorism and obstruction of justice.[343]

ZUBEIDAT TSARNAEV

The son gets married, the back of the mother bends;
the daughter marries, it becomes straight.

The mother's anger is like snow:
quick to come and quick to go.
–Chechen Proverbs

While a person is sitting, no one can tell if he's lame.
While a person is sleeping, no one can tell if he's blind.
While a person is dining, who'll say if he's bold or tame?
While a person is silent, no one can tell his mind.[344]
–Avar People's Poet of Dagestan, Rasul Gamzstov

"[I gave them] special love.
Who could know kids better than mother?"[345]
–Zubeidat Tsarnaev

Karny, an Israeli author who lived in and traveled extensively through Chechnya and Dagestan, related the following poignant anecdote when his mother died. Dr. Fakhruddin Daghestani sent flowers upon hearing of her death. This is because the mother plays perhaps the most significant role in the culture.[346] Yet honor killing of the female persists. They do not see the veneration of the mother and the murder of one of their own future mothers as paradoxical. They do not understand that this love–hate of the female is a problem arising from the male's terror of the female. They are in conflict and psychologically preoccupied, if not dominated, by this developmental deficit of being tied into their mothers. The love of the mother comes at the expense of killing off the female and others as in the case of jihad. Zubeidat Tsarnaeva provides a transparent caricature of this psychological relationship—the maternal drama that drives the volcanic iceberg mentality.

Zubeidat Tsarnaeva has been anything but quiet. She does not adhere to the words of her motherland Dagestan poet, Rasul Gamzstov: "While a person is silent, no one can tell his mind." Instead she seems to embody the Chechen proverb "The men are bigger and the women louder." In fact, Zubeidat Tsarnaeva preferred to identify herself as Chechen, thereby influencing her sons to identify with her husband's Chechen ethnicity. It also speaks to her inferiority complex of being a devalued Dagestani female. Zubeidat captured the attention of the global public with her denial of her sons' guilt.

Zubeidat elicits a kind of coulrophobic response. She is clownish in her denial of reality. Her excessive rage defends against the truth. The image of the clown fits with this maternal drama. She is creepy and disturbing because her denial is so pervasive:

> Clowns exaggerate for effect, distorting reality and proportion. They drive impossibly tiny cars and carry outsized gear, such as tricycles the size of elephants and hammers the size of logs. Nearly everything about a clown, including his or her speech, actions and clothes, are either too big or too small, and nothing about them is normal.
>
> Clowns are at once both instantly recognizable and yet totally anonymous. We don't know who is behind that makeup and red rubber nose: a kindly grandfather or a serial killer?[347]

As the Basque expert on ETA terrorism writes: "Words can easily be deceptive, not so the body. One can speak falsely or lie by omission, but it is not so easy for the face, the eyes, the voice to conceal the truth. The body can't help but betray by showing the truthful fears and desires of the subject."[348] Unconsciously lying provides a special mechanism of adaptation to protect a shame-filled self, a self that is quite depressed though perhaps not conscious of it or willing to admit it, a self beaten down by early abuse. Some lie so convincingly that they even delude themselves.[349]

Tsarnaeva has maintained her sons' innocence in interviews. She told BBC Sunday: "I am their mother. I give them the birth. I brought them up. I raised them by giving them love. Special love. We never talked about killing. The word killing in our house had no place. So of course I am sure that my kids never would do this."[350]

Zubeidat has been described as extremely controlling and hence emasculating. Her husband could not provide for the family, which needed food stamps and stipends to get by[351] A photo of her in the BBC Sunday article shows her pointing her finger in rage. Note the contradiction: Her body language spews rage and anger, and yet she is unwilling to admit her denial. Doesn't she realize how transparent she is? We see right through her defensive position, which attempts to cover over her own terror. Because of the merged personalities in this enmeshed family, the boys unwittingly and unconsciously become the carrier of her rage. And to a degree her impotent husband was the carrier of his mother's rage in the Chechen cultural cycle of shame-blame, along with a religion that devalues the female through advocating her beating to "educate" her properly. Who else can act out her murderous impulses than her sons? Because she lives in a culture of deprivation programmed to devalue all her feelings, she not only feels the rage, she becomes it, as do her sons. Like the psychotic patient on a locked ward who becomes an iceberg because of their terrors, Zubeidat and her sons become the terror. The photo of Zubeidat says it all. Rage is written all over her face, projected so intensely and toxically that the rage spews over to not only her sons but her daughters as well. This is the process of internalizing the raging storm that is the maternal drama.

Time and again we hear mothers of jihadis deny the involvement of their children in jihad. We can surmise that they were raised in a similar shame–

honor type of family. An example is John Nutall, a Canadian who became a terrorist along with his partner, Amanda Korody.[352] Morino [his lawyer] said he's spent time with Nuttall's mother. "As you can appreciate, like all mothers, she has trouble accepting that her son was involved in such a matter," he said.[353] The lawyer taps into the code of the maternal to elicit empathy for his client. Do only mothers of highly disturbed and detached sons and daughters come to their defense? Some mothers are well aware and concerned, such as one mother who wrote after Adam Lanza murdered twenty-three school children, worrying that her son could become such a terrorist.[354]

"It wasn't blood, it was paint" said Zubeidat Tsarnaev, who then went on to say that Tamerlan and Dzhokhar, had been framed by the police.[355] That is how she compensated for her flawed, psychotic thinking. The mother believes that the bombing scene has been staged. She is not in touch with reality. Imagery holds the key to her delusional thinking. The central underlying image is the template of the maternal cameo that encapsulates the maternal platform from which terrorists launch their attacks. Their attacks are dual in nature: The attack on innocent civilians is their conscious justification for jihad against the kufar (nonbelievers), while at an unconscious level it is an attack on the mother, who represents the other. The mother is publicly venerated as heroic, but she is unconsciously vilified and repudiated. We see this in Al Qaeda's signature truck bombings of U.S. embassies in Nairobi and Dar-Essalem in 1998. The facade of the buildings were sheared off. Consciously they claim that the attack was against the American oppressed and kufar, but unconsciously one can read it as an attack on the mother's body, specifically her face. Through the bombing they reattach through the fusion. This is the dual communication of the terrorists.

It is this psychopathology grounded in maternal attachment that remains the most fertile soil for radicalization during adolescence. Until then the attachment problem goes undetected by others. In *The Anatomy of Violence*,

Raine looks almost exclusively into the neuroscience that precipitates the actions of predators and violent criminals who commit serial killing, mass murder, rampage shooting, rape and murder, including domestic violence's murder–suicide. Even though Raine is not a psychoanalyst, he states that maternal attachment is a key ingredient for violence, a kind of tipping point if the relationship is of poor quality and abusive.[356]

In most cases the early mother-child relationship goes unaccounted for in the psychological profile of terrorist. Ironically, though, Zubeidat helps us see clearly the maternal jihadi launching pad. She was front and center, dominating the news when the story broke. She embodies the profile of an overbearing mother, and the media feeds her pathological malignant narcissism. The role of shame in relationship to the female that affected Zubeidat when she was a little girl has been virtually absent from the discussion. She, herself, was a devalued female in the clan of Avar in Dagestan, even though she might very well deny this. We can speculate that most likely she herself was abused precisely because she remains so out of touch with reality in her paranoid world. As a female in her clan, we can hazard a guess that she was the shock absorber of male hatred of the female and internalized male hatred of the female as self-hatred. The female has been the hidden, ongoing target of unrelenting hatred for the terrorist, who projects his murderous rage outward.

Zubeidat tasted her first sense of power and acquired "honor" within the shame–honor culture of the Avars when she gave birth to her first child, a male son. Subsequently she lived her life vicariously through her first-born son. He was her narcissistic object and hence she misused him as a baby. Prior to Tamerlan's birth she lacked status in the Avar clan as well as in her husband's clan. Zubeidat concretely represents the underlying problem in the production of terrorists. We speculate that because of her own history of devaluation and abuse, she could not adequately, healthily, and optimally bond with Tamerlan other than in an overbearing borderline, narcissistic way. She used him as her narcissistic prop, her badge of honor and treated him like an object just as she was treated like an object—as chattel and property. Terrorists relate to us only as objects in their unconscious world.[357]

Indeed, a democratic society will only be as healthy as its infant-mother bond. If a mother is overbearing and claims that blood is really only paint, we can surmise that she has trouble differentiating between reality and delusion. As Zubeidat grew up, she was constantly under attack—physically, emotionally and psychologically. It is not my intent to blame the abused female. She has merely continued the cycle, with the males in her clan maintaining control over her. Often the male will describe the female as "ruling the roost" or characterize her as fierce and loud. This is an overcompensation by the males, who feel powerless and smothered by their mothers. It is also fantasy because the female is not the one making political decisions, ruling countries, or heading terrorist organizations; she remains abused, manipulated, and subservient.

Even though Zubeidat may have greatly influenced the twisted, troubled minds of her jihadi sons, this dynamic needs to be contextualized as a factor of intergeneration transmission of trauma. Schützenberger, in *The Ancestor Syndrome*, discusses how trauma is unconsciously communicated across generations. Davoine and Gaudilliere in their *History Beyond Trauma* also underscore the impact of trauma, especially that of war across generations.[358]

Coupled with this transgenerational transmission are the writings of Abdelwahhab Bouhdiba about the Muslim mother. In the second part of his book *Sexuality in Islam* he details the mother-son relationship.[359] It is important to note that Bouhdiba does not concern himself with ethnic differences within the ummah. A Muslim is a Muslim. He does not bother to describe the cultural differences between groups. His critique remains informative for Chechen culture. Yet we can observe two interacting entities of culture and religion vis à vis shaming.

With the Tsarnaev, we see an enmeshed relationship with the mother and an inability to detach from her. Zubeidat described Tamerlan's body as an object—"a masterpiece."[360] This maternal perversion reflects her self-investment in her son in an incestuous manner. It shows he was misused and over-stimulated as a sexual object, an object of excitement for his mother. This kind of alleged veneration masks a deep-seated envy and fusion that is often experienced by the male as suffocating. Zubeidat Tsarnaeva fits the profile of whom Bouhdiba speaks and writes revealingly: "Of course everything is expressed in subtle terms and the status of women is certainly ambiguous, even in the Quran itself. Nevertheless, there is a progressive decline of the Muhammadan ethic of marital tenderness. It is as if the continuous training and domestication of love led to a negation of love—that is to say, in a male-worshipping society, to the negation of women."[361]

In the Afghan movie *The Patience Stone*, a young Muslim wife opens up to her paralyzed, husband about all the abuse she has endured as a female in the Muslim culture. Paraphrasing her aunt, she says "If men do not know how to love, they fight."[362]

ZUBEIDAT'S BLACK WIDOW'S FANTASY

One month after the Boston Marathon Bombings, on May 25, 2013, a female suicide bomber detonated in Makhachkala, Dagestan, where the Tsarnaevs had moved. Zubeidat, who was on the FBI's terrorist watch list,[363] rejoined her ex-husband in Dagestan after fleeing America to evade criminal prosecution for shoplifting and removal of anti-theft sensors.[364] Stealing emphasizes her neediness, deprivation, greed, and omnipotence; she believed that the luxe dresses and lingerie were owed her. Shoplifting lingerie points to her suppressed sexuality. While not all women who shoplift become jihadi terrorists, the peculiar mix of shame–honor culture and religion based on chronic abuse may have been a contributing factor to her behavior.

A news report described the jihadi uniform that Zubeidat adopted but not the dresses she tried to steal from Lord and Taylor: "Their mother is speaking to me just after returning to the Dagestani capital from Kizlyar, where she had been mourning the death of her brother (from natural causes). She is dressed from head to toe in layers of black. When she speaks—in English—of her sons, her large eyes blaze with passion."[365] Even though she is in mourning for her brother, the extreme to which she is shrouded hearkens to the image of the Black Widows of the Moscow Theatre Hostage Attack. The only differences are that her face is not covered in a veil and she is not wearing a suicide belt.

> Islamic militants are believed to convince 'black widows that a suicide bombing will reunite them with their dead relatives beyond the grave...Since 2000, at least two dozen women, most of them from the Caucasus, have carried out suicide bombings in Russian cities and aboard trains and planes. All were linked to an Islamic insurgency that spread throughout Dagestan and the predominantly Muslim Caucasus region after two separatist wars in neighboring Chechnya. [366]

However, how could Zubeidat be a Black Widow if her husband Anzor was not dead? Or could he be dead to her unconsciously? Her story of reconciling with her husband picks up on the subtheme of domestic violence that courses through the history of the family. Her son Tamerlan abused his former girlfriend and then his wife Katherine. Upon whom did he model his behavior? Anzor? Anzor minimized the domestic violence charges brought against his son. Boys learn to abuse partners by imitating their fathers. Anzor Tsarnaev fits the bill for being an abuser by encouraging his sons to box and wrestle under the guise of the Chechen cultural perception of wrestling as a manly sport and the national symbol of the Lone Wolf. To what degree was Zubeidat abused by Anzor? Could her jihadi posture be a defense against her sense of defenseless?

Her ardent denial of her sons' involvement in jihad could also be a perverse tactic of *taqiyya*, lying for the sake of Allah in jihad. This dissimulation tactic is well known in Islam. Not being able to be honest has been elevated to the pathological art form of lying for the religion. Such a perversion seems to be played out literally by her dressing in black, echoing an identification with and a fantasy of being a Black Widow. The perversion is exciting and filled with drama. Her demeanor embodies the volcanic iceberg mentality. She is as cold as ice. Her mind is frozen, yet boiling with rage. Yet the excitement of bombing is temporarily enlivening to someone who is so dissociated from reality. She is the opposite of compassionate. Zubeidat represents the extreme of a woman trying to mourn but who cannot. She yearns to connect through death. She is a failed suicide bomber.

Unwittingly Zubeidat discloses to us what has been unconscious all along in these shame–honor Muslim cultures of the Caucasus: the mother is married to her son in a psychologically incestuous relationship. She finds a perverse sense of honor through her pseudo identification as a Black Widow, a delusional wish to rejoin with her son, who was a replacement husband for her.

Zubeidat's run-ins with the law should have been immediate red flags for the police, just as jihadis who receive speeding and parking tickets, beat their women, and in general display a profound arrogance for Western law enforcement. Zubeidat's failure to appear in court is the most telling. The minds of the children have internalized the hostile, violent fantasies of the mother.[367]

THE SISTERS TSARNAEVA: BELLA AND ALINA

> The boy is happy to move around and the girl to sit still.
>
> –Chechen Proverb

The little girl is lowest on the clan totem pole, with the aggression rolling downhill. The Tsarnaev sisters slept on a *shared mattress on the floor* [emphasis mine] while their brothers slept in beds. [368] This nonverbal treatment reveals how devalued and fused they are. Not all Chechens, or Avars for that matter, would make their daughters sleep on the floor, but this kind of treatment is quite common in shame–honor oriented immigrant Muslim families. The brother comes first and is given special prerogatives that the sister does not have. Just as the mother was devalued, so are the sisters because of their sex, which is considered contaminating.

From birth on, girls are forced to take on subservient roles and submit to cultural demands. The little girl who has been brutalized by society has no freedom of movement. She is trapped, held hostage, and immobilized. These feelings are later communicated to her children unconsciously. The cycle repeats itself. This lack of freedom is translated into a political nationalistic separatist movement, a theme that runs through many terrorist organizations that call for the "liberation" of a territory. In shame–honor Muslim religio-social entities, the primary form of liberation needs to be understood as liberation from the abused, devalued mother, who is portrayed to the world as heroic. This cover-up masks the abuse of babies as objects by the heroic mother who herself was treated as an object.

Is it possible to break out of this cycle? Perhaps, if there were intervening positive factors in childhood such as good and caring teachers, and if the pain is great enough to cause one to work toward a psychological understanding of one's problems rather than blaming and hating the other. These factors offer a disruption of the cycle of violence and lack of empathy. We do not know a lot about the Tsarnaev sisters, but let us put together some of the pieces of information that we have. Indeed, as one journalist has put it, the women closest to the Tsarnaev brothers may hold an important key.[369]

The sisters modeled their financial behavior after their mother; they could not pay their rent. They were needy like their shoplifting mother.

Psychoanalytically, one view is that the shoplifting was an attempt to get what one did not receive during early childhood, which expresses a profound sense of loss and deprivation.[370] We can surmise that the mother's deprivation and inability to mourn this loss was communicated unconsciously to her daughters, who in turn felt financially and emotionally deprived. And they were in fact deprived. Both girls were ultimately evicted from their apartment for falling behind in rent.[371] We learn more about this sororal twinship:

> Jahar rarely spoke to his friends about his sisters, Alina and Bella, who, just a few years older than he, kept to themselves but also had their own struggles. Attractive, dark-haired girls who were "very Americanized," as friends recall, they worshipped Tamerlan, whom one sister would later refer to as her "hero"—but they were also subject to his role as family policeman. When Bella was a junior in high school, her father, hearing that she'd been seen in the company of an American boy, pulled her out of school and dispatched Tamerlan to beat the boy up. Friends later spotted Bella wearing a hijab; not long afterward, she disappeared from Cambridge entirely. Sometime later, Alina would similarly vanish. Both girls were reportedly set up in arranged marriages.[372]

However, they were able to get out of their marriages, according to the *Rolling Stone*'s article. Bella and Alina were both subjected to being placed under surveillance for potentially shaming the males in their family by desiring sexual freedom. While we do not know if they were at risk of being honor killed, nonetheless the chauvinistic honor code hung over their heads like the sword of *qital*.

Luis Vasquez, a Hispanic high school student who went to school with Tamerlan, had an interesting series of observations. Coming from a Latin culture himself, Vasquez picked upon on the Tsarnaevs' preoccupation with their Chechen/Avar concept of honor. Vasquez understood the Spanish concept of "*honra*" which had actually been inherited from the Muslims when they ruled Spain for 700 years. Vasquez witnessed Tamerlan monitoring his sisters, especially Bella: "He kept an eye on her literally…It was an honor thing. He was trying to keep her out of trouble," he said.[373] It remains unclear if Vasquez understood the depths of Chechen revenge honor killing, with Bella being at risk of being murdered if she deviated from the culture.

Zubeidat had opened a "spa" in her home, giving facials. Alyssa Lindley Kilzer sought treatments there until Zubeidat's anti-American rhetoric, conspiracy thinking, and rage "pushed" her out the door. Borderline personalities do that frequently. Their rage is so great that it wears on others to the point of their exiting the relationship. Kilzer was grounded enough in her sense of self that she drew a mental boundary and would not tolerate Zubeidat's paranoia. After all, the attack on America was also a veiled attack on Kilzer herself. Alyssa had this to say about the daughters:

> During this time first one of Zubeidat's daughters, and then the other, were set up in arranged marriages, and started having kids. This was something I found slightly disturbing, as one was just my age (18-19) and didn't seem to be happily married. Within two years I heard that she had been beaten badly and eventually filed for divorce, which was *at first against her mother's wishes* [emphasis mine]. Later Zubeidat said that she had accepted the divorce because it was an unhappy marriage. Her daughter then moved back into the house with her child. Her younger son, Dzhokhar, was often in the room or the room next door looking after his nephew while I was getting my facial. There were usually issues with parking on her crowded Cambridge Street. Sometimes she would have Dzhokhar go down to the street to put the visitor-parking pass into my car window (Yes, I gave him my car keys). Once he moved my car, which made me nervous, as the street was so crowded and parking spots so

> small. Dzhokhar was always friendly to me and seemed easy going. In 2010-11, there was a day when Dzhokhar wasn't home, so Zubeidat took the parking pass out to the street for me. I noticed that she first put on a hijab before going outside. She had never worn a hijab while working at the spa previously, or inside the house, and I was really surprised…[374]

Thus, one of the daughters is reported to have experienced domestic violence. The arranged marriage is an attempt at controlling the female. However, the daughters' Western high school experience made them familiar with the subject of intimate partner violence, and they knew that it was wrong. At least one sister was able to get out of an abusive marriage. They were successful in disengaging from the traumatic bonding to a degree.

How can we expect the daughters to develop a sense of altruism and empathy given their raging mother? Yet the sisters did muster a sense of remorse and managed to build into their life a sense of empathy. Perhaps this occurred because even though they were highly devalued, abused, and neglected in their parents' home, they were also partially raised in the West. There may have been better external supports such as identifications with teachers who might have helped them along the way. They also had their own sisterly twinning, which together might have made the domestic situation more bearable. We don't know for sure, but we can speculate about their predicament.

Alina and Bella demonstrated remorse when they released the following statement: "Our heart goes out to the victims of last week's bombing. It saddens us to see so many innocent people hurt after such a callous act. As a family, we are absolutely devastated by the sense of loss and sorrow this has caused. We don't have any answers but we look forward to a thorough investigation and hope to learn more. We ask the media to respect our privacy during this difficult time."[375]

We can give the two sisters the benefit of the doubt that their expression of remorse for the Boston Marathon Bombings is genuine, that they could identify with the victims because they themselves had been repeatedly victimized by their own brothers and parents as devalued females. They remind me of the young girls I observed in the mid-2000s in the Somali community in Minnesota, who thrive under the new-found freedoms of Western culture.

However, Alina's expression of remorse is typical of that of a borderline's "you-do-it-too" mindset, whereby she justified her sense of loss only by comparing it to her murderer-brother's death:

> When she spoke to reporters in the morning, Alina Tsarnaev was aware her one brother was dead.
>
> "I'm sorry for the families that lost their loved ones, the same way I lost a loved one ... This is very hurtful," she said.
>
> She balked when media asked if she was "okay."
>
> "No I'm not okay. No one is okay right now," she said.
>
> Though Tsarnaev said she hadn't seen her brothers in "a long time," she described Dzhokhar as "an amazing child."
>
> "He was a great person," she said of her dead brother. "I thought I knew him. I never would have expected that from him. He is a kind and loving man. The cops took his life away just the same way he took others' lives away, if that's even true. At the end of the day, no one knows the truth."[376]

Both sisters stood together as if fused when the first reports came out. Alina ultimately turned herself in and was subsequently released without bond because of her indigent status and the fact that she is a mother with one small child and was pregnant. She had a three-year-old warrant for her arrest for passing counterfeit money at an Applebee's Restaurant, with her car apparently used by diners whom the police were interested in. She skipped out on her initial court hearing and lives in a different state. According to her lawyer, she wants to be in good standing with the law. She left her mother's home and sought out a shelter because she felt her mother was too strict.[377]

Lingering in the background is what we do not know, which is to what degree the sisters' expression of remorse might be *taqiyya* or dissimulation for Allah's jihad. Time will tell if, in fact, they were involved at all in the Boston attack. Furthermore, we know nothing of their views on the triple homicide in Waltham and what they may have known.

KATHERINE RUSSELL: TAMERLAN'S WIFE

I place Katherine, or Katy as she is called, after the sisters because she is not a blood relative and her status, unbeknownst to her, is even lower than that of the sisters. She was at the mercy of her husband, who remained undifferentiated from his mother. Katherine also had to obey her mother-in-law and would have to become like her, deprived and abused.

> Katherine Russell, was a Protestant from a well-off family in Rhode Island. After high school, she'd toyed with joining the Peace Corps but instead settled on college at Boston's Suffolk University. She'd met Tamerlan at a club during her freshman year, in 2007, and found him "tall and handsome and having some measure of worldliness," one friend would recall. But as their relationship progressed, Katherine's college roommates began to worry that Tamerlan was "controlling" and "manipulative." They became increasingly concerned when he demanded that she cover herself and convert to Islam.[378]

Katherine took the Muslim name "Karima," meaning "precious, magnificent," another fantasized aspect of grandiosity. However, her life was anything but that once she became pregnant and dropped out of college. In June 2010, she and Tamerlan were married; not long afterward, she gave birth to their daughter. To have a daughter in a shame–honor culture is catastrophic, nearly bordering on bringing shame to the family.

Around this time, both her friends and family say, she "pulled away." She was seen in Boston, shopping at Whole Foods, cloaked and wearing a hijab. She rarely spoke around her husband, and when alone, recalls one neighbor, she spoke slowly with an accent. "I didn't even know she was an American," he says.[379]

The paradox was that Katherine came from an upper middle class, nominally Christian home, yet she became enmeshed in a dysfunctional immigrant family, becoming essentially a "slave to them." Even with her college education, she became a health care aide like her raging mother-in-law. She married "down" because she had no self-esteem. We can surmise that she was devalued in her parents' home because where else did she learn that she was worthless? This raises the question of whether her own mother was abused and controlled by her prominent physician husband, Katy's father. One never knows what goes on behind closed doors, but this is a common story for abused women. They think by marrying someone "different" and coming from a higher socioeconomic class they will have power over their future husbands. Instead they go from the fire into the frying pan. I write about this in *Penetrating the Terrorist Psyche*.

We have a hint at the degree to which Katherine must have been dissociated and highly traumatized. She became traumatically bonded to an abusive male from a foreign culture who was interested in hypnosis. (Tamerlan had an article in his possession on "How To Create an Instantaneous Sexual Attraction in Any Woman You Meet")[380] At first Katy may have found Tamerlan exotic and erotic, a sadomasochism of sorts. When he started to tighten control and abuse escalated, she submitted and regressed. Her fate was further sealed when she had a baby. We still do not know her story in detail, but she most likely experienced a position of devaluation in her childhood home. In borderline and narcissistic psychopathology. which can exist concurrently, the psychological configuration and biochemistry precipitates the shifting of self states, some of which may be dissociated and may have been a contributing factor for her to become swept up with Tamerlan.

Psychoanalysis, and especially Freud, have discussed love and its regressive state, which can be traced back to fusion occurring in the maternal attachment.[381] Freud initially used hypnosis. Most likely Katherine became even more regressed than one usually is when one falls in love, but in her case she may have felt terrified of Tamerlan from the start. The more severe a regression, the greater the indicator of traumatic bonding. Not having a family to go back to at this point would have aroused tremendous shame in Katherine that she had failed. She felt trapped. Dutton has written extensively on traumatic bonding and domestic violence.[382]

My colleague Joan Lachkar has written on "East-West" marriages and how fraught they are with cultural and psychological problems.[383] Katherine may have broken down mentally. This would have been compounded by fear that she would lose her young daughter, Zahara (meaning "shining" in Arabic) if she divorced under Sharia law because children belong to the father. On average, it takes an abused woman six times to get out of an abusive relationship.[384] Even the Vatican issued a document called *Erga migrantes caritas Christi* ("The Love of Christ Toward Migrants"), in which Catholic women were warned about marrying Muslim men:

> When, for example, a Catholic woman and a Muslim wish to marry … bitter experience teaches us that a particularly careful and in-depth preparation is called for. During it the two fiancés will be helped to know and consciously "assume" the profound cultural and religious differences they will have to face, both between themselves and in relation to their respective families and the Muslim's original environment, to which they may possibly return after a period spent abroad.
>
> If the marriage is registered with a consulate of the Islamic country of origin, the Catholic party must beware of reciting or signing documents containing the shahada (profession of the Muslim belief).
>
> In any case, the marriage between a Catholic and a Muslim, if celebrated in spite of all this, requires not only canonical dispensation but also the support of the Catholic

> community both before and after the marriage. One of the most important tasks of Catholic associations, volunteer workers and counseling services will be to help these families educate their children and, if need be, to support the least protected member of the Muslim family, that is the woman, to know and insist on her rights.[385]

While Katherine was not Catholic, a similar attitude abides in other religions. Only Muslim men can marry a Christian. If a Muslim woman wants to marry a Christian man, he must convert.[386] In fact, we know that the Tsarnaevs did not speak to one of their daughters, Alina, because she married out of their religion. Alina's husband was quoted as saying, "I'm not Muslim and they didn't accept me."[387] Marriage to a Muslim man is not a two-way street. The male dominates. He is inculcated through his religion to look down on non-Muslim females, even more so than his own Muslim sisters, because they are kufar. In Katherine's case, she did convert, but one wonders to what degree it was of her own volition since the abuse began before she married, according to reports from her college roommates. They expressed concern about Tamerlan abusing her, calling her "slut" and "prostitute" early in their courtship.[388] These kinds of accusations unmasking delusional jealousy of the partner are common symptoms of intimate partner violence. Judging by the experience of many abused women, Katherine was already doomed, and it would have been very difficult for her to extricate herself from the relationship because of the risk of being murdered. Many women leave and are murdered.

As noted, Tamerlan had a previous track record of abusing women. "In 2009, the aspiring Olympic boxer was busted for slapping around a different girlfriend, Nadine Asceucal."[389] His father minimized the behavior, saying he only slapped her.[390] Furthermore during this same time period Tamerlan grandiosely flew out to Washington state to allegedly "rescue" his sister, who was being abused by her husband, Elmirza Khozhugov, whom she subsequently divorced. Tamerlan was quoted as saying he wanted to "straighten his brains" for abusing his sister.[391] However, it is not so much about his sister being abused, but more about family honor. Khozhugov subsequently lost contact with his former brother-in-law but did describe Tamerlan as feeling guilty that he was having too much fun in America.[392]

By 2010, in addition to his background of domestic violence, Tamerlan also became radicalized. In 2012 he left his wife and traveled to Russia and Chechnya for six months. His appearance and behavior changed; he was wearing a five-inch beard and on two occasions shouted out extremist views at the Boston mosque he attended. But none of this was factored in, and the FBI still did not comprehend the degree to which he was a risk.[393] In the case of Tamerlan, it was a red flag that went unrecognized by the FBI and a missed opportunity for law enforcement intervention before the Boston Marathon Bombings.

ANZOR THE FATHER AS CAUSE OF THE DEVALUED FEMALE

It is fitting to place Anzor at the end of the cast of characters in this maternal drama because he is so astoundingly ineffective. Fathers are supposed to set limits for their sons, not encourage their aggression. But in Anzor's shame–honor culture linked to jihad, it is the opposite. He has been described as a nice guy mechanic and hard working. Raised in Chechnya, he claimed he was a lawyer by training. He came from a more well-to-do family than Zubeidat and was the "authentic" Chechen in the family, unlike Zubeidat, who appears to have been a want-to-be Chechen Black Widow.

Anzor minimizes the idea of domestic violence. He also adheres to the family party line that the boys were innocent and that they were framed.[394] He refuses to believe that his sons committed these acts of terror. Psychiatrist Keith Ablow noted how the entire family was a cauldron of denial.[395] Although the uncle, Ruslan Tsarni, called the brothers losers, yet even here the issue of

Chechen honor surfaces, as he professed that they had brought "great shame upon the Chechen people." While the uncle acted appropriately throughout, even assuming responsibility for burying Tamerlan, it remains unclear if he understands on a deeper level how Chechen shame–honor dynamics prime the pump for the Chechen jihadi. Ruslan was quoted as being ready to get down on his knees to ask forgiveness from the victims.[396] In fact, the boys' uncle came out staunchly against the behavior and showed remorse for the victims, not just for his own social group.[397] In stark contrast, the aunt living in Toronto, Canada, Maret Tsarnaev, made the same claim as Zubeidat, that her nephews had been set up—that it was a conspiracy and the bombing had been staged.[398]

Often it is assumed that the father plays the authoritarian role in these families. The father is not as powerful as one would think in terms of Western psychodynamics because he relinquishes his role to the first-born son to carry out the honor killing and do the dirty work, thereby training the son to be suspicious of and hate the female. The father generally is emotionally absent from the family. When present he abuses the mother, who in turn over-invests in the son, manipulating the son as her power source. It is her only playing card. This dilemma has described the father as an underlying cause of the devalued female.[399]

P.A. Olson has written on the absent father and the hunger for a stable, nonviolent limit-setting father.[400] Hendrika Freud continues along this line in her book *Men and their Mothers*, based on extensive clinic experience.[401] Not all men play out a classic Oedipal drama, fighting with their fathers for the love of their mothers. In some families the mother becomes the central figure for her son; the father is forced out of the triad or absents himself as in the practice of polygyny so that fantasies of patricide are replaced with fantasies of matricide. Abdel Wahhabi Bouhdiba claims that this is the case for Islam in his *Sexuality in Islam*.[402] In shame–honor cultures, especially those whose religion is Islam, this is the pattern: the mother dominates in a false manner and the son is never permitted to separate. Because Anzor never separated from his own mother, we can speculate that he turned to spousal abuse verging on matricide through projection. The male identity suffers because the man's development is stunted and he becomes either passive, dependent, or rageful.

SUMMARY

All of the dysfunctional familial relationships in this maternal drama of the Chechen/Avar jihadi offer the makings of a mentality that is as cold as ice on the surface. But lurking beneath is a murderous rage ready to explode. The devalued female is the underpinning of a dysfunctional, enmeshed group. Bion's concept of a regressed, destructive group applies to the Tsarnaevs.[403] The subgroups I have attached to the mother include daughters Bella and Alina, Tamerlan' wife, Katherine, and the ineffective father, Anzor. Katherine was the scapegoat of this dysfunctional Chechen totem pole, a slave to Tamerlan and his mother. Zubeidat and Anzor essentially killed off their son by encouraging jihad, while Dzhokhar, Tamerlan's "mini-me" narcissistic prop, literally killed his own brother by driving over him as he was fleeing from the police. Zubeidat claimed she gave them special love. Most people would call it rage and hatred.

CHAPTER 6

THE CHECHENIZATION OF JIHAD: THE CROSSOVER EFFECT

Rather than live like a chicken,
it is better to die like a cock.
A cock is valiant on his own dung hill.
Every dog is valiant at his door.[404]
– Chechen Proverb

The Chechen proverb above articulates the aggressive warrior stance that characterizes Chechen male culture in general and resonates with the Chechen jihadi volcanic iceberg demeanor. In the previous chapters we noted that the symbol and image of the Chechen jihad and even the Chechen brand continues to be emulated.

This is what I call the crossover effect, which is more than just routine imitative behavior. It speaks to a special kind of imitative behavior, which engages violence, aggression and murderous rage. The concept of a crossover effect facilitates conceptualizing how violence transverses theoretical categories such as domestic violence, domestic terrorism, and political violence to murder/suicide and maiming. It helps to clarify why "self-radicalization" is a bit of an oxymoron because it does not occur in a vacuum or as isolated incidents. As human beings we share a repository of images that are communicated daily. These artificially constructed linguistic categories can be linked together through underlying templates and similarities of violence. Those with a volcanic iceberg mentality identify with and emulate this type of violent behavior. This mentality focuses on nonverbal imagery and behavior that is coupled with a deep split in their psyches and a high degree of dissociation.

In Arabic there is a saying among Bedouins that he who imitates a group of people becomes one of them. This can be applied to the stray dog rampage shooter who becomes like all the other mass murderers and jihadis. Different kinds of violence influence and fuel the flames of other types. Even if not jihadis, those who harbor a history of criminality and murderous rage are influenced by violent attacks like the ones that occurred at the Moscow Theater or the Beslan school. Although it is difficult to provide concrete links from one to another, the unconscious is driven to seek this kind of toxic at-one-ment or symbiotic twinship to recycle the violence.

Even the loners who want to be part of a group but have superficial or poor interpersonal skills form this kind of reclusive bond through violence. What they all appear to have in common is faulty early developmental attachment bonds. Similar to the Tsarnaev brothers, they may seem functional but they are only marginally functional. They cannot compete in the modern world. Freud refers to this as unresolved oedipal conflicts. Those who cannot function in the real world need to compete and act out unleashed aggression, which results in endless pent-up frustration and rage erupting in violence. These rampage shooters and jihadis don military clothes and arm themselves with hard object weapons. They dress like men in an attempt to show the world they are combat-ready. Yet they are in reality more like the little boy who wants to be like father, but when he tries to wear his clothes finds that they don't fit.

The crossover effect bridges the unconscious dialogue of the volcanic iceberg mentality as the perpetrator of murder executes his or her maternal drama. The template represents the experience of fusion and fission within the first bond in life—that with the mother. Those in whom the early bond has been severely compromised via trauma or disrupted maternal attachment remain regressed and susceptible to psychologically absorbing the crossover effect of violent behavior. Imitation is a less developed psychological mechanism for modeling. Yalom and Leeszcz confirm the drawback of imitative behavior when it does not lead to a more highly evolved interaction with others based on empathy.[405]

There has been reluctance among counterterrorism experts to consider the crossover effect of violence and aggression as a link to terrorism, even though it has been known for a long time. It is important for them to note that unchecked aggression breeds further aggression and violence. Active shooter incidents such as those at Columbine, Sandy Hook Elementary School, and Santa Monica, defined as non-political terrorism, have become the new normal, along with more swarming attacks of political violence of jihad such as those that occurred in Mumbai in 2008 and at the Westgate shopping plaza in Nairobi in 2013. We cannot expunge these images from our collective unconscious.

Experts are finally beginning to take another look at how violence spreads. Jenkins, one of the leading experts in the United States on political violence, testified before the House Homeland Security Subcommittee on Counterterrorism and Intelligence on June 12, 2013. In his remarks, he referred to the Santa Monica shooting rampage carried out by Jonathan Zawahri in connection with a terrorist assault. The categories between rampage shooters and Islamic terrorism have begun to break down as the root problem of violence is increasingly viewed as beginning in the home. The categories of violence have outrun their course of usefulness in organizing the wanton lethal chaos of murder of the innocent. Writes Jenkins:

> It is ironic that as I am preparing this testimony, neighboring streets in Santa Monica, California, are blocked off because of a shooting rampage by a heavily armed lone gunman who killed five people and wounded four others before being killed by police. Insofar as we know now, political motives were not involved in this incident, *but the occurrence of such episodes in the*

United States demonstrates the possibilities of similar terrorist assaults and at the same time has resulted in police being better prepared to respond to what are referred to as "active shooter" situations [emphasis mine].[406]

Jenkins draws a parallel between rampage shootings and terrorist assaults, even if it is just a nod toward linking the two kinds of violence. There are definite similarities in domestic and global violence and the way in which violence easily jumps categories. In the crossover effect, imitative behavior becomes coupled with a murderous rage that exceeds murder itself. As Freud reminds us, aggression can become addictive. The perpetrator always craves more blood, more death. This is very crude, primitive violence. It is important for politicians, homeland security, the state department, and other government agencies to be aware of this little-mentioned crossover phenomenon in order to establish better modes of intervention. Thus far their strategic methods have been ineffective in stopping the march of violence.

A *USA Today* database of mass shootings (which, according to the FBI, are murders that occur within a short span of time and in which four or more people are killed) [407] over the past seven years shows that what Americans experienced over in calendar year 2013 is sadly typical. There were 14 such incidents between January and mid-July of 2013, while 2012 actually had a low for the reporting period: 22 mass killings. The high was 37 in 2006, the first year that these statistics were kept.

As Professor Matusitz has noted, culture shapes terrorism. The globalization of jihad has elevated the Chechen jihadi, and "Chechen" has become a brand for jihadi terrorism that competes in many ways with Arab terrorism. Chechnya has come to symbolize the violent spirit of warring that the country venerates. The Tsarnaev brothers quickly became the new poster boys for the Chechen brand and new heroes of global jihad. They were placed at the center of the jihadi whirlwind by the radical Turkestan cleric Abu

Dhar 'Azzam, who has appeared in many videos by Al-Qaeda affiliates under the name Abu Dhar Al-Pakistani or Abu Dhar Al-Burmi. His remarks were "deposited" into the global repository for jihadi, accentuating the uniqueness of the Chechen approach to jihad:

> 'Azzam begins his article by lamenting what he presents as the catastrophic situation of children in the Muslim world, who he says are targets for killing in Afghanistan, Burma, India and elsewhere. He faults the Muslim nation for neglecting its children not only physically but also culturally, by failing to give them a proper Islamic upbringing that will make them good believers and fighters for their religion. He writes: "If we neglect the jihadi, ideological and spiritual upbringing of the new youngsters and the new generation, history will not forgive us, and the disgrace of this treason will not be erased from our foreheads. The ummah is in dire need of children [who will be] slaughterers and fighters of the infidels and the devils – children who will be ascetics by night and knights by day, children who will fight the infidels and the leaders of polytheism…"[408]

This opening allows Abu Dhar to present the Tsarnaev brothers as a model of the kind of jihad fighters that the next generation of Muslims should be raised to emulate. He writes:

> "This city of Boston, where Iblis [Satan] practices, is the city from which the movement to liberate America from Great Britain began. In the very house of unbelief, two Chechen brothers destroyed the infidels' fortresses on April 16, 2013. During the [ensuing] search [by the authorities for the perpetrators], the elder brother died as a martyr in the field of glory and honor, Allah willing. The younger brother, Dzhokhar, remained, and told his dear nation: 'We did this operation as revenge for what America does in Palestine, Iraq, and Afghanistan.' He didn't mention his homeland Chechnya, since this jihad is a jihad of [an entire] nation, not [a campaign] for the liberation of a single land.... The Muslims' lands are one and their honor is one.

"I saw Dzhokhar's photo, the photo of a handsome young man in the prime of his youth. I thought to myself: Years ago, he was a child, and he saw the tragedies and catastrophes befall his beloved ummah, one after another. His older brother raised him on jihad and martyrdom-seeking. So, years later, he grew up to be a lion who demolished the fortresses of the infidels and massacred them, rocking the throne of the greatest tyrant on earth.

"Yes, this should be our model. In the very house of unbelief and misguidedness, in the city of Boston, the city of American universities that spread poison around the world – this is where Dzhokhar was raised; in an environment that ridicules and denies faith, Dzhokhar and his brother carried out an attack that pleases the believers and makes us content. By his act, he said to us: This is what you should do, oh pearls [the name Dzhokhar is derived from the Arabic jawhar, meaning pearl] of Muhammad, and weep not. Weeping is unbefitting for men.

"This is but one pearl, oh infidels. Our sacrificing nation will offer many more pearls, until glory and honor is restored to their rightful people—the Muslims… Peace on Dzhokhar and his brother, and on anyone who follows their example—an example from the pearls of an immortal nation…"[409]

IMITATIVE BEHAVIOR: AN UNSOPHISTICATED PRIMITIVE EMULATION

How jihadi behavioral patterns repeat and spread in the crossover phenomenon also can be referred to as the "Chechenization" of Jihad. One way to access and examine violence and crimes involving terrorism is through associative thoughts by way of fantasy, imagery, language, the culture's mythology, and identification with the maternal object. Carl Jung introduced the concept of the shadow and the collective unconscious, which explains how cultures throughout time repeat the same behaviors. Freud referred to this as repetition compulsion. Copycat behavior is considered to be primitive and not well mentalized, meaning thought that is experienced emotionally and connected to language.

Psychoanalytic thinking offers invaluable concepts such as dreams and free association or associative thinking. Our thoughts roam and crisscross and link into our emotions and fantasies, both conscious and unconscious. They help structure and give form to one another. Associative thinking is what make us human and creative and should not be restricted for the mind in fantasy since this may lead to many dark places, including the violence of the volcanic iceberg mentality. The primitive mind cannot differentiate the act of fantasy from the act of doing. Many of these unconscious enactments are an unmentalized experience, that is, as Bion would say, "thoughts without a thinker like idle whistling,"[410] meaning that the person remains disconnected from thoughts and experiences, from emotional life and reality. Primitive thinkers lack empathy and have a cognitive deficit that often leads to paranoia and anxiety. Paranoid thinking is built around delusions, illusions, and feelings of persecution common in shame–honor cultures, which are often expressed as betrayal, the delusion of impurity and unfaithfulness of the other. This paranoid anxiety arises in the first relationship in life between the mother and infant.

In *The Banality of Suicide Terrorism*, I describe how the little girl is the target and the chronic object of her mother's projections, She is turned into the collective shock absorber and victim/scapegoat on which the clan projects its cast-off hateful feelings, the parts of their unwanted selves. This warps her sense of reality, and it may take a long time to disconnect from all the toxic behavior and being targeted as the scapegoat. By the time she becomes a mother, typically at all too young an age, she is already prescripted to be devalued and experiences her own infant's needs as an attack on her. She sees her baby's needs as too demanding and distorted, when in reality they are healthy. But in a shaming environment such as that of the Chechen culture needs are bad. The woman and her baby both feel drained and eternally empty, although the mother may not be aware of these feelings and why she has them. If the female infant is treated like the hated object and the maternal attachment is jeopardized, the child grows up feeling devalued as if she doesn't exist, nameless.

On the other hand, the male infant, although also treated as an object, is a narcissistic object of empowerment because the mother is given honor through his gender. The male baby is not permitted to separate, whereas the female baby from day one is under a death threat of honor killing.

What might these strangulating relationships have to do with imitative behavior? These children are not permitted to play, have fun, or grow up in a nonviolent atmosphere. They are stifled emotionally because play is inhibited and they are not allowed to explore and discover, which helps to build their identities. They do not know how to relate to people. They may look like they are relating. They may even appear to be high functioning. But a lot of it is through imitative behavior, mimicking and shadowing the more self-sufficient individuals that they envy and attack. This is the hidden underside of the volcanic iceberg facade.

The copycat effect is the essence of imitative behavior. It is like the imprinting of a duckling on its mother. However, this imprinting has a negative dimension to it. It focuses on destructive behavior. Suicide in particular is prone to imitation in this copycat existence. When there is a suicide in high school, there is concern that there will be a cluster of suicides. The standard intervention is to bring students together for counseling and monitoring to detect who is at risk of getting swept up into a hysterical state and following in the steps of the classmate who committed suicide. It is a way of processing the "toxicity" of the self-murder and interrupt the contagion effect on other young, vulnerable kids. The intervention itself helps to break the cycle. One wonders if there are clusters of certain kinds of violence that are most likely to occur within a certain interval. To the best of my knowledge this kind of research has not been undertaken.

Terrorist behavior is extremely imitative. It functions around the use of hard objects such as weapons and explosives, and it finds its justification through violent ideologies. That is why, for example, if there is a terrorist event in Somalia, the police and counterterrorist experts will monitor what is happening in the Somali diaspora, such as in the Twin Cities of Minneapolis-St. Paul. Even here the copycat effect crosses over into other ethnic jihadi groups. The same can be said for the Boston Marathon Bombings and what was going on in the Caucasus.

The internet plays a major role in speeding up the transmission of the crossover effect. Could the Tsarnaev Brothers' bombing attacks have had a crossover effect on Jonathan Zawahri's Santa Monica rampage shooting? Why do some killers choose school rampage murders while others choose a jihadi-style rampage such as occurred in Mumbai, Boston, or at the Westgate in Kenya? We have just begun to scratch the surface in understanding the profiles of these perpetrators of violence. What we do know is that they lack empathy and murder in cold blood, and that they are similar in many ways. Can it only be the jihadi ideology that makes the difference, as many counterterrorist experts claim? Conversely, could not this clinging of experts to the jihadi ideology as cause for global violence be a defense against understanding the machinations of the psychological unconscious in similar mass murders—as senseless violence committed as an unconscious psychic adaptation to their psychotic inner world?

The discussion of politically motivated violence as in jihad and the criminal category of rampage shooting takes on new meaning when viewed as parallel types of violence that hold the potential to cross over from one category to another. The "background music" for all of these attacks is the "shaming" these violent individuals share and their inability to mourn loss, which acts as a tripwire, especially with regard to their paranoid maternal drama.

The most striking parallel in politically motivated violence and criminal mass murder is that these attacks violate places that are linked to the maternal object and are unconscious manifestations of the need to repudiate the mother. Even though this might seem paradoxical because Zawahri murdered his father and brother, he did so out of an ambivalent relationship with his mother. He murdered them when his mother was away. Perhaps if she had been there he would have murdered her too, though we will never know. He wanted to prove himself to be a protector of an abused woman, his mother, by committing a grandiose act of murder–suicide. Zawahri apologized to his mother, showing that he understood that what he was doing would offend her. This shows that it was an aggressive attack on her authority and being.

By comparing Jonathan Zawahri's murderous rage with the Tsarnaevs' murderous rage, we learn several things. The feeling of murderous rage is first experienced in the maternal relationship then projected outwards onto other targets who represent the maternal. The fantasy is made concrete and is acted out in reality. Jonathan Zawahri's rampage might look like a non-ideologically motivated killing spree on the surface of things, but what was going on in his unconscious?

Initially it was not known if Zawahri's rampage was a politically motivated act of jihad. This is often the case with breaking news, and places the media audience in an anxious limbo waiting to hear more details. The attack began as a domestic violence incident and then shifted into a rampage-killing spree. Jonathan Zawahri first murdered his father and brother, set their house on fire and then went on his rampage. This was strikingly similar to Adam Lanza's Sandy Hook Elementary School killing spree in December 2012. Lanza first murdered his mother and then went on a rampage, killing children and staff at the elementary school where his mother volunteered. This kind of violent spillage blurs the line between domestic violence and criminal acts of murder. The artificially constructed linguistic categories cannot contain the violence.

A comparison of these seemingly different forms of violence also shows how the killing spree exceeds murder itself because the murder of one or more family members is not enough to satiate the murderer. He must continue to murder, acting out violent fantasies by projecting them onto non-family members, who are a symbolic extension of his family, especially his mother. As we have noted, the school is a sacred space, like the inner sanctum of the family home. It is unconsciously connected to the maternal. The school becomes in loco maternis.

What's in a name? Zawahri offers another dimension of the parallel between domestic violence, rampage shooting, and jihad. In the Bible, Noah named the animals, and suddenly there was an identification: e.g., the elephant became the elephant. Psychologically speaking, it is not by chance that Jonathan Zawahri has the same name as Ayman Zawahiri. Most terrorists find leaders to identify with and idealize, which justifies and fuels their terrorist instincts. The same is true for rampage shooters, who thrive on violent videos and who, like Lanza, create spreadsheets of former incidents involving rampage shooters and mass murderers.[411] Police believe Lanza's score sheet was similar to those kept by video gamers, and that Lanza wanted to put his name at the top of the list.[412] Finding or unconsciously constructing an identification provides meaning and purpose for the volcanic iceberg personality. "Now I have a cause! Now I am somebody!" It also serves to justify one's murderous actions.

Could it be that Jonathan Zawahri was influenced by and unconsciously bonded with his famous Jihadi namesake Zawahiri, the leader of Al Qaeda? Such a coupling would represent the unconscious fantasy in his mind that he had to live out as his "personal" mission. Was he Zawahiri's Mini-Me in fantasy? If so, could this underlying fantasy have mobilized him to carry out his "personal" jihad for his mother, who had become like Allah to him? Did the Tsarnaevs' jihadi attack ignite a violent fantasy life through a copycat effect of suicide (in this case suicide by cop), which is commonly known to exist among students? Aggression breeds aggression if left unchecked. Even though there may be as many as 90,000 other people in the Middle East who share the same surname as Zawahiri or its variant Zawahri, most do not become jihadis. Nonetheless, after 9/11 having the name Zawahri would be like being named John bin Laden. Names shape our sense of purpose. Free association plays an important psychoanalytic role in tapping into the realm of unconscious fantasy. It would be a mere hop, skip, and a jump if your last name were Zawahri to associate it with Ayman Zawahiri.

Let us take a closer look at the commonalities between the violence that occurred in Santa Monica and Boston. The Santa Monica attack took place on June 7, 2013 while Boston began on April 15. Zawahri carried out his rampage less than two months after the Boston Marathon Bombings and seven months after the April 18 Sandy Hook school attack in Connecticut. There are several striking similarities between the Santa Monica and Boston incidents.

- Crime scenes ended with the death by cop killing of the respective rampage shooters—Jonathan and Tamerlan. This is reminiscent of Islamic martyrdom by the Filipino Moros, the Muslims living in the Philippines.[413]
- People were ambushed and shot to death.
- There were attempted or successful car hijackings.
- Immolation was involved, with Zawahri setting his father's residence on fire and the Tsarnaevs using explosives.
- There was domestic violence. Did Jonathan and the Tsarnaevs witness their fathers beating their mothers?
- Shooting took place at schools of higher education—Santa Monica College and MIT.

- The attacks were premeditated.
- Both mothers were out of the United States at the time of the rampages. The maternal absence could have been experienced as a mini-death by the killers, which may have acted as a tripwire. The killers may have felt abandoned, which may have loosened their control over their volcanic rage, since the mother provides a psychological anchor.
- Both mothers were residing in Muslim countries—Lebanon and Dagestan, respectively—when the rampages occurred. Even though Zawahri's mother is a Lebanon Christian, many Lebanese Christians more readily identify with Muslims. The work of Bat Ye'or on Dhimmitude has attested to the Christians in Lebanon and the broader region having been coopted by the Palestinian jihadi agenda.[414] The Tsarnaev brothers' mother had returned to Dagestan.
- Both women had been separated and divorced from their husbands, but Zubeidat Tsarnaev is thought to have reconciled with hers. There was a history of domestic violence for Jonathan's mother, and we speculate that Zubeidat was probably abused since Anzor minimized the domestic violence incident of Tamerlan, who undoubtedly modeled his behavior after his father's.
- In both attacks the younger brother killed the older brother either consciously, as in the case of Zawarhi, or semi-unconsciously, as Dzhokhar killed Tamerlan. Zawarhi shot his brother and father to death while Dzhokhar ran over his brother when he fled the scene after Tamerlan had been shot by the police, probably killing his brother.
- There was a question of mental illness. Jonathan Zawarhi had a documented history of mental impairment. So did Adam Lanza, who was diagnosed with Aspergers. As cited in the preceding chapter, a neighbor of Zubeidat Tsarnaeva raised the issue of

Tamerlan being mentally ill but his mother could not tolerate the idea that her perfect narcissistic object was flawed.

There are also some differences:

- Zawarhi gave no motive for the school shooting and apologized for killing his father and brother ,while the Tsarnaevs' motive was jihad and revenge for the killing of Muslims by American troops.
- The number of murdered and wounded was different. In Zawarhi's Santa Monica attack, five people were killed and four injured, while in the Tsarnaevs' Boston Marathon attack three spectators, including one child, were killed and an MIT police officer and 280 people were injured.
- The Tsarnaev brothers worked in tandem to carry out the Boston attack while Zawarhi acted alone.

Did Zawarhi identify with Dzhokhar and Tamerlan? Could this unconscious bond have internally justified his violence? Did the Santa Monica incident mimic the Boston Marathon Bombings with a carjacking and rampage shooting? Did Zawarhi also mimic the rampage shootings at Sandy Hook Elementary School and Columbine High School? While there are more questions than answers, the aim is to raise awareness among law enforcement, the military, and others working in counterterrorism, as well as the public about how associative thinking and identifications work. Even though I do not have access to the computer of John Zawahri, which may reveal his record of what he read, to whom he wrote, what violent computer games he played, and violent films he watched, we can still pose a series of other questions.

To what degree did being from a Lebanese Arab Christian background influence his awareness of Arab Muslim violence? While Christianity is constantly under attack in the Middle East, and Lebanon was essentially the only "Christian" country until its takeover by Hezbollah and Shi'ite Islam, were Zawarhi's family influenced by the violence or did it undergo a series of displacements that made it difficult to fit in? Jonathan shared with Tamerlan and Dzhokhar the immigration experience, which impacts greatly on identity formation in adolescence, a critical time where shame is experienced in a new culture and when rage can be uncapped. To be an immigrant is to feel a regression to earlier childhood vulnerabilities.

Professor Anwar Chejne, my dissertation advisor for aljamía, Old Spanish in Arabic script, was also a Lebanese Christian. He told me that although he was ethnically Christian, he identified with Islam and was an Islamophile. He wrote a 500-page history of Muslim Spain and never once mentioned jihad. Bat Ye'or has repeatedly emphasized that a large swath of Arab Christians formed an identification with Arab Muslims, particularly those in Lebanon.[415] "The Bride of the South," Sana'a Mehaidli, who claimed to be the first female suicide bomber, was Lebanese Christian.[416] Moreover, Ziad Jarrah, another Lebanese, was one of the 9/11 pilots who crashed his plane into Shanksville, Pennsylvania, killing all on board after a passenger uprising. He came from a secular Sunni Muslim family and had been sent to Catholic school in Beirut.[417] Thus, there has been crossover in religious identifications in Lebanon, which have been heavily tinged with jihadi violence, perhaps an overlay to the culturally sanctioned revenge and honor killings. This history was most likely known to John Zawahri.

A colleague of mine pointed out that a French psychiatric patient beheaded two nurses in Pau in December 2004.[418] He was not Muslim. She noted that one could assume that his fantasy world was shaped by the current custom of beheading occurring in Saudi Arabia, as well as throughout regions where jihad is being fought, such as Iraq. Figuring prominently were the Zarqawi rampage beheadings, which began in May 2004 with the beheading of Nichols Berg. As has been noted, Zarqawi began the beheadings directly after completing forty days of mourning for his mother, who died from cancer. In psychoanalytical terms, his beheading rampage, which held the attention of the global media, was a displaced matricide. In the case of the Pau, France, beheadings, one head was set on top of a television, nonverbally communicating its link to jihadi global beheadings via the media, referencing Zarqawi and Daniel Pearl's beheading in February 2002. Chechen jihadi Basayev beheaded many.[419]

Moreover, men and women have been swept up by the jihad conquest and turn into mujahedin. One doesn't have to be an ethnic Arab; one can pretend.[420] Just think of Lawrence of Arabia. This is evidenced by all the converts to jihad.[421] Furthermore the term "jihad" is often presented as being nonviolent, an allegedly personal struggle. Yet language does not work that way as its history is encoded in the term jihad, and in this case the term has a violent history that cannot be erased.

Aggression breeds aggression and violence gets spread by imitative, concrete behavior. However, this kind of violent behavior does not come out of nowhere. Psychoanalysis shows us that behavior and personality are formed early on. Jonathan Zawahri's rampage was premeditated, as most jihadi attacks are. Yet he had his first run-in with the law as a juvenile in 2006, which was during the height of post-9/11 concerns and amid increased awareness of the wars in Iraq and Afghanistan, to say nothing of Lebanon, from where Zawahri's family hailed. [422] An individual who has a cognitive deficit and does not know how to handle his violent fantasies in an appropriate way is at risk of being seduced into believing that violence will alleviate and resolve the internal conflict of impulses and anxieties that he is experiencing. Violent attachment is a psychotic adaptation. Even though we may not be sure what Zawahri was feeling and thinking, specifically at the onset of his rampage, it was his attempt to adapt to his psychotic reality.

The Tsarnaev brothers self-radicalized by going to The Islamic Society of Boston in Cambridge, listening to jihadi tapes, downloading videos, viewing parts of Nidal Hassan's rampage at Fort Hood, and apparently using the Al Qaeda downloadable e-zine, *Inspire*, where they learned how to make a bomb in the kitchen of their mother. All of this is in the public domain. The associations swirl and spread. For example, did the Boston Marathon Bombings carried out by these two half-Chechen brothers embolden the *qital* of the Woolwich attack that butchered Lee Rigby on May 22, 2013? At the very least, it helped increase global awareness of jihadi violence. And what about the Jewish man, known to be mentally challenged, who tragically was shot to death by an Israeli Druze Security man at the Western Wall in Jerusalem because he cried out "Allahu Akhbar"? [423] Another instance where the Tsarnaev case was mentioned in a Canadian jihadi plot is that of Nutall and Korody, also claimed to be self-radicalized:

> As in the Boston Marathon bombing, Nuttall and Korody were targeting a mass gathering. The pressure-cooker bombs were the same type Dzhokhar and Tamerlan Tsarnaev deployed, packed with rusty nails and bolts. But unlike the Boston attack, the authorities foiled the plot. No explosions, no injuries, no deaths, and two arrests.
>
> Wayne Ridout, an assistant commissioner with the Royal Canadian Mounted Police (RCMP) told reporters, "The suspects were committed to acts of violence and discussed a wide variety of targets and techniques." The RCMP described Nuttall as "inspired by al-Qaeda ideology" but not supported from abroad. What contact Nuttall and Korody may have had with terrorist organizations and websites remains an open question.[424]

Nutall and Korody are a reminder of the crossover effect and imitative nature of terrorism's violence. The concept of the "lone wolf" who engages in a terrorist act allegedly alone dovetails with the Tsarnaevs' having embraced Chechen warrior identity as the Wolf. This crossover involves a linguistic lethal pun by using the image of the wolf as predator in a concrete manner.

The national image of the wolf intersects with the mosque in their collective unconscious. While the Tsarnaevs may have been backed by a terrorist group commonly thought to be the Caucasus Emirate they concretized the term lone wolf by trying to embody being THE wolves of Chechnya. We see how the media picks up on this: "The common-law couple [Nutall and Korody] appears to be a pair of 'lone wolves,' like the Tsarnaev brothers who attacked the Boston Marathon using pressure-cooker bombs they learned to make from the Internet."[425] The concrete nature of terrorism's embodiment of language points to a cognitive deficit in their thinking and behavior, a characteristic of their volcanic iceberg mentality.

How does the crossover effect relate to the concept of the maternal cameo for the Tsarnaev brothers and their mother, or for other terrorists and their mothers? The argument put forth here is that the underlying unconscious pantomime of communication boils down to their paranoid fused state with their mothers. Besides the fact that this involves perversion, the jihadi violence unconsciously targets the elimination of the mother, the female.

A question that has not been asked is: If this is the case, could the crossover effect and the negation of the female in Islam, as Bouhdiba claims, efface women across the globe? It is reported that one third of all women experience violence at some point in their lives. And 95% of suicides in Afghanistan are carried out by women.[426] We don't have an answer to this question.

There also has been a jihadi crossover effect in the area of soccer. We know through the writing of anthropologist Alan Dundes[427] that in sports the opponent is feminized. It is also well known that a great deal of violence has been associated with soccer players and their crazed fans, who have been characterized as terrorist thugs. A twist on the Chechenization of jihad has been the case of the Israeli Jerusalem soccer team hiring Chechen soccer players. The Chechens were horribly received by Israeli Jewish soccer fans, who verbally assaulted them and were guilty of discrimination and blatant racism against them because they are Muslims.[428] The team had never before hired Muslims despite the fact that there is a Circassian community in Israel with ancestral ties to the Caucasus. The Chechen footballers returned to Chechnya.[429] James Dorsey explores at length the manipulation of soccer as politics in his *The Turbulent World of Middle East Soccer.*[430]

There is also a connection to the Chechens in the Jerusalem suburb of Abu Gosh, where the largest mosque in Israel is currently being built. By and large, relations are good with the Arab Muslim and Chechen Muslims who have donated to the mosque. Israel is a democracy and permitted the building of the mosque. There is freedom of speech and worship.

Yet, tracings of jihad and violence further infiltrate the arena of soccer in the case of the Italian team, which chose to take its name—Zassbollah—from Hezbollah, the Shiite terrorist organization.

> In another news story, published in the *Washington Times* in January 2008, it was reported that, in Italy, the Carioca amateur-league football club had adopted for its players' shirts the green assault-rifle logo of the Lebanese terrorist group Hezbollah(p.145); the team had also changed its name to 'Zassbollah"....the team had appropriated the Hezbollah logo in order to frighten its adversaries and to make them understand the extent to which it was prepared to fight to win a match.
>
> The branding employed by terrorist groups is an understudied subject. Current studies of terrorism are limited to discussions on the definition of the word, and the nature and scope of terrorist acts. These studies are predominantly carried out in a subjective manner, defining terrorism as a criminal act. While this approach offers a functional means of understanding the major common elements of terrorism and helps to counter it, it does not help us to understand the brand identities of terrorist organizations, nor how their

> visual communication works, why certain visual elements are preferred over others, and how and why they carry certain meaning, emotions and values.[431]

Did the beheading of a Brazilian soccer referee and having his dismembered head impaled on a stake and paraded in the middle of the field in front of a violent crowd mimic the beheadings of Nicola Berg, Daniel Pearl, as well as Zarqawi's notorious beheading rampage?[432]

SUMMARY

If one looks at the sequence of domestic and criminal violence, one can also see a linking phenomenon to jihad. Violence is self-perpetuating. The crossover effect, based on imitative behavior, that leads to the global spread of violence may be hard to pin down, and the influencing source for the these attacks is undoubtedly complex. However, the perpetrators of domestic, criminal, and political violence under the banner of jihad share one thing in common: the lack of empathy that begins with the maternal drama—their flawed bond with their mothers. For the Chechen jihadis the maternal drama haunts their actions, which justifies in their minds the psychotic decision to act out their repressed rage and hatred in an outburst of violence.

CONCLUSION

THE FEMALE AS LYNCHPIN IN STOPPING THE VIOLENCE

A dagger drawn by the fool is more dangerous than that drawn by the brave.
—Chechen Saying

The Chechen threat remains unabated, as manifested in a video clip posted online, which contained a report from the International Center for Counter Terrorism in Herzliya, Israel:

> Chechen rebel leader Doku Umarov urged his followers to attack the Winter Olympics, slated to be held in Sochi, Russia, in February 2014. In an operation in southwestern Chechnya, Russian special forces killed Rustam Saliyev, Doku Umarov's former bodyguard.[433]

Continued violence in the Chechen arena took place on September 16, 2013, when a suicide bombing killed law enforcement officers. This incident came five months before Putin's Olympics in Sochi,[434] creating another layer of worry for Russia and the United States, as well as for Olympic athletes and their families. This was followed by suicide bombings in Volgograd (formerly called Stalingrad) in October and December 2013.

Dealing with the Root Cause of Violence

We have examined the idea of skewed maternal attachment as the outcome of a shame–honor culture and its religion. The infant is bonded to the devalued female. Both experience violence growing up. The flawed maternal attachment and child-rearing practices that arrest psychic development make it very difficult for the child to move forward and separate in life, growing into a responsible adult. Instead the child remains frozen in time and infantilized. Needs and feelings are dirty and scary. Violence becomes the way to explain this psychotic world and the vehicle to extract oneself from a pathological maternal fusion.

Using the imagery of the maternal cameo, we have noted this fusion and the quest for a fission or splitting. Key to the split in the terrorist psyche is their misuse of the targeted object. Shamil Basayev's three most famous and brutal attacks—on a maternity hospital, theater, and school—were unconscious attacks on aspects of the maternal cameo. The mother looms large in the psyche of the Chechen jihadi, who are raised in a shame–honor culture similar to those whose religion is Islam. The suicide attacks are in essence an attack on the mother and a quest to re-fuse with her in death. This violent engagement with their target and victims provides a clue to their disturbed psyches. My argument leaves room for both the role of genetics and neuroscience. Quoting from noted neuroscientist D.F. Swaab, we see that the child is misused as an object through brainwashing to commit violence. Swaab comments on the violence that ensued after publication of the 2006 Danish cartoons making fun of Islamic Extremism. "The Muslim Brotherhood, Syria, the Islamic Jihad Union, interior ministers of Arab countries, the Organization of Islamic Conference, all behaved as if they were themselves models of tolerance toward other religions and demanded apologies."[435] He goes on to note the behavior of the Taliban, Hamas in the Palestinian territories, as well as Hezbollah, reminding us that this kind of violence is not exclusively a Muslim problem and that the key to the manipulation of the child lies in the early bonding experience.

The Tsarnaev family, with its history of domestic violence and its cauldron of psychosis and denial, exemplifies the volcanic iceberg mentality and fits the profile of a family rooted in a shame–honor culture. The Tsarnaev brothers used violence and destruction to try to make sense of their inner psychotic world and to find an identity separate from the flawed maternal attachment. Such is the case with all jihadis. The media has played a part in creating and spreading the Chechen brand of jihad, similar to the fascination we may find in nineteenth century novels with the erotic and exotic representation of the Chechen warrior.[436] However, the stakes are different and the reality of the romanticization and addiction to such violence is real. The Boston Marathon Bombing brought this tragically into view.

In these pages we have examined the phenomenon of the crossover effect—how when violence goes unchecked it breeds more violence and aggression. If we are to succeed in intervening and bringing a halt to the creation of the kind of volcanic iceberg mentality that creates these wagers of jihad, the issue of the maternal platform and its attachment must be addressed at all levels of society. The Chechen people have suffered miserably at the hands of the Russians, another shame–honor people. They do not deserve to be held captive to ancient clan customs that are interwoven with Islam's jihad and the tradition of warring, to see a continuation of violence destroy their people.

Like all of us, the Chechens want to put food on the table, educate their children, and provide them with the best possible medical care so that they may have a bright future. If they are to achieve these goals without the continuing threat of destruction, the treatment of the female in utero onward must change. The shame–honor cultures that overvalue the male baby must make a 180-degree about-face and learn that the female should be valued equally with the male. The successful end to violence lies with a healthily raised baby girl who finally is valued as she deserves to be and does not have to live her life under a death threat. This is how to arrest the cycle of violence spawned by a traumatic maternal attachment.

Sandor Breiner, an expert on the history of child sacrifice and a physician-psychoanalyst who was also my mentor, knew Arab Muslim culture well. He felt that the ineffective father is the symptom of the underlying problem in shame–honor cultures, especially Arab-Muslim culture. Often the authoritarian father is pointed to as the problem by experts in Islam (most of whom are male), but the claim is unfounded and does not account for the ramifications of targeting the female as an object of hatred. States Breiner:

> "When all is said and done, the most important person in our universe is the mother who can pass along her love, nurturing, security, and stability to her daughters, who will continue the cycle and pass along these characteristics to her children. The perfection for motherhood begins in infancy. Without this foundation in the first two or three years of life, the little girl will become impaired in her functioning as a mother. This means that the most important person in the world is a newborn female child. What a horrible tragedy that she has been the object, throughout history, of society's prejudice and abuse. Without that love from mother we flounder; without it, there is pain, violence, death—even war. The only hope our civilization has lies in changing our response toward women. They should not be treated as equal to men; they deserve better."[437]

The maternal drama is universal. Our link with our mothers is the key to changing the way we feel about ourselves and the way in which we interact with others. Mother is our first point of contact with the world. Only by working toward ensuring that this all-important maternal bond is healthy and nurturing rather than mired in shame and rage can we get to the root of the violence that increasingly pervades our global society.

APPENDIX A

The current most wanted Chechen terrorist is Doku Umarov. Umarov leads the Caucasus Emirate (CE), a Chechen group dedicated to bringing Islamic rule to much of southern Russia. The U.S. State Department named Umarov a Specially Designated Global Terrorist in 2010, and said subsequently that he was "encouraging followers to commit violent acts against CE's declared enemies, which include the United States as well as Israel, Russia, and the United Kingdom." The U.S. government is offering a reward of up to $5 million for information on his location.[438]

U.S. officials have been investigating whether the Tsarnaev brothers—who were blamed for carrying out the Boston Marathon Bombing in April 2013—had any links with Chechen militant groups. Nothing has surfaced connecting them with CE, whose main focus has been on attacking Russian institutions and civilian targets. In January 2011, CE bombed Moscow's Domodedovo airport, killing 36 people, and was responsible for the suicide bombings of Moscow subway stations in 2010, which killed 40 people.

Umarov was born in southern Chechnya in 1964, according to Chechen websites, and describes his family as part of the "intelligentsia." He came of age as the separatist campaign against Russian rule began to take root and joined the insurgency when Russian leader Boris Yeltsin sent troops into the region in 1994.

In a proclamation published on a Chechen jihadist website in 2007, Umarov declared, "It was my destiny to lead the Jihad... I will lead and organize Jihad according to the understanding given to me by Allah."

According to the findings of START, the National Consortium for the Study of Terrorism and Responses to Terrorism,[439] there were 1,415 terrorist attacks connected with the Chechens from January 1992 through

December 2011 in the Global Terrorism Database. The Chechen groups that have engaged in attacks are the Caucasus Emirate, the Armed Forces of the Chechen Republic of Ichkeria, Riyadus-Salikhin Reconnaissance and Sabotage Battalion of Chechen Martyrs, Dagestani Shari'sh Jamaat, Islambouli Brigades of al-Qa'ida, NVF, Chechen Lone Wolf Group, Special Purpose Islamic Regiment (SPIR), and other miscellaneous groups. To date no group has claimed responsibility for the Boston Marathon Bombing, although the Tsarnaevs did listen to audio tapes of the radical al Qaeda-affiliated Sheikh al-Awalki, who was also implicated in the Fort Hood Massacre perpetrated by the United States Army psychiatrist Major Nidal Hassan in November 2008.

Following are lists of the number of Chechen terrorist attacks by target type and by tactic type, as cited in the START report :

Attacks by Target Type:

- Police, 371
- Government, 271
- Private Citizens and Property, 199
- Military, 179
- Transportation, 102
- Business, 95
- Religious Figures/Institutions, 48
- Utilities, 36
- Journalists & Media, 14
- Educational Institution, 12
- Telecommunication, 12
- NGO, 11
- Airports & Airlines, 6

Attacks by Tactic Type:

- Bombing/Explosion, 749
- Armed Assault, 412
- Assassinassion, 133
- Facility/Infrastructure, 57
- Hostage Taking, 51
- Hijacking, 8

APPENDIX B

This short list of the major events in START's records further contextualizes the high degree of violence associated with the Chechens.

1995 Budennovsk Maternity Hospital Hostage Crisis hostage, June 14-19. An estimated 200 Chechen terrorists, described as separatists who became increasingly Islamized under the command of Shamil Basayev, attacked the southern Russian hospital.

1999 Vladimavkaz Bombing: This car bombing in a marketplace in North Ossetia killed 64 persons and injured 104. A Wahhabi group affiliated with Al Qaeda claimed responsibility. Osama bin Laden and/or the Jordanian Hattab Chechen field commander were said to have planned the attack.

1999 A series of apartment building bombings in Dagestan and Moscow killed 291 and wounded hundreds. Also the bombing of 18 apartment buildings in Vladikavkaz, North Ossetia killed 4.

2000 Argun Barracks Bombing killed 50 Russian soldiers, including special police units, and wounded 81.

2002 Moscow Dubrovka Theater Attack on October 23. Led by 25-year-old Movsar Barayev, 41 Chechen SPIR terrorists, including 18 women, attacked 850 theater goers, taking them hostage for three days. All terrorists and 130 hostages were killed when Russian forces used a gas to disable the terrorists and then storm the building.[440]

2004 Beslan School Siege, September 1, 2004, the single bloodiest attack by a Chechen terrorist group. Between 30 and 35 armed Riyadus-Salikhin

Reconnaissance and Sabotage Battalion of Chechen Martyrs took hostage approximately 1,200 children, parents, and teachers. During the three-day attack, Russian soldiers stormed the building with rockets and tanks. Of the 344 who died, 100 were children; 727 were wounded.

2005 Nalchik Assault on the Russian town in October including the Russian Corrections Department, with 85 killed and 150 wounded. Chechen rebels claimed responsibility.

2009 Bologoye Train Bombing derailed three cars with improvised explosive devices between Moscow and St. Petersburg, leaving 26 killed, 100 wounded, 18 unaccounted for. Caucasus Emirate claimed responsibility. The TNT bomb of 7 kg "left a crater of 1.5 meters in diameter" according to the START report.

2010 Moscow Subway Bombings. Two female suicide bombers, Black Widows, detonated at two subway stations, killing 40, wounding 90. One of the subway stations, Lubyanka, was located under the Russian Security Services.

2011 Airport Bombing. Suicide bombing at the arrival hall of Domodedovo Airport, killing 37 wounding 168. Dagestan Front of the Caucasus Emirate claimed responsibility.

A SELECTED BIBLIOGRAPHY

Ablow, K. 2011. *Inside the Mind of Casey Anthony*. New York: St. Martin's Press.

Ablow, K. 2007. *Living the Truth: Transform your Life through Honesty and Insight*. New York: Hachette Books.

Ablow, K. 2005. *Inside the Mind of Scott Peterson*. New York: St. Martin's Press.

Ablow, K. 2004. *Murder Suicide*. New York: St. Martin's Press.

Ahmed, A. 2013. *The Thistle and the Drone: How America's War on Terror Became a Global War on Tribal Islam*. Washington, DC: Brookings Institution Press.

Ahmed, S. Z. 1997. *Twilight on the Caucasus*. North Carolina/Strasbourg: A.E.R. [Assembly of European Regions] Publications.

Akhtar, S. 2005. *Objects of our Desire: Exploring our Intimate Connections*. New York: Harmony Books.

Akhtar, S. 1999. The Psychodynamic Dimension of Terrorism. *Psychiatric Annals*, 29(6), 350–355.

Akhtar, S., S. Kramer and H. Parens. 1996. *The Internal Mother: Conceptual and Technical Aspects of Object Constancy*. Northvale, NJ: Jason Aronson Press.

Alford, C.F. 1989. *Melanie Klein and Critical Social Theory*. New Haven: Yale University Press.

Alberto, P., L. Fredrick, M. Hughes, L. McIntosh and D. Cihak. 2007. Components of Visual Literacy: Teaching Logos. *Focus on Autism and Other Developmental Disabilities*, 22(4), 234–243.

Allen, W.E.D. and P. Muratoff. 1953. *Caucasian Battlefields*. Cambridge: Cambridge University Press.

Anderson, B. 1983. *Imagined Communities: Reflections on the Origin and Spread of Nationalism*. London: Verso.

Atran, S. 2010. *Talking to the Enemy: Faith, Brotherhood, and the (Un)Making of Terrorists*. New York: HarperCollins.

Baddeley, J.F. 1908. *The Russian Conquest of the Caucasus*. London: Longman.

Baiev, K. with R. and N. Daniloff. 2003. *The Oath*. New York: Walker.

Barakat, H. 1993. *The Arab World: Society, Culture, and State.* Berkeley: University of California Press.

Bashear, S. 1997. *Arabs and Others in Early Islam.* Princeton, NJ: The Darwin Press, Inc.

Bartell, D. and Gray, D. 2012. Hezbollah and Al Shabaab in Mexico and the Terrorist Threat to the United States. *Global Security Studies*, 3(4), 100–114.

Bat Ye'or. 2002. *Islam and Dhimmitude: Where Civilizations Collide.* Teaneck: Fairleigh Dickinson University Press.

Bauman, Z. 2000. *Liquid Modernity.* Cambridge: Polity.

Benslama, F. 2009. *Psychoanalysis and the Challenge of Islam.* Minneapolis: University of Minnesota Press.

Bergmann, M.S. 1992. *In the Shadow of Moloch.* New York: Columbia University Press.

Berko, A. 2012. *The Smarter Bomb: Women and Children as Suicide Bombers.* New York: Rowman and Littlefield.

Bick, E. 2011. *The Tavistock Model: Papers on Child Development and Psychoanalytic Thinking*, edited by M. Harris and M. Harris Williams.

Bion, W.R. 2000. *Experiences in Groups.* New York: Routledge.

Bishop, R. and T. Roy. 2009. Mumbai: City-as-Target, Introduction. *Theory, Culture & Society*, 26(7), 263–277.

Bitov, A. 1992. *A Captive of the Caucasus.* New York: Farrar Straus Giroux.

Blain, M. 2009. *The Sociology of Terrorism: Studies in Power, Subjection, and Victimage Ritual.* Boca Raton, FL: Universal Publishers.

Blanch, L. 1995. *Sabres of Paradise.* New York: Carroll and Graf.

Bloom, Mia 2005. *Dying to Kill: The Global Phenomenon of Suicide Terror.* New York: Columbia University Press.

Bodansky, Y. 2009. *Chechen Jihad: Al Qaeda's Training Ground and the Next Wave of Terror.* HarperCollins e-books.

Bouhdiba, A. 1998. *Sexuality in Islam.* London: Saqi Books.

Bouhdiba, A. 1977. The Child and Mother in Arab-Muslim society. In L.C. Brown and N. Itzkowitz eds. *Psychological Dimensions of Near Eastern Studies.* Princeton: Darwin.

Bowlby, J. 1982/1969. *Attachment and Loss*, vol. 1. New York: Basic Books.

Bowlby, J. 1988. *A Secure Base*. New York: Basic Books.

Brisard, J-C. 2005. *Zarqawi: The New Face of Al-Qaeda*. New York: Other Press.

Brothers, D. 2013. War, Peace, and Promise Making. Unpublished paper delivered at The Psychoanalyst in a Wounded World, Tel Aviv University, 25 April.

Bullough, O. 2013. The Roots of Chechen Rage. http://www.foreignpolicy.com/articles/2013/04/20/the_roots_of_chechen_rage?print=yes&hidecomments=yes&page=full

Bullough, O. 2010. *Let Our Fame Be Great: Journeys Among the Defiant Peoples of the Caucasus*. London: Penguin.

Burgess, M. 2003. *A Brief History of Terrorism*. Washington, DC: Center for Defense Information (CDI).

Burr, J.M. 2014. The Caucasus Snake Pit. The American Center for Democracy: Economic Warfare Institute, email 22 January 2014.

Cannon, C. M. 2012. *Forgiving the Unforgivable: The True Story of How Survivors of the Mumbai Terrorist Attack Answered Hatred with Compassion*. New York: SelectBooks.

Caputi, J. 1987. *The Age of Sex Crime*. Bowling Green, Ohio: Bowling Green State University Popular Press.

Carsten, J. 2000. *Cultures of Relatedness: New Approaches to the Study of Kinship*. Cambridge: Cambridge University Press.

Center for the Study of Political Islam. 2007. *The Submission of Women and Slaves: Islamic Duality*. CSPI Publishing, LLC.

Chejne, A. 1974. *Muslim Spain, Its History and Culture*. Minneapolis: University of Minnesota Press.

Chenciner, R. 1997. *Daghestan: Tradition and Survival*. New York: St. Martin's Press.

Clark, R. 1984. *The Basque Insurgents: ETA, 1952-1980*. Madison: University of Wisconsin Press.

Cleckley, H. 1988. *The Mask of Sanity*. Maryland Heights, MO: C.V. Mosby Co.

Cohen, I. and R. Corrado. 2003. A Future for the ETA? In Dilip Das & Peter Kratcoski (Eds.), *Meeting the Challenges of Global Terrorism: Prevention, Control, and Recovery* (pp. 271-288). New York: Lexington Books.

Colarusso, J. 2002. *Nart Sages from the Caucasus*. Princeton, NJ: Princeton University Press.

Coll, S. 2004. *Ghost Wars*. New York: The Penguin Press.

Collins, A. 2002. *My Jihad: The True Story of an American Mujahid's Amazing Journey from Osama Bin Laden.* New York: The Lyons Press.

Collins, R.1987. *The Basques.* New York: Basil Blackwell.

Conquest, R. 1970. *The Nation Killers: The Soviet Deportation of Nationalities.* London: MacMillan.

Cornell, S. 2002. Autonomy as a Source of Conflict: Caucasian Conflicts in Theoretical Perspective. *World Politics*, 54(2), 245–276.

Damasio, A. 1994. *Descartes' Error: Emotion, Reason, and the Human Brain.* New York: Avon Books.

Davoine, F. and J.M. Gaudilliere. 2004. *History Beyond Trauma.* New York: Other Press.

De Pauw, L. G. 1998. *Battle Cries and Lullabies: Women in War from Prehistory to the Present.* Norman, OK: Oklahoma University Press.

Dingley, J. and M. Marcello. 2007. The Human Body as a Terrorist Weapon: Hunger Strikes and Suicide Bombers. *Studies in Conflict & Terrorism*, 30(6), 459-492.

Dundes, A. Ed.1992. *The Evil Eye: A Casebook.* Madison: University of Wisconsin Press.

Dundes, A. 1997. *From Game to War and Other Psychoanalytic Essays on Folklore.* Lexington: University of Kentucky Press.

Dunlop, J.B. 1998. *Russia Confronts Chechnya.* Cambridge, UK: Cambridge University Press.

Eager, P. W. 2013. *From Freedom Fighter to Terrorists: Women and Political Violence.* Burlington, VT: Ashgate Publishing Company.

Evangelists, M. 2002. *The Chechen Wars.* Washington, DC: The Brookings Institute.

Fildes, V. A.. 1986. *Breasts, Bottles and Babies: A History of Infant Feeding.* Edinburgh: Edinburg University Press.

Fornari, F. 1974. *The Psychoanalysis of War.* Bloomington, IN: Indiana University Press with Doubleday.

Freud, H. 2013. *Men and Mothers: The Lifelong Struggle of Sons and Their Mothers.* London: Karnac.

Gall, C. and T. de Waal. 1998. *Chechnya: Calamity in the Caucasus.* New York: New York University Press.

Gambetta, D. Ed. 2004. *Making Sense of Suicide Missions.* Oxford: Oxford University Press.

Gammer, M. 2006. *The Lone Wolf and the Bear.* Pittsburgh: University of Pittsburgh Press.

Gammer, M. 1994. *Muslim Resistance to the Tsar: Shamil and the Conquest of Chechnia and Dagestan*. London: Frank Cass.

Gaylin, W.2003. *Hatred: The Psychological Descent into Violence*. New York: PublicAffairs.

Giduck, J. 2005. *Terror at Beslan*. Archangel Group Inc. http://www.terroratbeslan.com/

Ginat, J. 1987. *Blood Disputes among Bedouin and Rural Arabs in Israel: Revenge, Mediation, Outcasting and Family Honor*. Pittsburgh, PA: University of Pittsburgh Press in cooperation with Jerusalem Institute for Israel Studies.

Gilligan, E. 2010. *Terror in Chechnya: Russia and the Tragedy of Civilians in War*. Princeton, NJ: Princeton University.

Goltz, T. 2003. *Chechnya Diary*. New York: Thomas Dunne Books.

Gordon, J. 2014. Did Tamerlan Tsarnaev contact Jihadists near Sochi Site?, http://www.newenglishreview.org/blog_display.cfm/blog_id/51691 accessed 21 January 2014.

Griffin, N. 2003. *Caucasus: Mountain Men and Holy War*. New York: Thomas Dunne Books.

Gunawardena, A. 2006. *Female Black Tigers: A Different Breed of Cat?* Tel Aviv: The Jaffee Center for Strategic Studies.

Hall, C. and V. O'Sullivan. 1996. Tourism, Political Stability and Violence. In A. Pizam & Y. Mansfeld, Eds., *Tourism, Crime and International Security Issues*, pp. 175–186. New York: John Wiley.

Hamid, M. 1991. *Iman Shamil: The First Muslim Guerilla Leader*. Delhi: Adam Publishers.

Hammes, T. 2006. *The Sling and the Stone: On War in the 21st Century*. St. Paul, MN: Zenith Press.

Hassan, N. 2001, November 19. An Arsenal of Believers: Talking to the "Human Bombs." *The New Yorker*, 77, 36–41.

Heilbrunn, B. 1997. Representation and Legitimacy: A Semiotic Approach to the Logo. In Winfried Nöth, Ed., *Semiotics of the Media: State of the Art, Projects, and Perspectives*, pp. 175–189. Berlin: Mouton de Gruyter.

Higdon, H. 2013. 4:09:43-*Police Do Not Cross This Line*. Constellation, a Division of Perseus Books Group. Kindle edition.

Hoffman, B. 2006. *Inside Terrorism*, 2nd ed. New York: Columbia University Press.

Howell, E. F. 2005. *The Dissociative Mind.* Hillsdale NJ: Analytic Press.

Howie, L. 2011. *Terror on the Screen: Witnesses and the Reanimation of 9/11 as Image-Event, Popular Culture and Pornography*. Washington, DC: New Academia Publishing.

Hughes, T.P. 1994. *Dictionary of Islam.* Chicago: Kazi Publications, Inc.

Hunter, R. and D. Heinke. 2011. Radicalization of Islamist Terrorists in the Western World. *FBI Law Enforcement Bulletin*, 80(1), 24–31.

Inamdar, S.C. 2001. *Muhammad and the Rise of Islam: The Creation of Group Identity.* Madison, CT: Psychosocial Press.

Jaimoukha, A. 2005. *The Chechens: A Handbook.* New York: Routledge.

Jandt, F. 2010. *An Introduction to Intercultural Communication: Identities in a Global Community*, 6th ed. Thousand Oaks, CA: Sage.

Janes, R. 2005. *Losing Our Heads, Beheadings in Literature and Culture.* New York: New York University Press.

Jones, R. 2005. *Terrorist Beheadings: Cultural and Strategic Implications*. Carlisle, PA: Strategic Studies Institute.

Karny, Y. 2000. *Highlanders: A Journey to the Caucasus in Quest of Memory.* New York: Farrar, Straus Giroux.

Katz, J. 1988. *Seductions of Crime, Moral and Sensual Attractions in Doing Evil.* New York: Basic Books.

Khosrokhavar, F. 2002. *Suicide Bombers: Allah's New Martyrs.* London: Pluto Press.

Khoury, P.S. and J. Kostiner. 1990. *Tribes and State Formation in the Middle East.* Berkeley: University of California.

Kobrin, N. H. 2013. *Penetrating the Terrorist Psyche.* New York, NY: MultiEducator Inc.

Kobrin, N. H. 2010. *The Banality of Suicide Terrorism*: The Naked Truth about Islamic Suicide Bombing. Washington, DC: Potomac.

Kobrin, N. H. 2002 (first edition). Psychodynamic Treatment for PTSD in Foa, E. , T. M. Keane, M. J. Friedman, and J. A. Cohen eds. *Essential Treatments for PTSD.* New York: The Guilford Press.

Kobrin, N. H. 2008. Putting the Umm back in the Umma – Suicide Attack: Understanding the Terrorists' Deepest Terrors in *Suicide Bombers: The Psychological, Religious and Other Imperatives*, ed. by M. Sharpe. The NATO Science for Peace and Security Programme, vol. 41, pp. 151–160.

Kobrin, N. H. 1992. Freud's Concept of Autonomy and Strachey's Translation: A Piece of the Puzzle of the Freudian Self, *The Annual of Psychoanalysis*, vol. 21: 201–223.

Kouri, J. 2014. Black Widow terror threat linked to Islamist recruitment of women, http://www.examiner.com/article/black-widow-terror-threat-linked-to-islamist-recruitment-of-women accessed 22 January 2014.

Lachkar, J. 2011. *How to Talk to a Borderline.* New York: Taylor and Francis.

Lachkar, J. 2002. The Psychological Make-up of a Suicide Bomber: The World's Most Abusive Couple Ever, *The Journal of Psychohistory*, Volume 29, No. 4, Spring.

Lachkar, J. 1998. *The Many Faces of Abuse: Treating the Emotional Abuse of High-Functioning Women.* New York, NY: Jason Aronson Press.

Lachkar, J. 1983. The Arab-Israeli Conflict: A Psychoanalytic Study Doctoral Dissertation. Los Angeles, CA: International College.

Lankford, A. 2013. *The Myth of Martyrdom.* New York: Palgrave MacMillan.

Lentini, P. and M. Bakashmar. 2007. Jihadist Beheading: A Convergence of Technology, Theology, and Teleology? *Studies in Conflict & Terrorism*, 30(4), 303–325.

Lieven, A. 1998. *Chechnya: Tombstone of Russian Power.* New Haven: Yale University Press.

Lincoln, B. 2006. An Early Moment in the Discourse of "Terrorism:" Reflections on a Tale from Marco Polo. *Comparative Studies in Society and History*, 48(2), 242–259.

Lotman, Y. 2000. *Universe of the Mind: A Semiotic Theory of Culture.* New York: I. B. Tauris & Co.

Lorenz, K. 1963. *On Aggression.* New York: Harcourt, Brace & World.

Lule, J. 1991. Sacrifice and the Body on the Tarmac: Symbolic Significance of the U.S. News about a Terrorist Victim. In Yonah Alexander & Robert Picard, Eds., *In the Camera's Eye: News Coverage of Terrorists Events*, pp. 30–48. Washington: Brassey's.

Mahler, M. S., F. Pine, and A. Bergman. 1975. *The Psychological Birth of the Human Infant.* New York: Basic Books.

Mansdorf, I., and M. Kedar. 2008. The Psychological Asymmetry of Islamist Warfare. *Middle East Quarterly*, 15(2), 37–44.

Manfield, P. 1992. *Split Self/Split Object: Understanding and Treating Borderline, Narcissistic and Schizoid Disorders.* London: Aronson.

Martin, G. 2010. *Understanding Terrorism: Challenges, Perspectives, and Issues.* Thousand Oaks, CA: Sage.

Martin, W. and R. Zacharias. 2003. *The Kingdom of the Cults.* Grand Rapids, MI: Bethany House.

Matusitz, J. 2012. *Terrorism & Communication: A Critical Introduction.* Thousand Oaks, CA: Sage.

Meddeb, A. 2003. *The Malady of Islam.* New York: Basic Books.

Meier, A. 2003. *Chechnya: To the Heart of the Conflict.* New York: W.W. Norton & Company.

Meese, M. 2006. *The Islamic Imager Project: Visual Motifs in Jihadi Internet Propaganda.* West Point, NY: Combating Terrorism Center at West Point.

Mernissi, F. 1975. *Beyond the Veil: Male-Female Dynamics in a Modern Muslim Society.* Cambridge, MA: Schenkman Publishing Company.

Moore, N.-J., M. Hickson, III, and D. Stacks. 2010. *Nonverbal Communication: Studies and Applications*, 5th ed. Los Angeles: Roxbury Publishing Company.

Murphy, P.J. 2004. *The Wolves of Islam: Russia and the Faces of Chechen Terror.* Dulles, VA: Brassey's Inc.

Murphy, P.J. 2010. *Allah's Angels: Chechen Women in War.* Annapolis, MD: Naval Institute Press.

Nacos, B.L. 2007. *Mass Mediated Terrorism: The Central Role of the Media in Terrorism and Counterterrorism.* New York: Rowman and Littlefield Publishers.

Nandy, A. 1983. *The Intimate Enemy: Loss and Recovery of Self under Colonialism.* Delhi: Oxford India Paperbacks, University Press.

Nekrich, A.M. 1978. *The Punished People: The Deportation and Fate of Soviet Minorities at the End of the Second World War.* New York: W.W. Norton & Company.

Nivat, A. 2001. *Chienne de Guerre: A Woman Reporter Behind the Lines of the War in Chechnya.* Trans. S. Darnton. New York: Public Affairs.

Olson, L., C. Finnegan and D. Hope. 2008. *Visual Rhetoric: A Reader in Communication and American Culture.* Thousand Oaks, CA: Sage.

O'Ballance, E. 1979. *Language of Violence: The Blood Politics of Terrorism.* San Rafael, CA: Presidio Press.

O'Shaughnessy, N. and P. Baines. 2009. Selling Terror: The Symbolization and Positioning of Jihad. *Marketing Theory*, 9(2), 227–241.

Pape, R. 2005. *Dying to Win: The Strategic Logic of Suicide Terrorism.* New York: Random House.

Pedahzur, A. Ed. 2004. *Root Causes of Suicide Terrorism: The Globalization of Martyrdom.* New York: Routledge; American Free Press.

Peristiany, J.G. Ed. 1974. *Honor and Shame: The Values of Mediterranean Society.* Chicago, IL: The University of Chicago Press.
Perlmutter, D. 2011. The Semiotics of Honor Killing & Ritual Murder. *Anthropoetics*, 17(1), 22–34.
Perlmutter, D. 2005. Mujahideen Blood Rituals: The Religious and Forensic Symbolism of Al Qaeda Beheading. *Anthropoetics*, 11(2), 10–21.
Petersen, A. 1999. *Dictionary of Islamic Architecture.* New York: Routledge.
Pick, D. 2012. *The Pursuit of the Nazi Mind: Hitler, Hess, and the Analysts.* Oxford: Oxford University Press.
Piontelli, A. 1999. *From Fetus to Child: Observational and Psychoanalytic Study.* New York: The New Library of Psychoanalysis.
Politkovskaya, A. 2001. *A Dirty War: A Russian Reporter in Chechnya.* Transl. J. Crowfoot. London: The Harvill Press.
Pope, N. 2011. *Honor Killings in the Twenty-First Century.* New York: Palgrave Macmillan.
Pryce-Jones, D. 2002. *The Closed Circle: An Interpretation of the Arabs.* Chicago: Harper & Row.
Putin, V. 2000. *First Person.* New York: PublicAffairs Reports.
Rabasa, A., R. Blackwill, P. Chalk, K. Cragin and C. Fair. 2009. *The Lessons of Mumbai.* Santa Monica: RAND.
Radnitz, S. 2006. Look Who's Talking! Islamic Discourse in the Chechen Wars. Nationalities Papers: *The Journal of Nationalism and Ethnicity*, 34(2), 237–256.
Raine, A. 2013. *The Anatomy of Violence.* New York: Random House.
Richards, D. 6 May 2013. *Boston Marathon Photos, Facts And Trivia: Including Terrorist Attacks* (30 Ways And Tips Series), [Kindle Edition], South Star Media.
Rigstad, M. 2008. The Senses of Terrorism. *Review Journal of Political Philosophy*, 6(1), 10-21.
Ro'i, Y. 2000. *Islam in the Soviet Union: From the Second World War to Gorbachev.* London: Hurst & Company.
Rubin, U. 1999. *Between Bible and Qur'an: The Children of Israel and the Islamic Self-Image.* Princeton, NJ: The Darwin Press, Inc.
Schaefer, R.W. 2011. *The Insurgency in Chechnya and the North Caucasus: From Gazavat to Jihad.* New York: Praeger.
Schaffer, I.1973. *Charisma: A Psychoanalytic Look at Mass Society.* Toronto: University of Toronto Press.
Scharff, D.E. 1997. *Object Relations Theory and Practice.* Northvale, NJ: Jason Aronson.

Schement, J. R. 1993. An Etymological Exploration of the Links between Information and Communication. In Jorge Reina Schement & Brent Ruben, Eds., *Information and Behavior.* Vol. 4. Piscataway, NJ: Transaction Publishers.

Schmitt, A. and J. Sofer, Eds. 1992. *Sexuality and Eroticism among Males in Moslem Societies.* NY: Harrington Park Press.

Schützenberger, A.A. 1999. *The Ancestor Syndrome.* Trans. by A. Trager. London and New York: Routledge.

Schweitzer, Y. Ed. August 2006. Female Suicide Bombers: Dying for Equality? Memorandum 84. Tel Aviv: Jaffee Center for Strategic Studies, Tel Aviv University.

Segal, H. 2003. The Mind of the Fundamentalist. http://www.psychoanalysis.org.uk/fundamentalist mind.htm accessed 14 May 2013.

Seierstad, A. 2008. *The Angel of Grozny: Orphans of a Forgotten War.* New York: Perseus.

Seifert, K. 2006. *How Children Become Violent.* Boston, MA: Acanthus Publishing.

Seifert, R. 1994. War and Rape: A Preliminary Analysis. In Alexandra Stiglmayer (Ed.), *Mass Rape: The War against Women in Bosnia-Herzegovina,* pp. 54–72. Lincoln, NE: University of Nebraska Press.

Shott, Susan (1979). Emotion and Social Life: A Symbolic Interactionist Analysis. *American Journal of Sociology,* 84(6), 1317-1334.

Silverman, K. 1983. *The Subject of Semiotics.* New York: Oxford University Press.

Smith, S. 2001. *Allah's Mountains: The Battle for Chechnya.* London: I.B. Tauris.

Speckhard, A. 2013. The Chechen Black Widows Female Terrorists in Al Qaeda and the Tsarnaev Brothers, 14 May 2013. http://www.familysecuritymatters.org/publications/detail/print/the-chechen-black-widowsfemale-terrorists-in-al-qaeda-and-the-tsarnaev-brothers

Speckhard, A. 2012. *Talking to Terrorists: Understanding the Psychosocial Motivations of Militant Jihadi Terrorists.* McLean, VA: Advances Press.

Speckhard, A. and K. Akhmedova. 2006. The New Chechen Jihad: Militant Wahhabism as a Radical Movement and a Source of Suicide Terrorism in Post-War Chechen Society. *Democracy and Security,* 2(1), 103–155.

Speckhard, A. 2006. *Black Widows: The Chechen Female Suicide Terrorists.* Tel Aviv: The Jaffee Center for Strategic Studies.

Sroufe, A., B. Egeland, E.A. Carlson and W.A. Collins. 2005. *The Development of the Person*: The Minnesota Study of Risk and Adaptation from Birth to Adulthood.

Stein, A. 2007. *Prologue to Violence: Child Abuse, Dissociation and Crime.* Mahwah, NJ: The Analytic Press.

Steiner, J. 1993. *Psychic Retreats: Pathological Organizations in Psychotic, Neurotic and Borderline Patients*. London: Brunner-Routledge, published in association with the Institute of Psychoanalysis.

Stoller, R.J. 1979. *Sexual Excitement: Dynamics of Erotic Life.* New York: Pantheon.

Swaab, D.F. 2014. *We Are Our Brains: A Neurobiography of the Brain, from the Womb to Alzheimer's*. New York: Spiegel & Grau.

Szaszdi, L. 2008. *Russian Civil-Military Relations and the Origins of the Second Chechen War*. Lanham, MD: University Press of America.

Tierney, A.L. and C.A. Nelson III. Brain Development and the Role of Experience in the Early Years. http://main.zerotothree.org/site/DocServer/30-2_Tierney.pdf?docID=10001 accessed 22 January 2014.

Tishkov, V. 2003. *Chechnya: Life in a War-Torn Society*. Berkeley: University of California Press.

Tuovinen, M. 1973. Crime as an attempt at intrapsychic adaptation. Series D Medica No. 2, *Psychiatrica No. 1*, Finland: Unversity of Oulu.

Tuman, Joseph, 2009. *Communicating Terror: The Rhetorical Dimensions of Terrorism*, 2nd ed. Thousand Oaks, CA: Sage.

Tough, P. 2012. *How Children Succeed: Grit, Curiosity and the Hidden Power of Character*. New York: Houghton Mifflin Harcourt Publishing Company.

Van Creveld, M. 1991. *The Transformation of War*. New York: The Free Press.

Van der Leeuw, C. 1999. *Storm over the Caucasus*. Richmond, VA: Curzon.

Vidino, L. 2005. How Chechnya became a breeding ground for terrorists, http://www.meforum.org/744/how-chechnya-became-a-breeding-ground-for-terror accessed 3 September 2013.

Vinogradova, L. 2003. Deadly secret of the black widows, http://www.times-uk.com October 22.

Volkan, V., J. Demetrios and J. Montville. Eds. 1990. *The Psychodynamics of International Relationships: Unofficial Diplomacy at Work*, vol. I. Lexington, MA: Lexington Books.

von Uexküll, Jakob (1957). A Stroll through the World of Animals and Men. In Claire H. Schiller & Karl S. Lashely (Eds.), *Instinctive Behavior*, pp. 5–80. New York: International Universities Press.

Weimann, G. 2008. The Psychology of Mass-Mediated Terrorism. *American Behavioral Scientist*, 52(1), 69–86.

Weimann, G. and C. Winn. 1993. *The Theater of Terror: Mass Media and International Terrorism*. London: Longman Group United Kingdom.

Welner, M. 2007. Psychopathy, Media and the Psychology at the Root of Terrorism and Mass Disasters. In Matthias Okoye & Cyril

Wecht, Eds., *Forensic Investigation and Management of Mass Disasters*, pp. 189–220. Tucson: Lawyers & Judges Publishing.

Wright, L.2006. *The Looming Tower*. New York. Alfred A. Knopf.

Young, J. and C. Brunk. 2012. *The Ethics of Cultural Appropriation*. New York: Wiley-Blackwell.

Zulaika, J. 1984. *Basque Violence*. Las Vegas, NV: University of Nevada Press.

VIDEO CLIP

Volgograd Train Station Bombing, 23 January 2014. http://lifenews.ru/

ENDNOTES

1 J. O'Brien. New Icelandic volcano eruption could have global impact. http://www.bbc.co.uk/news/world-europe-15995845. accessed 29 November 2013.

2 E. Sokirianskaia, Winter Games, Caucasian Misery, http://www.nytimes.com/2013/12/06/opinion/winter-games-caucasian-misery.html. accessed 7 December 2013. Sokirianskaia further notes: At the eastern end of the Caucasus, a deep sectarian divide between Sufi and Salafi Muslims—exacerbated by state repression of the latter—has made Dagestan an epicenter of violence a nd the main exporter of terrorism. It was here that one of the Boston Marathon bombing suspects, Tamerlan Tsarnaev, visited in 2012, reportedly to make contact with jihadist groups.

3 M. Eckel. 21 October 2013. Russia identifies suicide bomber as woman from Dagestan, http://www.csmonitor.com/World/2013/1021/Russia-identifies-suicide-bomber-as-woman-from-Dagestan. accessed 21 October 2013. See also, Russia suicide bombing a test ahead of Sochi Olympics? http://www.cbsnews.com/8301-505263_162-57608636/russia-suicide-bombing-a-test-ahead-of-sochi-olympics. accessed 23 October 2013.

4 J. Matusitz. 2012. *Terrorism and Communication*. Thousand Oaks, CA: Sage Publications; see also How Culture Shapes Terrorism, http://www.youtube.com/watch?v=l4qFw6SGI_s accessed 29 June 2013.

5 N. Kobrin, 2009. U. Acosta, JM da Costa, M.D. What's Freud got to do with it? or How Ladino and Sephardic culture inform psychoanalysis and trauma studies, ed. D. Bunis; *Languages and Literatures of Sephardic and Oriental Jewry*, ed. by David M. Bunis, Yaakov Benttolila and Efraim Hazan. *Juried Proceedings of the Misgav Yerushalayim's Sixth International Congress*, pp. 306–318.June 11-16 2000. Jerusalem: The Hebrew University of Jerusalem Press.

6 A. Bouhdiba. 1998. *Sexuality in Islam*. London: Saqi Books; F. Benslama. 2009. *Psychoanalysis and the Challenge of Islam*. Minneapolis: University of Minnesota Press; S. Akhtar and A. Bergmann. 2012. *The Mother and Her Child*. New York: Routledge.

7 In an e-mail communication on 16 November, 2013, Anonymous writes: "She got a small stipend from the Witness organization in the US. She made the first documentary in the early 2000s. She was like 27 years old at the time. During the near-total annihilation of Grozny she stayed in the city, sleeping with the rest of them in basements and hoping that the building would not collapse on their heads. She ventured out during lulls in the bombing with a small video camera and recorded." http://www.youtube.com/watch?v=NjYCHgjExsA

8 29 January 2007, Analysis: Palestinian suicide attacks, BBC news.

9 Y. Schweitzer. 2003. *The Globalization of Terror.* Rutgers, NJ: Transaction Press.

10 N. Kobrin. 2013. *Penetrating the Terrorist Psyche.* New York: MultiEducator.com.

11 L. Kapteijns. 2013. *Clan Cleansing in Somalia: The Ruinous Legacy of 1991.* p.14: Daniel Compagnon's study influenced Kapteijns' understanding of the clan from a political science perspective, which is worth considering even though it is not psychoanalytic: The clan is conceived of "a political resource of 'political entrepreneurs' trying to maintain control over a patrimonial state." Kapteijns goes on to state that this influenced her understanding of clan-based violence. Unfortunately she does not delve into the developmental issue of shame-honor dynamics of clans.

12 http://blogs.timesofisrael.com/fbi-must-take-domestic-violence-seriously-in-its-profiling-of-jihadis 20 April; also The Mind of the Terrorist is the mind of the Mother, http://blogs.timesofisrael.com/the-mind-of-the-terrorist-is-the-mind-of-his-mother 23 April 2013

13 riehlworldview.com, http://riehlworldview.com/2013/04/tamerlan-tsarnaevs-amazon-wish-list-forged-ids-the-mafia-and-allahs-mountains-the-battle-for-chechnya.html accessed 21 June 2013.

14 It appears the Russian word Tzar or Czar is in the name Tsarnaev, but there is no connection, although one wonders if there could be an unconscious identification influencing an ambivalence regarding national and ethnic identities. A colleague who wishes to remain anonymous due to the sensitive issues involved with the shame-honor culture wrote the following when I asked about the origin of the name and its meaning: "Chechen surnames were given after the Russian conquest russified names, based on the name of the oldest known a ncestor. ...Tsarnaev comes from "Tsarni" - actually the name that the brothers' uncle chose, once he was in America....Tsarni comes from the word for home/house/fireplace: Tsarna. In several languages the fireplace is interchangeable with house, because it was the center of the house.... And Tsa or Tse means red, the color of fire." This etymological information leads back to our earlier discussion of the role of fire and immolation in terrorism in general and bombing in particular. The highly autistic behavior of making bombs holds a fascination with immolation. Yet at the same time the bomb maker is full of unconscious rage from which they are dissociated and project outward through bombing.

15 J. Reitman. 17 July 2013. Jahar's World. *Rolling Stone Magazine*, http://www.rollingstone.com/culture/news/jahars-world-20130717 accessed 4 December 2013.

16 L. Vidino. 2005. How Chechnya became a breeding ground for terrorists, http://www.meforum.org/744/how-chechnya-became-a-breeding-ground-for-terror accessed 3 September 2013.

17 A. Pereltsvaig, 20 January 2012, *Geocurrents*, http://www.geocurrents.info/cultural-geography/is-the-georgian-language-related-to-basque-another-european-outlier accessed 21 July 2013.

18 J.-P. Brisard, *Zarqawi: The New Face of Al Qaeda.* Cambridge, UK; Polity Press, p. 102.

19 A. Nekrich. 1978. *Punished Peoples: The Deportation and Fate of the Soviet Minorities at the end of the Second World War.* New York: W.W. Norton, p. 162.

20 A. Jolie, 18 October 2013. Putin's War on Terrorism, http://online.wsj.com/news/articles/SB10001424052702303680404579141213891936326 accessed 18 October 2013.

21 J. Leopold. Exclusive: Abu Zubaydah's journey from student to mujahedeen, Part 1 of The Secret Diaries of Abu Zubaydah reveals a troubled path from studying in India to battling in Afghanistan, 7 November 2013, sent by A. Gus in an email 11 November 2013; http://america.aljazeera.com/articles/2013/11/5/notebook-one-thesecretdiariesofabuzubaydah.html accessed 12 November 2013.

22 I wish to thank Dr. Joan Lachkar for the descriptive metaphor of the iceberg for psychotic behavior.

23 I think of the works of Estela Welldon. 2011. *Playing with Dynamite: A Personal Approach to the Psychoanalytic Understanding of Perversions, Violence, and Criminality.* London: Karnac; and Emilia Perroni and her forthcoming book, *Play: Psychoanalytic Perspectives, Survival and Human Development.*

24 J. Reitman. 17 July 2013. Jahar's World. *Rolling Stone Magazine*, http://www.rollingstone.com/culture/news/jahars-world-20130717.

25 G.A. Geyer. 2014. http://www.dispatch.com/content/stories/editorials/2014/01/27/theres-good-and-bad-news-about-sochi-olympics.html, accessed 27 January 2014.

26 pewforum.org http://www.pewforum.org/2013/04/23/most-muslims-in-region-reject-violence-against-civilians/ accessed 31 July 2013.

27 Franco Fornari wrote at length about warring as an elaboration of paranoia. See his 1974 opus: *The Psychoanalysis of War.* New York: Anchor Press.

28 L. Tolstoy. 2009. *Hadji Murad.* New York: Dover Publications, first published posthumously in 1912.

29 G. Fussell, In search of Chechen identity, 7 November 2013, http://www.newyorker.com/online/blogs/photobooth/2013/11/slide-show-davide-monteleones-spasibo.html#slide_ss_0=1 accessed 9 November 2013.

30 A. Nekrich. 1978. *The Punished People*, New York: Norton. p. 162.

31 Ibid. pp. 135-136.

32 C. Cini and FBI. 2013. The Boston Marathon Bombing FBI Investigation, J. Brooke, April 19, 2013, Chechen Brothers grew up as refugees, Voice of America.

33 Y. Karny. 2000. *Highlanders: A Journey to the Caucasus in Quest of Memory*, p. 207. New York: Farrar, Straus and Giroux.

34 Ibid. See also Y. Ro'i, 2000, section on the Sufi Orders and the Sects in the Northern Caucasus in *Islam in the Soviet Union: From the Second World War to Gorbachev*, pp. 405-421. London: Hurst & Company.

35 R. Schaefer. 2011. *The Insurgency in Chechnya and the North Caucasus: From Gazavat to Jihad*, p. 71. Santa Barbara, CA: Praeger.

36 N. Griffin. 2001. *Caucasus: Mountain Men and Holy War*, p. 80. New York: Thomas Dunne Books.

37 N. H. Kobrin, 2013. *Penetrating the Terrorist Psyche*, pp. 67-86. New York: MultiEducator Inc.

38 J.B. Dunlop, quoting Gammer, ft.102. 1998. *Russia Confronts Chechnya*, Cambridge, UK: Cambridge University Press.

39 Griffin, Foreword.

40 Griffin, p.81.

41 economist.com http://www.economist.com/node/7160644 accessed 12 November 2013.

42 I. Schiffer, 1973. *Charisma: A Psychoanalytic Look at Mass Society*. Toronto: University of Toronto Press.

43 C.J. Chivers, 27 August 2006, Missing Chechen Was Secret Bride of Terror Leader, http://www.nytimes.com/2006/08/27/world/europe/27chechnya.html?pagewanted=all accessed 14 September 2013; 7 see also BBC News, http://news.bbc.co.uk/2/hi/europe/5168984.stm accessed 14 September 2013.

44 R. Boudreaux, 18 June 1995, Hostages in Russia's Heartland: Defiance of Russians flows in the veins of lead hostage-taker: Guerrilla Shamil Basayev's family has long fought invaders. But the killings of his mother and two children preceded his raid on a city outside Chechnya,. L.A. Times http://articles.latimes.com/1995-06-18/news/mn-14600_1_shamil-basayev accessed 13 November 2013.

45 A. Dolnik, ICT Counter Terrorism World Summit, 11 September 2013, Herzliya, Israel.

46 N.H. Kobrin, *The Banality of Suicide Terrorism*, p. xvi.

47 A. Jaimoukha. 2004. *The Chechens: A Handbook*. London, New York: Taylor Francis, 2004, p. 3.

48 J.B. Dunlop. 1998. *Russia Confronts Chechnya: Roots of a Separatist Conflict*, p. 2. Cambridge: Cambridge University Press.

49 J.B. Dunlop, p.3.

50 M. Tsaroieva. 2005. *Ancients Croyances des Ingouches Et des Tchéchienes: Peuples du Caucase du Nord.* Paris: Maisonneuve et Larose, p.12.

51 Chechen national anthem as noted by A. Lieven, 1998. *Chechnya: Tombstone of Russian Power*, p. 358. New Haven: Yale University Press.

52 A. Lieven, p. 345.

53 P. Holinger, M.D, January 2014 Newsletter: Dr. Paul Holinger's Place for Parents and Children: Information, resources and tips about infant, child and adolescent development, email 9 January 2014. I am delighted to note that Dr. Holinger was my classmate at the Chicago Institute of Psychoanalysis and is currently Dean of the Institute. See his website for a more in-depth discussion of shame, http://www.paulcholinger.com

54 In an interesting article concerning psychological research done on shame–honor cultures, specifically Japanese, we learn that people seek to "remove" the shame experienced through a symbolic act. In less advanced shame cultures, the group resorts to a volcanic iceberg mentality by seeking revenge; this involves "cleansing" honor in a delusional manner, literally wiping the shame away by willfully spilling blood. See A. Lukits, 11 November 2013, Is the Antidote to Embarrassment in a Jar? People recalling embarrassing events want to apply face cream, *The Wall Street Journal*, http://online.wsj.com/news/articles/SB10001424052702304672404579184131796782664 accessed 11 November 2013.

55 D. Perlmutter, 2011, The Semiotics of honor killing and ritual murder, *Anthropoetics*, 17 (1), 22-34. While she does not discuss a psychoanalytic perspective, I consider psychoanalysis along with Kaja Silverman, the film semiotician as a subfield of semiotics. See also, J. Matusitz, Chapter 4: Symbolic Culture of Terrorism in *Symbolism in Terrorism*, unpublished ms., forthcoming by Rowland and Littlefield. There is no question that honor killing is ritualized murder yet this does not diminish the fact that it is also a non-western form of domestic violence, intimate partner of sibling/family violence. See, for example, P. Chesler, 2009, Are honor killings simply domestic violence? *Middle East Quarterly* xvi (2), 61-69. The reason why it is important to maintain the commonality between domestic violence's murder-suicide and honor killing is that they both represent at the most basic, unconscious level variants of traumatic bonding with the devalued female mother. It remains the important image of fusion to the other. This is poorly understood by most experts. Yet is accesses the nonverbal enactment of a volcano iceberg mentality.

56 See author's psychological anthropology, *Penetrating the Terrorist Psyche*, New York: MultiEducator, Inc.

57 N. Al Jallad, The concept of "shame" in Arabic: bilingual dictionaries and the challenge of defining culture-based emotions, http://elies.rediris.es/Language_Design/LD12/AL_JALLAD_N.pdf accessed 3 August 2013.

58 Ibid.

59 E-mail communication, Anonymous, 30 July 2013.

60 K. Cherry, Freud's Stage of Psychosexual Development: The Anal Stage, http://psychology.about.com/od/theoriesofpersonality/ss/psychosexualdev_3.htm accessed 17 January 2014.

61 I wish to acknowledge Dr. Joan Lachkar, who immediately picked up on the role of bathroom fantasies in this passage.

62 Lt. Col. J. G. Zumwalt, 4 September 2013, A Child's Death Rocks Islam's Teachings, http://www.familysecuritymatters.org/publications/detail/a-childs-death-rocks-islams-teachings#ixzz2dzZ5HEMH accessed 4 September 2013.

63 M. Klein, 1961. *Narrative of a Child Analysis: The Conduct of the Psychoanalysis of Children as Seen in the Treatment of a Ten Year Old Boy*, Issue 55 of International Psycho-analytic Library. London: Hogarth Press.

64 K. Ablow, How to build a terrorist, 30 April 2013, http://www.foxnews.com/opinion/2013/04/30/how-to-build-terrorist accessed 5 May 2013. See also J. Matusitz, 2013. Chapter 6 Terrorism as Social Construction of Reality in *Terrorism and Communication*, Los Angeles, Ca.: Sage Publications, Ltd.

65 I. Schiffer. 1973. *Charisma: A Psychoanalytic Look at Mass Society*, p. 28-30. Toronto: University of Toronto Press. It is during the separation individuation stage of early childhood that we begin to sense the imperfection or defect of the mother. In an early essay I connected the function of the heliotropism of the infant searching out for the mother through the senses, particularly vision. The heliotropism constitutes an aspect of maternal attachment or bonding. See Kobrin, Freud's Concept of Autonomy and Strachey's Translation: A Piece of the puzzle of the Freudian Self, *The Annual of Psychoanalysis*, 201-223, (1992) vol. 21: 201-223.

66 A. Jaimoukha. 2004. *The Chechens*, p. 213. New York: Routledge.

67 J. Colarusso. 2002. *Nart Sagas from the Caucasas: Myths and Legends from the Circassians, Abazas, Abkhaz, and Ubykhs*. Princeton: Princeton University Press. See also Karny, p. 100.

68 J. Colarusso, p.123.

69 Ibid, p. 295.

70 M. Evangelista. 2002. *The Chechen Wars*. Washington, D.C.: The Brookings Institute, p. 124.

71 A. Politkovskaya, 2001. *A Dirty War: A Russian Reporter in Chechnya*, pp. xxiii-xxiv. London: The Harvill Press.

72 Dunlop. 1998, p. 24.

73 Griffin, p. 21.

74 4 December 2013. Russian MPs brawl over monument to 19th-century Chechen conflict, http://rt.com/politics/russian-duma-golden-gun-689 accessed 4 December 2013.

75 Karny, p. 99.

76 Murphy, *Allah's Angels*, p. 7.

77 Tamerlan's aunt, Maret Tsarnaeva, appeared on Canadian TV and denied her nephews committed the terrorist attack. See Elias Groll, 23 April 2013, Your Guide to the Tsarnaev Family, http://blog.foreignpolicy.com/posts/2013/04/23/your_guide_to_the_tsarnaev_family?wp_login_redirect=0 accessed 14 November 2013.

78 K. Baiev with R. and N. Daniloff. 2003. *The Oath*, p. 85. New York: Walker.

79 Ro'i, p. 539-40.

80 Ibid, 546.

81 Op.cit., 542.

82 Karny, p. 99.

83 Ro'i, p. 546; see also my book, *The Banality of Suicide Terrorism*. Dulles, VA: Potomac, 2010.

84 Karny, p. 99.

85 Baiev, p. 86.

86 Ibid. p.96.

87 Personal communication from Anonymous, an authority who has direct contact with Chechens in Chechnya.

88 Ro'i, p.546.

89 P. J. Murphy. 2010. *Allah's Angels: Chechen Women in War*. Annapolis, MD: Naval Institute Press. Loc. 4881 of 5865.

90 J. Lachkar. 1998. *The Many Faces of Abuse: Treating the Emotional Abuse of High Functioning Women*. Lanham, MD: Littlefield and Rowman, A Jason Aronson Book.

91 A. Nivat. 2001, *Chienne de Guerre: A Woman Reporter Behind the Lines of the War in Chechnya*. New York: Public Affairs, p. 226.

92 Evangelista. *The Chechen Wars*. p. 105.

93 A. Meier, p. 13 ft.3.

94 A. Lieven, p. 355.

95 J. Matusitz, *How Culture Shapes Terrorism*, http://www.youtube.com/watch?v=l4qFw6SGI_s accessed 29 June 2012. See also his *Terrorism and Communication*. Thousand Oaks, CA: Sage Publications.

96 A. Raine. 2013. *The Anatomy of Violence.* New York: Random House, p. 14-15.

97 J. Matusitz, *How Culture Shapes Terrorism*, and *Terrorism and Communication.*

98 H.F. Stein, 1986. *Developmental Time, Culture and Space: Studies in Psychogeography.* Norman, Oklahoma: University of Oklahoma Press.

99 N.H. Kobrin, *The Mosque as Mother,* http://www.familysecuritymatters.org/publications/detail/the-mosque-as-mother

100 A. Harrod. Many things rotten in Denmark, 13 November 2013, *Frontpage Magazine,* http://www.legal-project.org/4204/many-things-rotten-in-denmark accessed 13 November 2013.

101 Raine. 2013. *The Anatomy of Violence.* New York: Pantheon, p. 78.

102 Ibid, p. 21.

103 A. Speckard. 2012. *Talking to Terrorists: Understanding the Psychosocial Motivations of Militant Jihadi Terrorists.* McLean, VA: Advances Press. Loc. 245, 564, 1061, 2021, 2022.

104 P.J. Murphy. 2010. *Allah's Angels: Chechen Women in War.* Annapolis, MD: Naval Institute Press: "How many women suffer from psychological disorders? Dr. Baiev says that "the whole [Chechen] nation is suffering from post-traumatic stress." Loc. 4891.

105 Ibid. Loc 4894 of 5865.

106 A. Meier. 2003. *Chechnya: To the Heart of the Conflict,* New York: W.W. Norton & Company p. 52.

107 Y. Bodansky. 2009. *Chechen Jihad: Al Qaeda's Training Ground and the Next Wave of Terror.* No place of publication cited: HarperCollins ebook p. 236.

108 Baiev, p.150.

109 Gammer, p. 145.

110 Personal communication, Yitzhak Reiter, 20 June 2012.

111 D. Markosian, 29 April 2012,Washington Times http://p.washingtontimes.com/news/2012/apr/29/chechen-women-in-mortal-fear-as-president-backs-ho/print/ accessed 30 July 2013.

112 Ibid.

113 A. Lankford. 2013. *The Myth of Martyrdom.* New York: Palgrave MacMillan.

114 M. Feldman, 1 August 2011, Dr Hanna Segal: Psychoanalyst who was inspired by Melanie Klein and contributed hugely to the field of cultural studies, http://www.independent.co.uk/news/obituaries/dr-hanna-segal-psychoanalyst-who-was-inspired-by-melanie-klein-and-contributed-hugely-to-the-field-of-cultural-studies-2329542.html accessed 18 November 2013.

115 H. Segal, The mind of the fundamentalist, 2003, http://www.psychoanalysis.org.uk/fundamentalist mind.htm accessed 14 May 2013.

116 M. Mahler, M. S., F. Pine, and A. Bergman. 1975. *The Psychological Birth of the Human Infant.* New York: Basic Books.

117 Various authors. 2013. *Chechnya: The Land, The People & The Conflicts.* New York: Simon and Schuster. Back cover. See also, Chechen Folklore. Proverbs and sayings, http://mashar.free.fr/proverbs.htm accessed 21 September 2013.

118 countertransference, http://en.wikipedia.org/wiki/Countertransference accessed 5 September 2013.

119 Griffin, p.155.

120 Baiev, p.95.

121 n.a., Russia kills nine militants in Dagestan, 21 August 2013, http://news.msn.co.nz/worldnews/8709536/russia-kills-nine-militants-in-dagestan accessed 21 August 2013.

122 Griffin, p. 36.

123 R. Solash, Are Sounds Of The Caucasus Shaped By The Mountains Themselves? *Radio Free Europe,* 8 July 2013, http://www.rferl.org/articleprintview/25039081.html accessed 10 July 2013.

124 Griffin, p. 44-45.

125 Karny, p. 265.

126 See J. Lachkar. *The Psychopathology of Terrorism: A Cultural V-spot,* http://www.joanlachkarphd.com/index.php/published/articles-essays accessed 17 January 2014.

127 Gammer, p. 108.

128 Lieven, p. 324.

129 Ibid, p. 345.

130 Ibid, p. 355.

131 rightlivelihood.org, 23 June 2013. http://www.rightlivelihood.org/csmr.html

132 Baiev, p.114.

133 Collins. *My Jihad.* Caption to picture, Scenes from a Chechen field hospital, no page number cited.

134 Ibid., p.138.

135 Baiev, p.118.

136 email communicaton with A. Lankford, who shared with me that female colleagues had also complained about sexism in the field of counterterrorism.

137 R. Paine, 2012. *Everyday Terrorism: How Fear Works in Domestic Abuse,* p. 3-38. United Kingdom: Center for Social Justice and Community Action, Durham University and the Scottish Women's Aid.

138 John Steiner. 1993. *Psychic Retreats: Pathological Organizations in Psychotic, Neurotic and Borderline Patients,* vol. 19. London: The New Library of Psychoanalysis.

139 Interview with Keith Ablow, M.D., How to build a terrorist, 30 April 2013, http://www.foxnews.com/opinion/2013/04/30/how-to-build-terrorist/ accessed 16 June 2013.

140 Assassin: from Arabic hashishiyyin "hashish-users," A fanatical Ismaili Muslim sect of the time of the Crusades, under leadership of the "Old Man of the Mountains," with a reputation for murdering opposing leaders after intoxicating themselves by eating hashish. The plural suffix -in was mistaken in Europe for part of the word. http://www.etymonline.com/index.php?term=assassin accessed 20 November 2013.

141 D. Semmelhack and L. Ende, The Psychotic Element in Everyday Group Thinking: Reflections on the Salem Witch Trials, Radical Psychology http://www.radicalpsychology.org/vol7-1/semmel.html accessed 25 September 2013.

142 A.L. Tierney and C.A. Nelson III. Brain Development and the Role of Experience in the Early Years in *Zero to Age Three*. http://main.zerotothree.org/site/DocServer/30-2_Tierney.pdf?docID=1001 accessed 22 January 2014.

143 J.-F. Ratelle. 2014. A Power Shift in the Caucasus Emirate: The Vilayat Dagestan Threat and Its Implications for the Sochi Olympics, http://www.huffingtonpost.com/jeanfrancois-ratelle/a-power-shift-in-the-cauc_b_4637724.html accessed 25 Jan 2014

144 START Background Report, Terrorism and the North Caucasus: An Overview, April 2013, p.1, http://www.start.umd.edu/start/publications/br/STARTBackgroundReport_TerrorismAndNorthCaucasus_April2013.pdf

145 Ibid. p.2.

146 Op. cit., p.3.

147 Op.cit., p.3.

148 Op.cit., p.4-5.

149 Matti Tuovinen. 1973. Crime as an attempt at intrapsychic adaptation, Acta Universitatis Ouluensis, Series D Medica No. 2 *Psychiatrica* No. 1, p.32.

150 J. Matusitz. *Symbolism in Terrorism*, unpublished ms., p. 204.

151 Ibid., pp. 219-221. Matusitz notes that revenge killing is deeply ingrained in Chechen culture and links it to the Black Widow.

152 Egypt "worst for women"' out of 22 countries in Arab world, updated 12 November 2013, http://www.bbc.com/news/world-middle-east-24908109 accessed 19 November 2013.

153 H. Barakat, 1993. *The Arab World: Society, Culture and the State*. Berkeley: University of California Press, p. 118.

154 Interview with Mia Bloom on female terrorists, 6 September 2013, http://www.isn.ethz.ch/Digital-Library/Articles/Detail/?lng=en&id=168648 accessed 6 September 2013.

155 Nightwatch email, 27 August 2013.

156 L. Vidino. 2005. How Chechnya became a breeding ground for terrorists, http://www.meforum.org/744/how-chechnya-became-a-breeding-ground-for-terror accessed 3 September 2013.

157 L. Loewenthal Marcus, Attack sporting events online jihadi Mein Kampf instructed, http://www.jewishpress.com/news/attack-sporting-events-online-jihadi-mein-kampf-instructed/2013/05/02/0/ accessed 6 May 2013.

158 J.C. Brisard. Zarqawi: *The New Face of Al Qaeda.*

159 Brisard, p.173.

160 Ibid., p.174.

161 A. Schutzenberg. 1998. *The Ancestor Syndrome.* London: Routledge.

162 N. H. Kobrin. 7 August 2013 http://blogs.timesofisrael.com/fire-detecting-the-undetectable-in-liquid-explosives

163 S. Imas, Japanese designer who uses Israeli technology to 3d print futuristic garments, *No Camels*, http://nocamels.com/2013/09/japanese-designer-uses-israeli-tech-to-3d-print-futuristic-garments accessed 8 September 2013.

164 H. Cleckley. 1976 *The Mask of Sanity.* Maryland Heights, MO: C.V. Mosby Co.

165 David Van Dyke, Ph.D. articulation analyst, coined this concept, email communication 29 September 2013.

166 Matusitz, pp. 299, 250, 260.

167 See Adrian Raine for neurocriminology and the wide and diverse field of early childhood development. I especially acknowledge the work of Margaret Mahler (and her notion of maternal symbiosis) and Alessandra Piontelli. See M. Mahler, M. S., F. Pine, and A. Bergman. 1975. *The Psychological Birth of the Human Infant.* New York: Basic Books; E. Bick. 2011. *The Tavistock Model: Papers on Child Development and Psychoanalytic Thinking*, edited by M. Harris and M. Harris Williams.

168 Interview, Can brain scans explain crime?, Washington Post online, http://js.washingtonpost.com/opinions/can-brain-scans-explain-crime/2013/06/07/c88056de-cde8-11e2-8f6b-67f40e176f03_story_1.html accessed 20 June 2013.

169 See, for example, E. Heineman. 2000. *Witches: A Psychoanalytic Exploration of the Killing of Women.* London: Free Association Books; also, E. Welldon. 1988. *Madonna and Whore: The Idealization and Denigration of Motherhood.* London: Karnac; S. Cashdan. 2000. *The Witch Must Die: The Hidden Meaning of Fairy Tales.* New York: Basic Books.

170 Kathleen Taylor, Neuroscientist, Says Religious Fundamentalism Could Be Treated As A Mental Illness, http://www.huffingtonpost.com/2013/05/31/kathleen-taylor-religious-fundamentalism-mental-illness_n_3365896.html?utm_hpref=mostpopular accessed 22 June 2013.

171 A. Stein. 2007. *Prologue to Violence: Dissociation, Child Abuse and Crime.* New York: The Analytic Press.

172 "Cameo". 1971/1984. *The Compact Edition of the Oxford English Dictionary*, vol. I, Oxford: Oxford University Press.

173 Matusitz, pp. 170, 191, 214, 255.

174 B. Clune. 20 June 2013. I am not a good mother, *The Guardian*, http://www.theguardian.com/commentisfree/2013/jul/30/being-good-mother?CMP=EMCNEWEML6619I2&et_cid=43691&et_rid=7277627&Linkid=http%3a%2f%2fwww.theguardian.com%2fcommentisfree%2f2013%2fjul%2f30%2fbeing-good-mother accessed 1 August.

175 See Kobrin, *The Banality of Suicide Terrorism* concerning the maternal cameo, p. 14.

176 There are Muslim psychoanalysts who, like atheists, generally wish to remain anonymous, especially in Lebanon. Fethi Benslama, Salam Akhtar, Masud Khan, Vamik Volkan, and Afaf Mahfouz, to name only a few, concur with Bouhdiba that the negation of the female is a challenge for the religion as well as the political movement. This is due to the fear of being labeled an apostate and subject to death threats. See timesofisrael.com, http://www.timesofisrael.com/arab-atheists-though-few-inch-out-of-the-shadows accessed 4 August 2013.

177 Google search: definition of object, https://www.google.com/search?q=definition+of+object&ie=UTF-8&oe=UTF-8&hl=en&client=safari accessed 6 September 2013.

178 S. Orgel. 1974. Sylvia Plath: Fusion with the victim and suicide, *Psychoanalytic Quarterly*, 43:272-273.

179 Albert Axell and Hideaki Kase. *Kamikaze: Japan's Suicide Gods*. London: Longman. Japanese kamikaze pilots were given manuals advising them to "exert supernatural strength" and keep their eyes open, 7 September 2009, The Guardian, http://www.theguardian.com/world/2009/sep/07/japanese-kamikaze-pilots-second-world-war accessed 7 December 2013; see also "Crashing bodily into a target is not easy," http://www.warbirdforum.com/tokko.htm accessed 21 November 2013.

180 Kobrin, p. 14.

181 Purdue University, http://www.cla.purdue.edu/english/theory/psychoanalysis/definitions/object.html accessed 6 September 2013.

182 Both Jung and Freud contemplated fire in the history of mankind's evolution. Philosopher Gaston Bachelard quoted Jung in his 1938 La Psychanalyse de Feu. The subject matter of fire came into focus during times of social crisis and impending war—World War II and the raging '60s in America. G. Bachelard. A. Ross, *The Psychoanalysis of Fire*, translated in 1968 by A. Ross. New York: Beacon Press.

183 Rachel Ehrenfeld, Fire Wards, http://acdemocracy.org/fire-wars-june-2013 accessed15 June13.

184 A. Campbell, 2 May 2013, http://www.huffingtonpost.com/2013/05/02/dzhokhar-tsarnaev-planned-july-4th-attack_n_3204633.html accessed 21 November 2013.

185 N. Kobrin. *The Banality of Suicide Terrorism*, p. 85, 92-98.

186 Murphy, *Allah's Angels*, Loc 827 of 5865.

187 A. Collins. *My Jihad*, p. 122. New York: Star Pocket Book.

188 *Allah's Angels*, Loc 945-946 of 5865.

189 *Allah's Angels*, Loc 947 of 5865.

190 For the importance of play, see V.G. Paley. 2005. *A Child's Work: The Importance of Play*. Chicago: University of Chicago and the forthcoming M. Akhtar, 2014. *Play and Playfulness*. New York: Rowland and Littlefield.

191 Matusitz, *Symbolism in Terrorism*, pp. 70, 190, unpublished ms. D. Perlmutter, 2005. Mujahideen Blood Rituals: The Religious and Forensic Symbolism of Al Qaeda Beheading. *Anthropoetics*, 11(2), 10-21 does not draw a link to the mother and her beheading buried in the jihadi attack.

192 *Allah's Angels*, Loc 1324 of 5865.

193 Lachkar, The Psychological Make-up of a Suicide Bomber, *The Journal of Psychohistory*, Volume 29, No. 4, Spring 2002, http://www.joanlachkarphd.com/images/PDFs/Suicide_Bomber_by_Joan_Lachkar_PhD.pdf accessed 5 December 2013.

194 *Allah's Angels*, Loc1341 of 5865.

195 N. Kobrin and J. Lachkar. Cutting off your nose to spite your face.10 August 2010. *Family Security Matters*, http://www.familysecuritymatters.org/publications/id.7000/pub_detail.asp accessed 7 December 2013.

196 *Allah's Angels*, Loc 1157 of 5865.

197 Bodansky, p. 243.

198 Breast bombers, Doctors trained to plant explosives inside chest of female bombers, *The Daily Mirror*, 14 May 2012, http://www.mirror.co.uk/news/world-news/doctors-trained-to-plant-explosives-inside-832010 accessed 14 September 2013.

199 G. Bleich. 2009. Bio. http://bleikh-art.gala-studio.com/bio.php accessed 31 July 2013.

200 Israelity.com, http://israelity.com/2009/09/04/another-madonna-controversy-in-israel accessed 10 July 2013.

201 J. Zuleika. 2009. *Terrorism: The Self-Fulfilling Prophecy*, Chicago: University of Chicago, p. 75 loc. 744.

202 Kobrin, pp. 37-38.

203 Matusitz, p. 124. See also R.J. Lifton. 1961. *Chinese Thought Reform and the Psychology of Totalism.* New York: Norton; Anthony Robbins, & Barrie-Anthony. (2002). Cult and Anticult Totalism: Reciprocal Escalation and Violence. *Terrorism and Political Violence*, 14(1), 211-240; Manfield, Philip (1992). *Split Self/Split Object: Understanding and Treating Borderline, Narcissistic and Schizoid Disorders.* London: Aronson.

204 M. Mamakayev. *An Anthology Of Chechen-Ingush Verse.* 1959. Moscow: The State Publishing House of Belle Lettre Literature.

205 M. Levitt. 21 November 2013. New Strategies for countering homegrown violent extremism, Analysis of Near East Policy from the Scholars and Associates of the Washington Institute, Policy forum Report, PolicyWatch 2172, http://www.washingtoninstitute.org/policy-analysis/view/new-strategies-for-countering-homegrown-violent-extremism accessed 22 November 2013.

206 I would be remiss if I did not mention this important development. Chechen president Kadryrov enacted a law on 7 December 2013 prohibiting Chechens from going to Syria to fight jihad for fear of their returning, http://english.farsnews.com/newstext.aspx?nn=13920916000280 accessed 8 December 2013.

207 Bodansky, p. 228 of 444, Loc 3975 of 8828.

208 S. Katz. 1992. *The Hunt for the Engineer.* Guilford, CT: The Globe Pequot Press.

209 Murphy, *Allah's Angels*, Loc 178 of 5865.

210 G. Feifer, 10 July 2006, Chechen rebel dies in explosion, http://www.npr.org/templates/story/story.php?storyId=5546797 accessed 5 December 2013.

211 J. Lachkar. 2004. The Psychological Make-Up of the Suicide Bomber. *Journal of Psychohistory*, 29(4), 349–367.

212 wikipedia.com, http://en.wikipedia.org/wiki/Budyonnovsk_hospital_hostage_crisis accessed 25 November 2013.

213 "Mastermind of Russian school siege killed; Report: Chechen warlord dies in blast set by Russian agents". *CNN.* 10 July 2006. Retrieved 23 May 2010.

214 Bodansky, p. 241 of 444, Loc 4200 of 8828.

215 N. Kobrin, p. xv.

216 Fighting reported at Mumbai Jewish Center, CNN, http://edition.cnn.com/2008/WORLD/asiapcf/11/27/india.attacks/index.html accessed 6 September 2013.

217 J. Zulaika. 2000. *Basque Violence: Metaphor and Sacrament.* Reno: University of Nevada.

218 Others have called it the "Missing Mother Syndrome"; however they do not link it to terrorism, per se. See Cama Zacharias-Miller's work. http://www.missingmother.com/the-syndrome accessed 25 November 2013.

219 J. Shay. 1995. *Achilles in Vietnam: Combat Trauma and the Undoing of Character.* New York: Simon and Schuster.

220 G. Weimann and C. Winn. 1993. *Theater of Terror: Mass Media and International Terrorism.* London: Longman Group United Kingdom.

221 Newman, Fox, Mehta and Harding, 2004, p. 330, quoted by Lankford. A. Lankford. 2013. *Justice Quarterly*,. Mass Shooters in the USA, 1966–2010: Differences Between Attackers Who Live and Die, http://dx.doi.org/10.1080/07418825.2013.806675 accessed 20 September 2013, p. 2.

222 Chechen warlord claims responsibility, http://news.bbc.co.uk/2/hi/europe/2388857.stm accessed 15 September 2013 and Russian Lawmakers Vote to Curb News Media – Terrorism Reporting Restricted After Crisis, Peter Baker, *Washington Post*, November 2, 2002, A.18, accessed 15 September 2013.

223 A. Geifman, 2010. *Death Orders*, p. 72. Oxford, UK: Praeger, Greenwood Publishing Group.

224 See J. Stokes, Stokes and Jolly Ltd., *The Unconscious at Work in Groups and Teams Contributions from the work of Wilfred Bion*, http://www.academia.edu/1150053/The_Unconscious_at_Work_in_Groups_and_Teams_contributions_from_the_work_of_Wilfred_Bion accessed 23 October 2013.

225 S. L. Carter, 18 April 2013, Boston and the Terrible Theater of Terrorism, http://www.bloomberg.com/news/2013-04-18/boston-and-the-terrible-theater-of-terrorism.html

226 A. Dolnik and R. Pilch. 2003. The Moscow Theatre Hostage Crisis: The Perpetrators, Their Tactics and the Russian Response. *International Negotiations* 8, 578-79.

227 A. Berko, 2012. *The Smarter Bomb: Women and Children as Suicide Bombers.* New York: Rowman and Littlefield.

228 Bodansky, p. 257 of 444.

229 Bodansky, p.258 of 444.

230 Bodansky, p. 259 of 444.

231 Anonymous, email 23 September 2013.

232 *Allah's Angels*, Loc 98 of 5865.

233 *Allah's Angels*, Loc 1962 of 5865.

234 See *The Banality of Suicide Terrorism.*

235 R. Pape. 30 March 2010. What makes Chechen women so dangerous? *New York Times*, http://www.nytimes.com/2010/03/31/opinion/31pape.html?pagewanted=all&_r=0 Elsewhere I have noted that Pape comes close to understanding the phenomenon. While he points to political liberation, unfortunately he does not take it to the next level, which is a quest for

psychological liberation from the mother, who is regrettably embedded in a shame–honor culture. The same is the case for the Tamil Tigers. I lectured to Sri Lankan military and police in Colombo and was in rebel territory in 2004. An additional difference is the religious ideology of Islam, which is much more polarizing in black and white binary oppositions than the Tamil Tiger experience.

236 T. Parfitt. 20 July 2003, Meet Black Widow Fatima – she programs women to kill, http://www.telegraph.co.uk/news/worldnews/europe/russia/1436622/Meet-Black-Fatima-she-programmes-women-to-kill.html accessed 25 November 2013.

237 Bodansky, p. 268.

238 Ibid.

239 Amanta Nagayeva & Satsita Dzhebrikhanova, http://www.globaljihad.net/view_page.asp?id=1030 accessed 25 November 2013.

240 Bodansky, p. 242. See also P. W. Eager. 2013. *From Freedom Fighter to Terrorists: Women and Political Violence*. Burlington, VT:Ashgate Publishing Company, p.. 202.

241 Bodansky, p. 308.

242 *Allah's Angels*, Loc 3156-57 of 5865.

243 See *The Banality of Suicide Terrorism*, p. 40, 42, 53, 54, 158.

244 *Allah's Angels*, Loc 1971 of 5865.

245 A. Geifman. 2010. *Death Orders*, p. 158. Santa Barbara, CA: Praeger.

246 Ibid. p. 159.

247 Geifman, p. 170.

248 Wikipedia gives a list of worldwide attacks on schools: http://en.wikipedia.org/wiki/List_of_attacks_related_to_primary_schools

249 D. Perlmutter, Postmodern Iconoclasm: Violence in the School Yard, http://www.religion.emory.edu/affiliate/COVR/perlmutter.html accessed 25 November 2013.

250 Ibid.

251 Perlmutter quotes James Gilligan, M.D., 1996. *Violence, Our Deadly Epidemic and Its Causes*, p. 133.. New York: G.P. Putnam's Sons.

252 Perlmutter, "Unfortunately there was no shortage of examples to choose from while researching this paper. In the past five years there have been more than a dozen school yard shootings that ended in murder. In this paper the focus will be on three recent separate incidents each of which entailed the murder of students and teachers by adolescents ages eleven through sixteen. These were all highly publicized events in which you will most likely recognize the names of the towns if not the names of the children. On March 24, 1998, in Jonesboro, Arkansas eleven-year-old Andrew Golden and thirteen-year-old

Mitchell Johnson dressed in camouflage, stole a van, stole handguns and rifles, secured a site in the woods, pulled a fire alarm and then proceeded to open fire on their schoolmates killing four girls, one teacher and wounding ten others. On October 1, 1997, in Pearl Mississippi, sixteen-year-old Luke Woodham stabbed his mother to death went to school and opened fire with a rifle killing two of his classmates and wounding seven. On December 1, 1997, in West Paducah, Kentucky, fourteen year old Michael Carneal opened fire with a .22 caliber semi automatic pistol on a prayer meeting that had assembled at the school killing three girls and wounding five, one of which will remain in a wheelchair the rest of her life." http://www.religion.emory.edu/affiliate/COVR/perlmutter.html

253 The Boston Marathon Bombing: An Orgonomic Analysis, *The Journal of Psychiatric Orgone Therapy*, http://www.psychorgone.com/tag/terrorism accessed 3 June 2013.

254 Y. Bodansky, 2010. *Chechen Jihad*, p. 419. HarperCollins e-books. His predictions are strikingly similar to those I made at Rand Corporation in Santa Monica in May 2008 when presenting on the Somali community of Minneapolis-St. Paul, where I said that there would be jihadi attacks arising from this community. Indeed, in October 2008 the first American suicide bomber detonated in Puntland. There are many parallels that can be drawn between Somali jihad and Chechen jihad. The Somalis and Chechens trained together, have clans embedded in a shame–honor culture, devalue the female. Also there is significant domestic violence in both cultures, and both find camaraderie with their Turkish Sunni brothers. Moreover, both countries experienced two civil wars and tremendous bloodshed They are not Arab but venerate them because Saudi Arabia is the home of the Haj and birthplace of the Prophet Muhammad. I write about the prison interviews I conducted with the Somalis in *Penetrating the Terrorist Psyche.*

255 Interestingly, Islam's arrival into the Caucasus region occurred in Dagestan, preceding its arrival in Chechnya by several centuries. Thus, it could be argued that Dagestanis have been Muslim longer and have a deeper tie to the religion and jihad.

256 Note that the idea of the genie comes from Arabic culture. In Islam there are many spirits or jinns. In fantasy they are extensions of a needy self. Recall also the expression that you can't put the genie back in the bottle. This unleashing of power is a signal of a repressed culture.

257 R.R. Lee, n.d. Archaic twinship and projective identification. http://www.eapsp.org.au/files/archaic_twinship_and_projective_identification.pdf accessed 21 September 2013. See also H. Kohut.1984. *How Does Analysis Cure?*, p. 204, ed. A. Goldberg and P. Stepansky. Chicago: University of Chicago Press.

258 H. Kohut. 1971. *Analysis of the Self.* NY: International Universities Press, quoted by J. Reid Melroy. 2004. *The Psychopathic Mind: Origins, Dynamics, and Treatment*, p. 329. Lanham, Maryland: Rowman & Littlefield Publisher, a Jason Aronson Book.

259 M. Andrews and C. Freeman. Yemen's hunt for master bomb maker Ibrahim al-Asiri. 10 August 2013. http://www.telegraph.co.uk/news/worldnews/middleeast/10235147/Yemens-hunt-for-master-bomber-Ibrahim-al-Asiri.html accessed 9 December 2013.

260 http://matthewaid.tumblr.com/post/56775054326/profile-of-al-qaedas-top-bombmaker-ibrahim-al-asiri accessed 19 August 2013.

261 N. Kobrin. 2010. *The Banality of Suicide Terrorism*, p. 53.

262 According to Brill—Watt, W. Montgomery. Mu'ākhāt." Encyclopaedia of Islam, Second Edition, edited by: P. Bearman, Th. Bianquis, C.E. Bosworth, E. van Donzel, W.P. Heinrichs. Brill Online, 2013. Reference. http://www.encquran.brill.nl/entries/encyclopaedia-of-islam-2/muakhat-SIM_5267 19 August. See also http://www.classicalislamgroup.com/index.php?view=tafseer/s48-v27to29-3, accessed, 26 November 2013.

263 Ibid.

264 J. Lachkar.2011. *How to Talk to a Borderline*, p. 138. New York: Taylor and Francis.

265 Y. Bodansky. The Mujahedin Factor, http://www.freeman.org/m_online/bodansky/chechnya.htm accessed 26 November 2013.

266 Bodansky, p. 237, loc 4126 of 8828.

267 Bodansky, p.237 of 444 Loc 4130 of 8828.

268 See "Murder," Arabic qatl [the root for qital], Thomas Patrick Hughes, *Dictionary of Islam*, p.420-422.

269 n.a., Inside the dark world of Woolwich Boys: ,The 300-strong gang of Somalis linked to Rigby murder suspect targeted by terror groups looking for jihadists of future, http://www.dailymail.co.uk/news/article-2334488/Inside-dark-world-Woolwich-Boys-The-300-strong-gang-Somalis-linked-Rigby-murder-suspect-targeted-terror-groups-looking-jihadists-future.html?ito=feeds-newsxml 1 June 2013.

270 N. Kobrin. 25 May 2013. "Blood on his hands": Woolwich and the Mother, http://blogs.timesofisrael.com/blood-on-his-hands-woolwich-and-the-mother

271 The Waltham Triple Homicide: A Jihadi Initiation Rite? Federal Prosecutors File Documents Implicating Deceased Tsarnaev Brother in 9/11/11 Triple Murders, http://www.newenglishreview.org/blog_display.cfm/blog_id/50773 accessed 23 October 2013.

272 L. J. Sweet, O. Johnson and A. Planas, 23 May 2013, http://bostonherald.com/news_opinion/local_coverage/2013/05/slain_russian_ibragim_todashev_intimidated_former_neighbors accessed 26 November 2013.

273 M. Schneider. 13 August 2013. Abdulbaki Todashev, Ibragim Todashev's Father, Speaks Out On Son's Fatal Shooting, http://www.huffingtonpost.com/2013/08/13/abdulbaki-todashev-ibragim-father-son-shooting_n_3748432.html accessed 26 November 2013.

274 J. Reitman. Jahar's World, *Rolling Stone Magazine*, 17 July 2013, accessed 18 July 2013.

275 A. Tailghman, 12 January 2004, Saudi pleads guilty to killing Jewish friend here, http://www.chron.com/news/houston-texas/article/Saudi-pleads-guilty-to-killing-Jewish-friend-here-1567401.php accessed 26 November 2013. See also D. Pipes, 23 May 2013, Muslim Acts of Beheading in the West, http://www.danielpipes.org/blog/2013/05/muslim-acts-of-beheading-in-the-west accessed 26 November 2004.

276 J. Gordon. 22 April 2013. When Tamerlan Got Religion, Might He Have Decided To Slit The Throats Of Jews? It's Happened Before. Wicked Local Indeed, Or, The Unsolved Throat Slittings In Waltham, *The New English Review*, http://www.newenglishreview.org/blog_display.cfm/blog_id/48685 accessed 27 November 2013. Are the ritual murders of Ariel Sellouk in Houston and Sebastien Selam in Paris linked to Takfir Wal Hijra? See "I have killed my Jew," http://www.militantislammonitor.org/article/id/353 accessed 27 November 2013.

277 K. Curran, 22 April 2013, http://m.wcvb.com/news/Marathon-Bombing-suspects-stopped-several-times-by-law-enforcement/-/17428308/19851436/-/ergrjgz/-/index.html 22 April 2013.

278 E. Goode and S.F. Kovaleski. April 19, 2013. Boy at Home in U.S., Swayed by One Who Wasn't." *New York Times*. http://www.nytimes.com/2013/04/20/us/details-of-tsarnaev-brothers-boston-suspects-emerge.html?pagewanted=all&_r=2& accessed 27 November 2013.

279 See Kobrin *The Banality of Suicide Terrorism* and *Penetrating the Terrorist Psyche*.

280 See J. Marozzi, 2006. *Tamerlane: The Sword of Islam, Conqueror of the World*. Cambridge, MA: Da Capo Press.

281 D. Sontag, D.M. Herzenhorn and S.F. Kovaleski. 27 April 2013. A battered dream turned violent. *New York Times*. http://www.nytimes.com/2013/04/28/us/shot-at-boxing-title-denied-tamerlan-tsarnaev-reeled.html?_r=0 accessed 9 December 2013.

282 *The Banality of Suicide Terrorism*, p. 167.

283 T. Goltz, Is there a Chechen connection to the Boston Bombings? http://www.thenation.com/print/article/174026/there-chechen-connection-boston-bombings#axzz2XtVdkW00 accessed 2 July 2010.

284 A. Cullison, personal communication by email, 11 September 2013. See also A. Cullison, 6 August 2013, Boston Bombing Suspect Was Steeped in Conspiracies, http://online.wsj.com/article/SB10001424127887323420604578649830782219440.html

285 Reitman, 2013.

286 Ibid.

287 Karny, p. 300.

288 Personal communication, Y. Reiter, 5 February 2014.

289 T. Seibert, 2 February 2014, Sochi Olympics gives boost to Circassian identity, http://www.al-monitor.com/pulse/originals/2014/02/turkey-olympics-cicassian-identity-ethnicity-chechen.html accessed 2 February 2014.

290 Brisard. p.12.

291 Ibid., p.14.

292 Op.cit., p.150.

293 Brian Michael Jenkins, ICT World Summit on Terrorism, September 11, 2013, Herzliya, Israel. See his Stray Dogs and Virtual Armies: Radicalization and Recruitment to Jihadist Terrorism in the U.S. since 9/11. Santa Monica, CA: Rand, 2011, p. 21. Concerning lone wolf threats, see J. Khouri, 12 September 2013, Radical Muslim groups give way to radicalized Muslim individuals: http://www.examiner.com/article/radical-muslim-groups-give-way-to-radicalized-muslim-individuals-report accessed 12 September 2013.

294 Brisard, p.173.

295 Ibid., p.174.

296 A. Schussenberg. *The Ancestor Syndrome.*

297 L. Meixler, 16 September 2004, Chechen groups go underground for funds, http://groups.yahoo.com/neo/groups/chechnya-sl/conversations/topics/40375 accessed 2 September 2013.

298 J. Reitman. Jahar's World. *Rolling Stone Magazine.*

299 Ibid.

300 Op cit.

301 I was asked by his defense lawyer to be an expert witness at the trial. I had to recuse myself since I was working with the Army at Fort Irwin preparing for deployment to Helmand Province, Afghanistan on a Human Terrain Team.

302 A. Lankford. 2013. Mass Shooters in the USA, 1966–2010: Differences Between, *Justice Quarterly*, http://dx.doi.org/10.1080/07418825.2013.806675 sent by author in email 20 September 2013. See also A. Lankford and N. Hakim, From Columbine to Palestine: A comparative analysis of rampage shooters in the U.S.A, and volunteer suicide bombers in the Middle East. *Journal of Aggression and Violent Behavior*, 16, 98-107.

303 Ibid, citing Malphurs, J. E., & Cohen, D. 2002. A newspaper surveillance study of homicide-suicide in the USA. American Journal of Forensic Medical Pathology, 23, 142-148.

304 Reitman, 2013.

305 Ibid.

306 Baiev, p. 2, 19, 21, 43.

307 Reitman, 2013.

308 Nacos, B. L. 2007. *Mass-Mediated Terrorism: The Central Role of the Media in Terrorism and Counterterrorism.* New York: Rowland Little.

309 The Jerusalem Post online, http://www.jpost.com/Breaking-News/Accused-Boston-marathon-bomber-to-make-1st-court-appearance-319340 accessed 10 July 13.

310 C. Moore. 20 April 2013. Analysis: Chechnya Casts a Long Shadow Over the Boston Marathon Bombings. Cerwyn Moore of the University of Birmingham looks at the troubled history of Russia's Muslim republics. http://www.telegraph.co.uk/news/worldnews/europe/russia/10008084/Analysis-Chechnya-Casts-a-Long-Shadow-Over-the-Boston-Marathon-Bombings.html accessed 28 November 2013.

311 Photo of the day, http://europe.wsj.com/home-page accessed 13 July 2013.

312 W. Bion, 1962. A theory of thinking. *International Journal of Psycho-Analysis*, 43(4-5).

313 A. Beifuss and F. Trivini Bellini, Foreword by S. Heller. 2013. *Branding Terror: The Logotypes and Iconography of Insurgent Groups and Terrorist Organizations*, p. 61. New York: Merrell.

314 Ibid. See also n.a. 2010. *Arabian Swords*. Manama, Kingdom of Bahrain: Alwaraqoon Publishers.

315 Beifuss, p. 043.

316 J. Kaufman. 2013. The affable psychopath. Pajamas Media, http://pjmedia.com/blog/the-affable-psychopath/?singlepage=true accessed 23 July 2013..

317 Reitman. Jahar's World. He was a charming kid with a bright future. But no one saw the pain he was hiding or the monster he would become..July 17, 2013. http://www.rollingstone.com/culture/news/jahars-world-20130717?print=true accessed 18 July 2013.

318 Ibid.

319 L. Italie, Times of Israel, 18 July 2013, http://www.timesofisrael.com/bomber-on-rolling-stone-cover-sparks-outrag accessed 18 July 2013.

320 Op.cit.

321 Ibid.

322 Doug Stanglin, Rolling Stone defends Tsarnaev glam cover amid outcry, *USA Today*, 17 July 2013, http://www.usatoday.com/story/news/nation/2013/07/17/dzhokhar-tsarnaev-boston-marathon-bombing-rolling-stone/2523891 accessed 18 July 2013.

323 J. Wolfson, The Real Face of Terror, Boston Magazine online, http://www.bostonmagazine.com/news/blog/2013/07/18/tsarnaev accessed 19 July 2013.

324 Associated Press, Boston bombing: more leaked photos published, August 27, 2013. http://www.theguardian.com/world/2013/aug/28/boston-bombing-more-leaked-photos?

325 E. Pilkington. 2013. Dzhokhar Tsarnaev: dramatic new pictures of Boston suspect's capture, http://www.guardian.co.uk/world/2013/jul/18/dzhokhar-tsarnaev-new-pictures-rolling-stone accessed 19 July 2013.

326 J. Wolfson, The Real Face of Terror, Boston Magazine online, http://www.bostonmagazine.com/news/blog/2013/07/18/tsarnaev accessed 19 July 2013.

327 Reitman. See also, Twitter, https://twitter.com/J_tsar/status/209119289763053569 accessed 5 February 2014.

328 A. Campbell, 19 April 2013, Dzhokhar Tsarnaev tweets read alleged tweets by suspect@J "Tsarnaev, who is still at large and considered armed and dangerous, reportedly tweeted at 10:43 p.m. on Tuesday, "I'm a stress free kind of guy." That was his last tweet.

329 N. Kobrin, Tag Mehir The Israeli Jewish Terrorist Organization, 22 December 2011, http://www.familysecuritymatters.org/publications/id.11095/pub_detail.asp accessed 29 November 2013.

330 Reitman, 2013.

331 Ibid.

332 Ibid.

333 Kamp. 2013. Kazakh Men Indicted in Boston Bombing Probe, Wall Street Journal online, http://online.wsj.com/article/SB10001424127887323477604579000862784073816.html accessed 9 August 2013.

334 n.a., Marathon suspect's friends deny obstruction charge, 14 August 2013. http://www.myfoxboston.com/story/23120247/2013/08/13/two-friends-accused-of-covering-tsarnaevs-tracks-arraigned

335 http://www.hattiesburgamerican.com/usatoday/article/2649309, accessed 14 Aug 2013.

336 n.a., 10 July 2013. Action against Kazakh suspects in Boston Marathon bombings case delayed. http://rbth.ru/news/2013/07/10/action_against_kazakh_suspects_in_boston_marathon_bombings_case_delayed_27958.html, accessed 11 July 2013.

337 D. Leinwand Leger, 8 August, Dias Kadyrbayev and Azamat Tazhayakov indicted, http://www.ksdk.com/news/article/391864/28/Grand-jury-indicts-friends-of-Boston-bombing-suspect accessed 9 August 2013.

338 n.a., Kazakhstan students kept in small individual cells in US, Tengri News, http://en.tengrinews.kz/crime/Kazakhstan-students-kept-in-small-individual-cells-in-US-22142 accessed 28 August 2013.

339 E. Moskowitz. 25 April 2013. Carjack victim recounts his harrowing night, http://www.boston.com/metrodesk/2013/04/25/carjack-victim-recounts-his-harrowing-night/BhQWGzarWee8MZ6KtMHJNN/story.html accessed 29 November 2013.

340 Ibid.

341 J. Van Dkye. April 2013. The birth of Chechen Muslim radicals. http://www.cbsnews.com/news/the-birth-of-chechen-muslim-radicals accessed 10 December 2013.

342 M. Hogenboom, 25 July 2013, Psychopathic criminals have empathy switch, http://www.bbc.co.uk/news/science-environment-23431793 accessed 25 July 2013.

343 H. Foster, 19 August 2013, Boston arrests show that the 'help your buddy' mentality doesn't play well in some countries, http://en.tengrinews.kz/opinion/403 accessed 20 August 2013.

344 High in the Caucasian Mountains live the peoples of Daghestan, translated by Julius Katzer, http://gamzatov.ru/mydageng.htm accessed 4 July 2013.

345 http://www.newstalkzb.co.nz/auckland/news/nbint/1500061055-boston-bomber-suspects%E2%80%94mother-in-denial, accessed 25 June 2013.

346 Ibid., p. 300.

347 Why clowns are scary, 20 September 2013, http://www.csmonitor.com/Science/2013/0919/Clown-terrorizes-town-Why-are-clowns-scary accessed 20 September 2013.

348 J. Zuleika. 2009. *Terrorism: The Self-Fulfilling Prophecy*, p. 82. Chicago: University of Chicago Press.

349 D. Goleman. 1985. *Vital Lies, Simple Truths*, p. 52. New York: Simon and Schuster. See also H. Kohut and E. Wolf. Disorders of the Self and their Treatment, *International Journal of Psychoanalysis*, 59: 413-425.

350 http://www.metro.us/newyork/news/national/2013/06/24/mother-of-boston-bombing-suspect-plans-to-come-to-u-s-for-sons-court-appearance/#sthash.z5NIt3GP.dpuf, accessed 25 June, 2013

351 Reitman.

352 L. Dickson, 9 July 2013, Times Colonist http://www.timescolonist.com/mr-big-sting-used-by-police-in-legislature-bomb-plot-arrests-defence-lawyer-says-1.432382 accessed 11 July 2013.

353 T. Zytaruk, 9 July 2013, Alleged Surrey terrorists' bail hearing, Vancouver Sun, http://www.vancouversun.com/news/Alleged+Surrey+terrorists+bail+hearing/8637076/story.html accessed 5 February 2014.

354 Alexandra Petri, Washington Post, http://www.washingtonpost.com/blogs/compost/wp/2012/12/18/after-i-am-adam-lanzas-mother accessed 10 July 2013.

355 L. Warren and L. Boyle. 25 April 2013, Daily Mail, http://www.dailymail.co.uk/news/article-2314663/Boston-bombers-crazed-mother-Zubeidat-Tsarnaeva-says-marathon-carnage-play-paint-instead-blood.html accessed 10 December 2013.

356 Raine, p. 190-191.

357 A note on environmental forces affecting genetics and biology: It is not within the scope of this book to discuss epigenetics, the field of study concerning the cultural environmental influence on gene expression. Raine raises this important issue, and my mentor, Sander Breiner, M.D. who was the leading authority on the history of child sacrifice, also had a particular interest in epigenetics, believing that it played a significant role in perpetuating the violence.

358 F. Davoine and J.-M. Gaudilliere. 2004. *History beyond Trauma.* New York: Other Press.

359 A. Bouhdiba. 1998. *Sexuality in Islam.* London: Saqi, 212-229.

360 D. Sontag, D.M. Herszenhorn and S.F. Kovaleski. 2013. A battered dream, then a violent path, *New York Times.* http://www.nytimes.com/2013/04/28/us/shot-at-boxing-title-denied-tamerlan-tsarnaev-reeled.html?pagewanted=all

361 Ibid., 213.

362 A. Rahimi. 2013. *The Patience Stone.* Film.

363 K. Deutsche and M. Chayes. 26 April 2013. Bombing suspects' mother on U.S. terrorist watch list, *Newsday*, http://www.newsday.com/news/nation/bombing-suspects-mother-on-u-s-terror-watch-list-1.5144463 accessed 5 February 2014.

364 27 April 2013, Boston bombing. http://www.independent.co.uk/news/world/americas/boston-bombing-suspects-mother-zubeidat-tsarnaeva-was-added-to-terror-database-18-months-before-bombing-officials-say-8590901.html accessed 20 August.

365 T. Franks, 23 June 2013, Dagestan and the Tsarnaev brothers: The radicalisation risk, http://www.bbc.co.uk/news/magazine-23004244 accessed 29 September 2013.

366 One person died in the attack. AP, May 25; AFP, May 26, http://www.ctc.usma.edu/posts/recent-highlights-in-terrorist-activity-42 accessed 25 June 2013.

367 N. Kobrin, 23 April 2013, The Mind of the Terrorist is the Mind of the Mother, http://blogs.timesofisrael.com/the-mind-of-the-terrorist-is-the-mind-of-his-mother

368 *Rolling Stone* http://www.rollingstone.co.za/opinion/item/2650-jahar-s-world accessed 28 September 2013.

369 J. Ford. 22 April 2013. http://pix11.com/2013/04/22/women-close-to-tsarnaev-brothers-could-hold-important-clues-for-investigators. accessed 1 December 2013.

370 W. Cupchik, W.and Atcheson, D.J.. Shoplifting: An Occasional Crime Of The Moral Majority (1983). *The Bulletin of the American Academy of Psychiatry and the Law*, 11 (4): 343–54.

371 *Daily Mail.* http://www.dailymail.co.uk/news/article-2311939/Sisters-Boston-bombing-suspects-nearly-evicted-home-rent-bickered-constantly--federal-agents-question-sister-home.html In addition, there is a known relationship between kleptomania and pyromania, setting fires. The sons engaged in explosives and the mother stole. Both behaviors indicate poor impulse control. See B. Sadock and V. Sadock. 2008. Kaplan and Sadock's Concise Textbook of Clinical Psychiatry, p. 365.. Philadelphia: Wolters and Kluwer/Lippincott Williams and Wilks.

372 Reitman. The family was not really considered to be Chechen: "Anna Nikeava was unaware the girls had even left Boston, and suspects the parents never talked about it for fear of being judged. "Underneath it all, they were a screwed-up family," she says. "They weren't Chechen." They had not come from Chechnya, as she and others had, "and I don't think the other families accepted them as Chechens. They could not define themselves or where they belonged. And poor Jahar was the silent survivor of all that dysfunction," she says. "He never said a word. But inside, he was very hurt, his world was crushed by what was going on with his family. He just learned not to show it."

373 A. De Carbonnel and S. Simon. 23 April 2013. Special Report: The radicalization of Tamerlan Tsarnaev, http://www.reuterscom/article/2013/04/23/us-usa-explosions-radicalisation-special-idUSBRE93M0CZ20130423 accessed 5 February 2014.

374 A. Lindley Kilzer, 21 April 2013,The Tsarnaevs and Me, http://www.salon.com/writer/alyssa_lindley_kilzer accessed 20 August 2013.

375 http://foxnewsinsider.com/2013/04/23/read-ailina-and-bella-tsarnaev-sisters-bombing-suspects-release-statement, accessed 20 June 2013.

376 Boston Jihadis' Brother-in-law. 20 April 2013. http://atlasshrugs2000.typepad.com/atlas_shrugs/2013/04/boston-jihadis-brother-in-law-im-not-muslim-and-they-didnt-accept-me.html accessed 1 December 2013.

377 Laurel J. Sweet, 16 October 2013, Tsarnaev's sister released without bail, http://bostonherald.com/news_opinion/local_coverage/2013/10/tsarnaev_s_sister_released_without_bail 17 October 2013.

378 Sontag.

379 Reitman.

380 M. Hartmann. 8 June 13. Tsarnaev Delved Into Right-Wing Conspiracy Theories, With Help From an Unlikely Friend, http://nymag.com/daily/intelligencer/2013/08/tsarnaev-delved-into-right-wing-conspiracies.html accessed 1October 2013.

381 M. Newman. The Psychoanalytic Concept of love, n.d. http://www.freud-sigmund.com/psychoanalytic-concept-love accessed 1 October 2013.

382 D. Dutton. 2007. *The Abusive Personality*. New York: Guilford Press.

383 J. Lachkar, 2012. *How to Talk to a Borderline*, pp. 129-140. New York: Routledge.

384 S. Rubin Erdeky, Why I finally left my abusive relationship, http://www.goodhousekeeping.com/health/wellness/domestic-abuse-battered-woman accessed 28 September 2013.

385 D. Pipes, 16 May 2004 updated 7 August 2013, http://www.danielpipes.org/blog/2004/05/advice-to-non-muslim-women-against-marrying accessed 1 October 2013.

386 Ibid.

387 Boston Jihadis' Brother-in-law. 20 April 2013. http://atlasshrugs2000.typepad.com/atlas_shrugs/2013/04/boston-jihadis-brother-in-law-im-not-muslim-and-they-didnt-accept-me.html accessed 1 December 2013.

388 P. Caulfield, 23 April 2013, http://www.nydailynews.com/news/national/tamerlan-tsarnaev-abused-katherine-russell-taunts-slut-prostitute-courtship-roommates-article-1.1325216, accessed 26 April 2013.

389 Ibid.

390 D. Sontag, D.M. Heszhenhorn, S.F, Kovaleski, 27 April 2013, A battered dream, then a violent path, http://www.nytimes.com/2013/04/28/us/shot-at-boxing-title-denied-tamerlan-tsarnaev-reeled.html?pagewanted=all&_r=0 accessed 28 April 2013.

391 28 April 2013, The Tsarnaev Brothers' troubled trail to Boston, http://www.latimes.com/news/nationworld/nation/la-na-boston-suspects-20130428-dto,0,15030.htmlstory accessed 28 April 2013.

392 Sontag.

393 Ibid.

394 D. Kenner. 19 April 2013. Who is Tamerlan Tsarnaev? http://blog.foreignpolicy.com/posts/2013/04/19/who_is_tamerlan_tzarnaev. accessed 5 December 2013.

395 K. Ablow. 30 April 2013. How to build a terrorist. http://www.foxnews.com/opinion/2013/04/30/how-to-build-terrorist accessed 10 December 2013.

396 Dzhokhar and Tamerlan have shamed all Chechens, family says, 19 April 2013, http://www.theguardian.com/world/2013/apr/19/tamerlan-dzhokhar-tsarnaev-family-chechens, accessed 20 August 2013.

397 Ruslan Tsarni 'losers' interview video: Uncle says Dzhokhar, Tamerlan Tsarnaev were 'losers' on NBC, http://www.wptv.com/dpp/news/national/ruslan-tsarni-losers-interview-video-uncle-says-dzhozkar-tamerlan-tsarnaev-were-losers-on-nbc#ixzz2WkWwUnKK accessed 20 June 2013.

398 http://www.huffingtonpost.com/2013/04/19/maret-tsarnaev-aunt-bombing-suspects-staged_n_3118044.html, accessed 20 June 2013.

399 N. Kobrin, *Penetrating the Terrorist Psyche*; Breiner, S., February 8, 2010, personal email communication.

400 P.A. Olson. *The Malignant Pied Piper.*

401 H. Freud. 2013. Men and Mothers: *The Life Long Struggle of Sons and their Mothers,* p. 25. London: Karnac.

402 A. Bouhdiba. 1998. *Sexuality in Islam.* London: Saqi Books.

403 W. Bion. 1980. *Experiences in Groups.* London/New York: Tavistock/Routledge, p. 164-165.

404 This proverb must precede Islam's arrival to Chechnya since dogs are considered unclean in Islam.

405 Yalom, I. D., & Leszcz. 2005. *The Theory and Practice of Group Psychotherapy*, p. 60. New York: Basic Books.

406 B.M. Jenkins. The Threat of a Mumbai-Style Terrorist Attack in the U.S. http://www.rand.org/content/dam/rand/pubs/testimonies/CT300/CT391/RAND_CT391.pdf?utm_source=Al+Qaeda%27s+offsprings+in+Terror+Upswing&utm_campaign=ACD%2FEWI+BLOG&utm_medium=email, June 12, 2013, accessed 24 September 2013.

407 M. Hoyer, USA Today, http://www.freep.com/article/20130715/NEWS06/307150125/aurora-movie-theater-shooting-one-year-later accessed 16 July 2013.

408 Email 6 September 2013, MEMRI's Jihad and Terrorism Threat Monitor (JTTM). "In a recent article published in Issue 13 of Turkestan Al-Islamiyya, the Turkestan Islamic Party's journal, an Al-Qaeda cleric praised the Boston Marathon bombing's Tsarnaev brothers."

409 Ibid.

410 W.R. Bion. 1962. *Learning from Experience.* London: William Heinemann. Reprinted London: Karnac Books. See also Bion 1967. *Second Thoughts*, London: William Heinemann. Reprinted London: Karnac Books 1984. In a paper on Bion, Grostein suggests that Bion may have suffered from post traumatic stress. I agree. See J. Grostein. Bion's Transformation in 'O'" and the Concept of the 'Transcendent Position. http://www.sicap.it/merciai/bion/papers/grots.htm accessed 2 December 2013.

411 H. Koplowitz. 18 March 2013. Adam Lanza Spreadsheet: Sandy Hook Shooter Compiled Extensive List Of Mass Murderers, http://www.ibtimes.com/adam-lanza-spreadsheet-sandy-hook-shooter-compiled-extensive-list-mass-murderers-1133557 accessed 2 December 2013.

412 Lupica: n.d. Morbid find suggests murder-obsessed gunman Adam Lanza plotted Newtown, Conn.'s Sandy Hook massacre for years, http://www.nydailynews.com/news/national/lupica-lanza-plotted-massacre-years-article-1.1291408?print accessed 2 December 2013.

413 J.R. Arnold. 2011. *The Moro Wars: How America Battled a Muslim Insurgency in the Philippines*. New York: Bloombury Press.

414 Bat Ye'or. 2002. *Islam and Dhimmitude: Where Civilizations Collide*. Teaneck, NJ: Fairleigh Dickenson University Press, p. 41.

415 A. Chejne. 1974. *Muslim Spain: Its History and Culture*. Minneapolis: University of Minnesota Press. Bat Ye'or. 2002. *Islam and Dhimmitude: Where Civilizations Collide*., pp. 182-186. Teaneck, NJ: Fairleigh Dickinson University Press.

416 She attacked an Israeli convoy in southern Lebanon on April 9, 1985. She was a member of the Syrian Socialist Nationalist Party. B. Khrais.24 April 2010. Lebanon's Women Warriors. 2010. http://www.aljazeera.com/programmes/general/2010/04/2010413115916795784.html accessed 3 December 2013.

417 See *The Banality of Suicide Terrorism*, p. 48.

418 J. Henley. 20 December 2004. France shocked by double murder and beheading at psychiatric hospital, http://www.theguardian.com/world/2004/dec/20/france.jonhenley accessed 24 August 2013.

419 Y. Bodansky. 2008. *Chechen Jihad: Al Qaeda's Training Ground and the Next Wave of Terror*, p. 37, reprint ed.. HarperCollins.

420 N. Poller, personal communication, 3 July 2013.

421 See *The Banality of Suicide Terrorism*, pp. 93-98.

422 Chief says Santa Monica killings were premeditated, 7 June http://www.actionnewsjax.com/news/national/story/Chief-says-Santa-Monica-killings-were-premeditated/5GiZQTGU4kiZZdR35_s6zg.cspx accessed 24 August.

423 S. Schwartz. 21 June. http://www.theblaze.com/stories/2013/06/21/security-guard-kills-jewish-man-reportedly-shouting-allahu-akbar-at-jerusalems-western-wall accessed 24 August 2013.

424 Canada's Terrorist Take-down, http://www.aina.org/news/20130708150723.htm accessed 9 July 2013.

425 http://www.thestar.com/opinion/commentary/2013/07/09/converts_can_find_meaning_and_radicalism_in_religion.print.html, accessed 11 July 2013.

426 T. Majidy, 11 September 2013. http://www.tolonews.com/en/afghanistan/11886-women-comprise-95-percent-of-suicides-in-afghanistan-officials accessed 16 October 2013.

427 Alan Dundes, 1997. *From Games to War and Other Psychoanalytic Essays on Folklore*. Lexington: University of Kentucky.

428 http://www.haaretz.com/news/sports/hundreds-of-beitar-jerusalem-fans-walk-out-after-chechen-player-scores.premium-1.506981, accessed 24 August 2013; J. Rudoren, http://www.nytimes.com/2013/01/31/world/middleeast/some-fear-a-soccer-teams-racist-fans-mirror-israel.html?pagewanted=all&_r=0 accessed 24 August 2013.

429 Personal communication, Mundar Khalayle, spokesperson for Sakhnin Professional Football team, 20 Nov. 2013 at the conference: Shared Living in Mixed City, Jerusalem.

430 J. Dorsey. 2014. *The Turbulent World of Middle East Soccer.* London: C Hurst & Co Publishers Ltd. forthcoming; see his blogs http://mideastsoccer.blogspot.co.il, also Beitar Jerusalem and Egypt's President Morsi: two vignettes of racism, 30 January 2013.

431 Beifuss, p.011. However, since the publication of his book, Jonathan Matusitz has delved into the function of branding in his forthcoming book, *Symbolism in Terrorism.*

432 http://www.guardian.co.uk/football/2013/jul/07/brazilian-referee-decapitated-stabs-player/print, accessed 8 June 2012.

433 http://www.ict.org.il/ResearchPublications/DatabaseReports/tabid/380/Articlsid/1221/currentpage/1/Default.aspx accessed 15 September 2013.

434 The Jerusalem Post, http://www.jpost.com/Breaking-News/Suicide-bomber-kills-three-police-in-Russias-Chechnya-326237 accessed 16 September 2013.

435 D.F. Swaab. 2014. *We Are Our Brains: A Neurobiography of the Brain, from the Womb to Alzheimer's.* New York: Spiegel & Grau, loc. 4433 of 6120.

436 M. Ziolkowski. 2005. *Alien Visions: The Chechens and the Navajos in Russian and American Literature.* Newark: University of Delaware Press.

437 S. Breiner, M.D. Adapted from *Slaughter of the Innocents.*

438 T. Lister, 9 October 2013, CNN, http://www.wptv.com/dpp/news/world/ayman-al-zawahiri-nasir-al-wuhayshi-ibrahim-al-asiri-most-dangerous-terrorists-list-compiled accessed 10 October 2013.

439 START, Terrorism in the North Caucasus: An Overview, April 2013.

440 Meier. P. 125.

www.ingramcontent.com/pod-product-compliance
Lightning Source LLC
LaVergne TN
LVHW010054110826
845155LV00028B/338
* 9 7 8 1 8 8 5 8 8 1 1 3 7 *